Sing to Me
and
I Will
Hear You–
A Love Story

Elaine G. McGillicuddy

Caritas Communications Caritas Communications Thiensville, Wisconsin

Dedication

For Rowan

Duet

I

"As death approaches me," you said,
"even if I seem beyond your reach,
sing to me and I will hear you."
I sang. You heard.

Bereft of your voice after you died,
I turned to you with the same request:
"Sing to me, please – and I will hear you!"
You do. I hear.

II

Where did you go, my love?
I know you're not gone, not disappeared.
You live, you're alive! You're here!

The you who is here is the you transformed
as a seed in the earth dies to bear fruit.*
Descended into earth, the new you lives on!

When Great Mystery beckoned, you entered Her depths,
but left the door ajar for me.
Now I can hear you sing!

*John 12:24

Sing to Me and I Will Hear You – The Poems

Table of Contents

Acknowledgements

I give thanks to my publisher, David Gawlik, for his unfailing support and ready collaboration. My editor, Mike O'Connor, poet, writer, and translator of Chinese literature, deserves to be recognized for his keen insights and trustworthy judgments. I acknowledge also those who, after reading part or all of this manuscript in draft, made helpful observations and suggestions: Jack Estes, publisher of Pleasure Boat Studio; William Bridges, a poet and journalist; and writer-friends: Berry Manter, Judi Rice, and Eleanor Morse. I thank, too, the many friends who supported me by expressing interest in the progress of my writing. My gratitude is also owed to Dr. Anthony T. Padovano, a Catholic Theologian, and Reverend Bill Gregory, a retired minister of the United Church of Christ, for their initial and ongoing support.

Foreword

Commitments Costing Not Less Than Everything

At the heart of this remarkable memoir is the mystery of fidelity.

The Latin root of the English word "fidelity" is trust. The story of Elaine and Francis is a search for what it is in life that we ultimately trust.

The protagonists in this narrative are two generous and sensitive pilgrims of love who search for God and find each other.

Nothing meaningful in life is easy. Elaine and Francis discover this not only in the elegant simplicity that leads them to pledge continence and chastity to God as a charism or gift. The object of this donation has abstinence from sexual love as its immediate consequence. Its further intention, however, is a life of freedom to serve others and an opportunity to focus on God intensely. Committed chastity is, of course, about relationships and love. It never works unless it leads to a bonding with the community and the people one serves as well an experience of God's love. This experience of God's love is analogously made clear through the language of marital and sexual love, not, of course, that it replicates them, but rather because it suggests intimacy and totality, inseparability and a fused life together. All of these are essential to chastity's validation. If these elements are missing, then, all one has is an institutional and obligatory burden, a confinement of the spirit, a violation of the heart.

When Elaine and Francis meet, something mystical and sexual comes together, not as a metaphor but as a lived experience. It is then their task and their calling to put together into the mosaic of their love the scattered pieces that they fear at times will not match. Both of them were taught, from their early years, the incompatibility of what they now try to make whole and, indeed, the infidelity of even trying to do this.

Elaine writes her story after the death of Francis. She does this as a tribute to him and of all they had together. She does it also as a witness, not to what she was taught, but to what she actually experienced in life. Indeed, she offers it as a pronouncement to us of a lesson we might learn from their journey.

As I read these pages, I was often startled at the beauty of Elaine's poetry and inspired by the lines of their correspondence with each other.

What Elaine and Francis reveal is something we must come to see and hear if we choose not to live lesser lives.

Quite simply, the central portrait they paint together shows us that commitments have seasons and continuities, and transferabilities that institutional systems cannot measure, and that arthritic theologies and doctrines cannot comprehend or verbalize. Allow me to explain what I am saying here.

Commitments come in seasons. There is a time when a commitment fits, when all the majesty of one's donation is evident and all the totality of one's gift is absolute. In such a season, love and God and the self and the community one serves blend into a symphony of joy and intersect in a tapestry of beauty. There may be discordant moments, of course, dark corners that resist being woven into light and color. There is no human journey of value without missteps and insufficiencies. Nonetheless, if the season is right for the commitment one makes, God never seems far away, love is near, and we experience completeness in our lives and a sense of the sacred.

These pages Elaine writes show us, however, that there are other seasons of life and that they require of us other responses. If one has loved a commitment deeply and genuinely, one may yet find that, in another season, this commitment can become problematic and a new commitment is the only way God seems to summon us. A new commitment may be necessary not because there are difficulties or darkness in the former commitment. There are always these experiences in all our lives and we are obliged to live through them. A new commitment comes from a deeper place, a sense that something more is imperative and that it cannot happen in the previous commitment. The anguish this brings is poignantly illustrated in these pages. Two people who loved passionately what they were doing now love passionately in a new way. And, tragically, the institutional structure of the Church they love will not allow what the Gospel itself permits.

A catholic response to all this is required, one total enough to see the continuity between the commitment of one season and the commitment of the next. If this continuity cannot be found, then we lose our way. Is it possible to deny nothing substantial from one's past and yet reverse the way one is going, retracing steps to a fork in the road which is still the road one is travelling?

Elaine and Francis ask each other and God and friends whether they are deluded or self-indulgent, whether they rationalize and equivocate. This is not an easy terrain. The sign-posts and markers are not as clear as one would prefer.

And yet, such a journey may emerge as imperative. It may come with demands as urgent as those experienced in the previous journey one had taken. At stake now is one's identity and self-respect; at stake now is one's relationship with God and community; at stake now is the difference of living a life that is authentic; at stake now is the decision to not miss the gift the future offers in place of the past that one still treasures.

And so a continuity is created keeping God and love central, making the vows of an earlier time the vows of a new age and season. All this is possible because so many have found this new way and because others who have never walked such a road are able to see the rightness of such a journey.

Vows and commitments have transferabilities. The surface may seem different, the music may sound discordant, and so one works to reach the depths so that elegance and harmony are fashioned with deeper experiences until one finds all that was most profound and most intended in earlier commitments. This is what is carried through to the next season.

How does one know one has gotten such a calling right? One knows by the fruits that come from this. If compassion and generosity continue and, indeed, are magnified so that a return to the past seems less giving, then the life one is living is the life one should not have missed. If service and care for others lead to new intensities, then it is good that one is where one is. We carve sign-posts with our lives so that other wayfarers may know they are not alone in the perilous and magnificent journey they are taking.

The newer commitment is not necessarily a judgment on the former commitment as a lesser calling for those who follow such a path. In like manner, the choice and continuance of a life of celibacy was not a judgment that marriage was a lesser calling for those who were summoned there and loved their lives there. Elaine and Francis beckon us in these pages to walk with them and become their companions. Who would not want to follow?

Anthony T. Padovano
Catholic Theologian

Preface

The Preface to my first book *Sing to Me and I Will Hear You – The Poems*, written after my husband's death early in 2010, sketches Francis' and my love story. I promised then to tell more of the story in prose. This is that book.

Among reasons cited why I wanted to write it, I highlight three. The wonder of what happened to Francis and me never faded. Throughout the years, we were aware that the love given us was bigger than both of us. And so, it's a love story meant to be shared – with those who love love.

And with my goddaughter, too. Even at nine, being slight of stature, Rowan still sits on my lap while I read her stories. She is bright enough to read this one now, but she will understand it better as an adult, or after she herself falls in love.

Rowan was seventeen-months old when she first came up to *pepere* in the kitchen and asked him to pour maple syrup on her pancakes. She was five-years old when she sat next to him on his hospital bed, raising and lowering its upper end as he encouraged her to do. I dedicate this book to her because since his death, she has somehow absorbed and reflected some of my love for Francis.

I was deeply moved while writing about Francis. *Sing to Me and I Will Hear You – A Love Story* is my tribute to him. Further, I want to uphold the example he gave – of extraordinary patience, courage, and grace in dealing with pain and in facing the unknown.

The reader will learn how Francis' life was influenced by his patron saint, St. Francis of Assisi. As he approached his own death, Francis A. McGillicuddy (with the "A" referring to "Assisi") did not directly use his namesake's expression, "Welcome Sister Death," but he went out to meet her with the same attitude. And with love on his lips.

CHAPTER ONE
Through the Third-Way

I was a nun, and he, a priest, when Sister Aimee introduced us in her principal's office. Yet I was predisposed to notice the handsomeness of his tall frame, his dark hair, and his smiling eyes. Each of us had been newly assigned that September, 1968, to Waterville, Maine – Father Francis A. McGillicuddy as assistant pastor at Sacred Heart Church, and I, Sister Maureen (the name I had chosen as my religious name) – as eighth-grade teacher in the school he would oversee. I was thirty-three and Francis, forty-one.

I felt more inclined to notice how Father McGillicuddy looked because after the winds of change initiated by Pope John XXIII had blown across the world, the idea of the "third-way" was in the air. Not just for me, but for other nuns and priests.

The third-way might be likened to platonic friendship, but coming from

Fr. McGillicuddy, when they met.

1

French philosopher, Jesuit priest, and visionary, Teilhard de Chardin, it held richer overtones and a unique application. By the time I met Father McGillicuddy, my understanding of the third-way had translated itself to "celibate love." Meeting him, the third-way readily came to mind.

OCCASIONS TO MEET

From the beginning, Father McGillicuddy's duties and mine over-lapped, bringing us into frequent contact. It was expected that the assistant parish priest would occasionally join the faculty in the lunchroom below the classrooms. One reason Father Mac (as he was soon affectionately called by the students) may have come to lunch more often than duty called for, was not just my presence, but my other job. In addition to teaching at his parish school for that first year, I had also been assigned as Campus Minister at Colby College located close by, just up Mayflower Hill Drive. The Mount Merici Convent site where we nuns lived in community was positioned next to the high school "Academy" by the same name.

Sitting together at table in the lunchroom, we discovered we had a lot in common, whether we were dressed in black or not. Father McGillicuddy's clerical white collar distinguished his black suit as priestly garb. My Order had modernized our nun's habit by abandoning the old-fashioned headpiece (bandeau and guimpe) I had worn during "formation," the Novitiate and Ju-niorate days of my earlier years. These starched linen pieces of cloth pinned together had then covered my forehead, neck, shoulders, and chest.

Now, a simple white collar and a short veil allowed my neck, entire face, forehead, and hair to show. In the past, the black serge dress was gathered at the waist with a leather "cincture" which looped through a metal buckle and hung down close to the hem of the habit, near the ankles. The sleeves of the modern habit, on the other hand, were no longer double – with outer, long, wide sleeves hanging over the wrists covered by narrower under-sleeves – but rather, one set of standard-shaped long sleeves. Even the shoes, though black, looked modern. I didn't look out of place, therefore, taking on a second job at the college, but just clerical enough to signify my position as a campus minister. And now, there was more of my person for Father McGillicuddy to see.

CONCERN ABOUT WAR IN VIETNAM

Sr. Maureen, when they met.

I wasn't surprised to learn Father McGillicuddy regularly read *National Catholic Reporter* (*NCR*), the progressive independent lay newspaper, the same one I had read in our community library since its founding eight years earlier. With the Vietnam War raging, it made sense he wanted to share with me the *New Yorker* articles focused on widespread protests against this war held on college campuses all over the United States. He pointed out in particular an article on the Berrigan brothers. Both were priests – Daniel, a Jesuit, and Philip, a Josephite. In sharing this reading, he was assisting me to better understand the situation into which I was thrust. Because of this, and because Father McGillicuddy joined CALCAV (Clergy and Laity Concerned About Vietnam), which I also joined, we had even more opportunities to meet.

Father Leopold Nicknair, an outgoing, friendly priest with whom I worked as campus minister, was also a member of CALCAV. Along with several Colby College professors and other leaders in the community, we three were key parts of that team.

During one of our meetings, we learned why Father McGillicuddy had joined CALCAV. It was "a natural" for him, he said, because two years earlier, in 1966, he had spoken up in court in support of two young men who felt in conscience they couldn't go to war. That experience, he explained, made him politically aware. "I recognize now that governments sell war-making to citizens and that in war, the first casualty is truth." We could see he was still moved by that event, likely because Judge Edward Gignoux' ruling was in the offing. Soon after, in 1969, those first Catholics in Maine who had requested it were granted conscientious objector status.

Between discussions during lunch about the war in Vietnam, and meetings of CALCAV at Colby College, Father McGillicuddy and I were becoming very good friends. I couldn't help notice we kept getting "thrown together." For example, we were both members of the diocesan Liturgical Committee. A photo of this committee of eight was published in the diocesan weekly newspaper, *Church World*. I cut it out and saved it.

It wasn't surprising, therefore, that the thought insinuated itself, in my mind, at least: "Perhaps this relationship is developing into the third-way." So I let it happen. I wondered if he wondered, too, though of course, I didn't speak of it.

FIRST INKLINGS

Almost four months after we met, the Christmas Messiah Sing at Colby College added to the momentum of our growing relationship. In the Lorimer Chapel, Father McGillicuddy and I were seated in the same pew, but there were a few people standing between us. Noticing his cough, I pulled out a tissue and reached past them to give it to him. That's when, once he took it, my heart flipped. I couldn't help thinking: "This must be the third=way!"

Father McGillicuddy, as I probably still addressed him, then telephoned me one day to ask if I would be willing to befriend a young woman he was trying to help who had attempted suicide. He thought seeing a nun, a woman, would be good for her. I was happy to agree, but even more so when we chanced upon each other at the hospital. "How good of you to visit her!" he said, a smile spreading on his face as he rounded a corner. He was leaving as I was arriving. But we stood for a while in the corridor as Father McGillicuddy brought me up to date on her state of mind. As he walked out of the hospital, I walked on to find her room. I was joined with him in our concern for her.

Then the two of us were interviewed on television. Standing by his side with the mike handed from one to the other to describe the Confraternity of Christian Doctrine program for Catholic youth attending public schools in the area – I was concerned my attraction to him might show. So I tried to hide it by trying to look more serious than usual.

In reality, although by then I indeed thought the third=way was happening to us, I was also conflicted. "How am I going to handle this?" I worried. "What do I do about the growing magnetism that draws me to him, and even, it seems, him to me?"

For my part, even though I knew very well there was no sin in feeling attracted to Father McGillicuddy, I nevertheless mentioned it to my confessor, Father Raymond Picard, when I went to church for the Sacrament of Reconciliation (or "confession" as we referred to it before Vatican II). I did that to get a handle on it, I told myself, trying to tame it, I suppose. But trying to tame it didn't work, perhaps because deep within, I didn't really want to tame this attraction.

VIETNAM MORATORIUM

Our joining CALCAV came none too soon, because during these times of "We Ain't Gonna Study War No More," it seemed the world was seething and aglow. In the spirit of college students across the country, the students at Colby College occupied Lorimer Chapel. One Sunday morning when Father Nick and I arrived to celebrate mass, the students, sweeping out and tidying up the chapel for us after their overnight sleep-in, greeted us cordially. We were personal friends with several of those who had organized it, for example Peggy Elkus and Marshall Knapp.

For the nationwide "Vietnam Moratorium" protest on October 15, 1969, our CALCAV contingent was in the vanguard of the Colby College students and Waterville citizens. We marched from the campus heights past Mount Merici convent and the Academy and on down Mayflower Hill Drive to the town square where peace demonstrators had gathered for the rally. Father Nick, Father Francis, and I walked alongside John Cole whose progressive weekly newspaper *Maine Times* kept us abreast of latest developments on the peacemaking front.

ON THE PERSONAL FRONT

I was caught by surprise one day while upstairs in my "cell," the monastic name for our small private rooms. Seated at my desk near the window beyond the sink, closet, bed, and rocking chair, I was either preparing for a class at school, or a panel discussion at Colby College, or maybe even writing in my journal, trying to deal with the attractive force that was drawing me toward Father McGillicuddy. Suddenly, I heard my name announced over the intercom.

It was not a visiting Sunday when my parents might come, nor was I expecting a student – or anyone – to call on me. But here it was: "Sister Maureen, please come to the parlor."

As I walked into our nuns' parlor to the right of the entryway, tall, dark, and handsome Father McGillicuddy rose to greet me with a broad smile, his sparkling eyes meeting mine as he grasped my hand in a warm, firm handshake. My heart was racing as I adjusted my chair to face him.

Here he was, calling on me, for no reason I knew. And without advance notice! This was more than unexpected; it was out of the ordinary. This was not a meeting at Colby College, nor a pulling up of chairs in the teacher's lunch room, nor a meeting with any of the other groups to which we belonged. I was accustomed to those. But this was new. This making contact with me individually, and especially here, where I lived, in the convent – this felt very personal.

He immediately explained, "I've signed up for a course at the University of Maine in Orono" (the campus, a one-hour drive north), in psychology," he added. "And it's such a good course, I wanted to tell you about it." So it was personal! The undertone itself spoke more loudly than our voices. With this visit, our first deliberately open personal meeting, the deepening of our third-way friendship became a plunge.

REVEALING LETTERS

I wrote to him within the hour. "I think we could become very close friends," I began. "But I remember e.e. cummings' line: 'Be of love more careful than of everything.' Your referring to the fact that suffering comes principally through human relations also puts me on guard; I wouldn't want to hurt you. I wouldn't want to mislead you."

I continued: "I could love you; in fact, perhaps I already do." There it was – I had said it! – yet, true to third-way thinking, I added: "But I would not want you to think I have doubts about celibacy; I do not. . . . A better way to characterize my attitude toward celibacy, rather than the word 'doubt' is to say, that because I have always preferred taking risks in order to grow, I am open to possibilities of growth wherever they may lead." I went on. "But, as far as I can see now, the gift of celibacy which has always been a positive experience in my life, will probably, please God, still be offered to me in that future I cannot foresee – because I want to be fully faithful to the Lord each step of the way. . . . Under these circumstances," I explained, "I hope we will become friends. I am not afraid. I feel free to be your friend. But I sense that you are even more sensitive than I. And I would not want to hurt you! Knowing all this, take the initiative in a way that is best for you. For my part," I concluded, "I see friendship as compatible with celibacy. I think it must be a gift – rare, precious, fragile." I had signed off: "Peace, Elaine."

In the P.S. I had invited him: "Do call me just 'Elaine,' unless you prefer 'Sister Maureen'," adding: "Do you mind if I call you 'Francis'?"

TWO WORLDS

These times were passionate for us on at least two fronts. While we were caught up in anti-war fervor that swept the country, our personal relationship was growing. I felt as if I had a foot in two worlds. The contrast was stark between living in the convent and teaching at its nearby Academy on the one hand, and, on the other, working among the students at Colby College.

For my second school year in Waterville, I had been reassigned from the 8th-grade parish school to the high school Academy. Now I would no longer have the opportunity to see Father Francis at lunchtime. I wondered if this move had anything to do with my relationship with him.

My involvement as a campus minister engaged me with students in a variety of ways. I regularly joined them for evening meals on certain days. For example, as part of a welcoming program for incoming college freshmen, I was asked to be on a panel discussing Archibald MacLeish's drama J.B.

Peace songs filled the airwaves, and I was singing and humming some of them while driving in the campus minister car: "Where Have All the Flowers Gone?" – "To Everything, Turn, Turn, Turn . . ." I would return from Colby on fire with the movement's work for peace only to get it dampened by convent conversation focused on changes in the religious habit. Here were my sisters considering whether we would wear blue habits, instead of black!

Surely, they cared about the war, but since they were removed from the college campus scene I experienced, I began to feel like an outsider. There was no doubt the life of prayer and silence still appealed to me. Yet, convent life, in general, was beginning to feel too limiting for my comfort. I felt less and less at home there. My doubts increased – whether I should stay in the convent, or not. Those doubts deepened, because of the following development.

TELEPHONE CONVERSATIONS

In early November, 1969, Francis and I began having long, daily telephone conversations. I would leave my cell on the third floor, descend two flights of stairs, and slip into the privacy of the chaplain's office on the first floor which Father Nick and I frequented by day, to call Francis. Although the content of our conversations is lost, one of my letters to him mailed on November 25 touches on one part of it: "I tend to go almost too deeply into things," I told him. "I verbalize and analyze a lot. In other words, just as you said about yourself, I've got that 'introspective, neurotic streak' in me, too." It was personal talk.

Our stealth-in-the-night conversations must have satisfied my heart enough to encourage me about one month later to send Francis this special card. The front flap reads: "A FRIEND" and the inside message, also in lovely calligraphy, finishes the sentence: "IS THE HALF OF MY SOUL." "St. Augustine" is in fine print. The only writing in my own hand, in black ink, reads: "12.9.69 henceforth and always."

The telephone blossomed our love. With mainly our voices as the medium to express ourselves, we could speak more freely, and at leisure.

As the nights wore on, our conversation became even intimate.

MOUNTING TENSION

In my mind, Francis and I had reached a stage that had all the earmarks of the third=way, the way of celibate love, but he had not yet verbalized that to me. My doubts about remaining in the convent were deepening, but it was a much more complex, nuanced, and agonizing matter than simply realizing I no longer belonged there, if indeed I did not. After all, "third=way celibate love" was celibate; the convent allowed that.

Like me, Francis was struggling to understand his own situation. "I am torn between loyalty to what I really consider to be outdated structures of the Church of my fathers and of my childhood," he wrote in his journal, "and the demands which personal growth, risk and search have imposed on me." A big admission came next: "I probably originally took refuge in the ecclesiastical system because it protected me from being vulnerable and open to persons." A kind of recent "breakthrough" had happened to him, he noted, after which – now – he had begun to be "increasingly person oriented."

Reflecting on the findings of a survey of eighty priests, seminarians, and laity conducted at the University of Alberta, Canada, to discover why many priests had personal problems, especially problems of identity, Francis wrote: "They may never have discovered themselves as persons because they had veered away from deep, personal, human involvements in their lives." And then he had added, "We find our identity in our relationships with others. The deeper and more intimate the relationships, the more secure the identity."

Francis clearly wanted what I was seeking – a deep, intimate relationship, something much like a third-way relationship. We were both, as he wrote, "anguished by this tension between structure and person." For my part, since I was lurching back and forth because of it, I knew I was up against something serious. It would require thorough analysis and deliberation. It was then I sought professional help.

PROFESSIONAL COUNSELING

The psychologist on staff in the Diocese, a Dr. Staffieri, lived in Portland, a ninety-minute drive from Waterville, so I took a round-trip bus ride there to consult with her. After our initial meeting, I sent her a list of "thirteen weighty reasons" I was considering why I should leave the convent.

A second letter, however, signals a shift. I wrote: "Very much has happened in a short time. One factor has changed the whole picture for me." Having cleared up a misunderstanding because of Francis' "great respect for my freedom," I wrote Dr. Staffieri that I had now "discovered to my deepest joy, that this celibate love is mutual. Now, everything falls into place!" – meaning that I was deciding to stay in the convent after all.

In reaffirming his commitment to me, Francis had made clear his intention to remain in the priesthood. I explained in my letter to her: "I can put up with the absence of deep relationships in the convent, since this one relationship breaks through my isolation."

The letter concludes on this note: "We can survive without genital sexuality. I won't say 'sexuality' in general, because sexuality pervades all human activities, but," I pointed out, "I can survive the convent with *this* relationship," hastening to add the important point: "If it were broken, I would leave the convent." In any case, I told Dr. Staffieri "this is my new balance sheet, the decisive one."

The third=way's celibate love was what mattered to me. I belabored the point in my letters to her: "Will this person whose love injects new meaning in my life, be the value according by which I will order all other values, taking for granted that love of Him, the Lord, is the ultimate meaning and source of our celibate love?"

I admitted: "For fifteen and a half years, I have been able to experience celibacy as fulfilling. That is a mature basis on which to build a new, and newly fulfilling relationship of celibate love, I think. In fact I firmly believe in it. It rests on a very finely attuned affinity of soul fed by our sharing of ideas and thoughts, and one another's persons, all via the telephone." I even dared to assert, "Through this man – the person whom I love (the priest I told you about) – I know God's Love more deeply than I ever have (and I have known love) before."

PIONEERS

The "new balance sheet" turned out, however, not as decisive as I had thought. Use of the word "survive" in my letter to Dr. Staffieri could have predicted that. But it worked for a while, because I had what meant everything to me – "this one relationship that breaks through my isolation."

Both of us seemed at one point confident our relationship could survive within the structures in which we lived, in spite of the tension between structure and person Francis had mentioned.

But then those tensions reappeared. I stated in a December letter to Francis: "I'm so full of thoughts I don't know where to start . . . I have all kinds of questions!" Apparently alluding to the third=way, I wrote, "I cannot toy with this idea, nor allow it to develop into a languishing kind of regret that I am celibate."

There was this new, stronger word, languishing. Some invisible wise hand must have guided my own to write it, warning me what could happen if I didn't stay alert. Would I want to remain in the convent languishing with regret for remaining celibate? I needed courage to look straight into the eye of our situation.

It was not a straight line Francis and I projected for ourselves on our way out. There were advances and retreats and forks in the road from which we returned to try another way. In the late sixties and early seventies something new was afoot, and we, a legion of us who left the convent, clerical priesthood, and religious life – were pioneers in its ranks without realizing it.

Pioneers like us would find one another in 1974, banding together to form a nation-wide community of "married priests" known as *CORPUS*. But in that time I'm portraying, five years earlier, in 1969, when our own tension was mounting, Francis and I, in Waterville, Maine, found ourselves having to scramble through the thickets, alone.

TRIDUUM RETREAT

Providentially, the end of the year had arrived when we Ursuline nuns made our annual "Triduum," or three day retreat. This was just what I needed – time to think things through, but especially to listen during those days of silence which ended on New Year's Day. It was a silence full of reflection. By this time, having gone back and forth between "I must leave!" and "No, I can stay now, since with this relationship I can survive," I looked into the face of the new awareness: "But what about this other thing – the languishing?"

By nature a person who probes her thoughts, which for weeks had me active in analyzing them, I trusted this retreat would put me in a new frame of mind for receptivity. Pondering the past would be the kind of non-activity that simply stops to look and listen – to be attentive. I was grateful for this opportunity at a juncture like this in my life. I wondered: "Do I really want to leave? Would I regret it?" I became keenly aware: "Here before me stands a life-changing choice, a personal decision with far-reaching consequences." I trusted Silence would speak to me.

REFLECTING ON MY PAST

I had invested in the convent over fifteen years of my life, but in an extended sense, I had also spent a year living in a nun-like way.

13

To their credit, the Ursuline nuns whose community I entered had required that aspirants complete one year of college beforehand. It was a way for the potential nun to make a more mature decision. Fresh out of high school, then, even though I had a boyfriend whom I invited to my freshman prom during the year preceding my entry into the convent, I spent time in daily meditation.

I rose early to go into the chapel at Mount Saint Mary's (in Hooksett, New Hampshire), just as the Sisters of Mercy, our teachers, did. Seated alone in the empty pews up front (with the nuns seated in the back) until the students' walked in for mass, a special book sat on my lap: *L' abandon à la Divine Providence* (also translated as *The Sacrament of the Present Moment*) by Jean Pierre de Caussade. It had been recommended to me by Mother Celine Pratt, the Ursuline nun who acted as my advisor during this year of preparation.

A good bit of time had been invested, I understood, in following this first vocation of mine. It had seemed to me the goal, if not the culmination, of my yet young life. I had embarked upon this vocation two months short of my nineteenth birthday. In the convent, I had found a great Love. Since a child, I had felt drawn to something more – through the calls of the loons at the lake, and the seamless chanting of the locusts in the still unspoiled meadow of our backyard.

My ruminations continued in this vein: Yes, I thought, and I also found more during my two and a half years of apprenticeship in the Novitiate (in Missouri.) I had fallen in love with the Psalms, ancient songs that united centuries of seekers in call and chant, and with the Gregorian chants. I had also been given the privilege one year, of proclaiming in Latin the birth of Jesus on Christmas Eve. In this dramatic, once-a-year chant from the "Roman Martyrology," the cantor's voice progressively rises as the proclamation situates the Nativity of Christ within the context of salvation history. By making reference to biblical events as well as to the Greek and

Roman worlds, the coming of Christ at Christmas is seen as the summit of both sacred and secular history. It still had a draw on me.

In the Juniorate, too, I had found more. During my studies at the College of New Rochelle, the study of Ontology had enthralled me. It was taught by an inspiring professor who didn't use a book. (The truth was, his own lectures surpassed anything in books.) I had taken copious notes in that course. Literature and poetry were also at the head of my list of loves. I could still visualize the wisteria hanging over our porch on Meadow Lane. When the towering apple tree on the other side of the gravel road was in full bloom, Keats' poems had uplifted my spirit. I lingered, too, over how John Donne's sonnet had played in my soul like an organ with all the stops pulled out. (We had been told that as nuns, we were the brides of Christ. For me, then, this had been, as it remained – wedding music.)

> Batter my heart, three person'd God; for, you
> As yet but knocke, breathe, shine, and seeke to mend;
> That I may rise, and stand, o'erthrow me, 'and bend
> Your force, to breake, blowe, burn and make me new.
> Take me to you, imprison me, for I
> Except you enthrall me, never shall be free . . .
>   "Holy Sonnet XIV"

As poignant as Donne's sonnet is, I had also found in the "Regnum Mundi" chant sung on my religious profession day in 1960 – a chant that, simply in remembering it now, moves me still. The day we pronounced our vows, the sisters in my "band," or group, and I had chanted in unison - *Regnum mundi, et omnem ornatum saeculi contempsi propter amorem Domini nostri Jesu Christi*. Translated it reads: "I have turned down the kingdom of the world and all worldly honors, for the sake of the love of the Lord Jesus Christ."

15

NEW UNDERSTANDINGS

During this Triduum Retreat, like the slow rising of the sun, a new truth rose before me: For all its riches, the spirituality in which I had been trained as a young nun was, nonetheless, confining. For example, the film *The Nun's Story* illustrates how women religious were treated by the male clergy. The Bishop in the film, true to ritual, addresses the young nuns receiving the religious habit with the words: "Come, my children." Unaware that the Women's Liberation Movement was developing at this time, I was nonetheless keenly aware of wider visions created by our own Vatican II Council: Women religious, consequently, would no longer abide being kept subservient to an all-male clergy.

Moreover, instead of living by a narrow spirituality by which I saw myself as God's bride (Hosea 2:19), for another example, I began espousing a more expansive spirituality which announces we are *all* God's bride. (Ephesians 5:32) The metaphor (in Revelation 21:2) depicts this micro truth as a truth of macro proportions. A spirituality that put clergy and religious on a higher plane than the laity, I had begun to realize, was unhealthy.

In the Novitiate I had read *The Pope Speaks*, believing as I had then, that God spoke through the pope. After religious studies at Providence College, I knew something was awry. Reading Dutch theologian Hans Kung's views told me why. The Vatican's hierarchal structure had arisen from Constantine's imperial Rome, after he had become a Christian. The early church which Jesus' example had inspired, on the other hand, was a prophetic community.

In the light of my retrospect on the Vatican II Council held only four years earlier, I pondered my own future. I had come to understand that for me, a convent life mainly centered on the ethereal world (the way I had been living it) would not do. It could not hold the expansive God of unending discoveries and infinite, sumptuous diversity revealed in the world

16

which now called me.

As my Triduum intuitions grew stronger, a seed of urgency got planted: I must leave the convent to explore for myself what that prophet of our time, Teilhard de Chardin, had announced – that we do in fact live in The Divine Milieu. One does not have to be a nun to experience God as Lover, I was realizing. That experience might be even more richly expressed as a married woman.

AMBIVALENT ABOUT CELIBACY

I had to admit I was also ambivalent about celibacy. Why else would I have brought with me to Waterville an *NCR* interview with Charles Davis, a well-known, highly respected priest? The news of his leaving the clerical priesthood and marrying had recently added to the ferment among progressive Catholics.

It's a "difficult and dangerous vocation," Davis had told the interviewer – unless celibacy is "really met by a love of God that is mystic." He explained how easy it is for the celibate to "remain in a state of a self-protective kind of selfishness, not in the crude sense, but in the sense of isolation that can be present together with very great self-sacrifice in helping others." I myself had used the word "isolation" in reporting to Dr. Staffieri when I wrote about Francis: ". . . this one relationship breaks through my isolation."

Davis' other argument applied to me also: "Helping others is not quite the same as living fully yourself with another person whom you love." The reason "the celibate is cut off from the spiritual discipline inherent in marriage," namely, being truly vulnerable to another "in the safety of love," Davis explained, "is that he is cut off from that kind of intimacy." In the context of this retreat, his conclusion forcibly struck me – that the celibate, therefore, can be "preserved" from a true revelation of him or herself. Now *that* was something to wonder about. No, it was even something to *worry* about!

I began to view the marriage vocation in the grander, more noble context it deserves, as the great sacrament it is. Marriage is not only a visible sign of an invisible reality, but it is a metaphor referring to the relationship between God and humanity. (Ephesians 5:32; Revelations 21:9) This possibility was actually what I was secretly, unknowingly desiring (I was shocked to realize) – a marriage union with *Francis* that would be a small but clear mirror of the love God Is.

MUTUAL CHRISTMAS CARDS

In my Triduum retreat, the "mature relationship" theme haunted me anew. Francis had sent me, just a few weeks earlier, a Christmas card of the Annunciation, painted by Roger van der Weyden, a Flemish master. It portrayed the Angel Gabriel addressing Mary in prayer. In my response, I had sent him my own unconventional Christmas card. In my best handwriting in black ink on four sheets of parchment paper, I had copied from the Hebrew scriptures (or "Old Testament") book, Song of Songs, carefully selected passages from chapters one through eight. I prefaced them with this explanation to Francis: "For several years now, these words have expressed my relationship to the Lord better than any, from any other source. But now they're for you too. I found myself spontaneously turning to these words to express my love for you."

I continued disclosing how I experienced our third-way relationship: "I know, Dear, that you cannot reach the deepest depths where lies the incommunicability which constitutes the very person; only the Lord God Creator can do that." Here is the bold part: "But your only barrier is human limitation itself; I will put up none, ever. Wherever the Lord may enter, and I have always been fully open to Him, you may, because I love you, Francis, beyond expression. My Christmas gift to you is my self, my love, and my promise that they be a lasting offer. Forever."

Is there a different tone in the audacity of this letter? Since it is so intimate, does it teeter on the edge of impropriety coming from a nun close to the eve of her grasping she must leave the nunnery? Is it an expression of the exclusiveness I had mentioned in a letter to Francis which I saw as "incompatible with celibate love?" Does it inadvertently reveal an evolution in my desire, a leaning toward marriage itself? Or, since it was innocently chaste in its understanding, does it express third-way experience at its deepest?

In what direction did my Christmas card point, I still cannot say for sure. Projecting myself back that many years, as well as examining it now, I could go back and forth in my interpretation.

Among my four pages of quotes from Song of Songs, I share this one. I had copied nineteen separate verses from this book of the Bible. At the end of the passage from 3:4: "I found him whom my soul loveth: I held him and I will never let him go. . ."* (with "never" underlined) I had attached an asterisk. At the bottom of the page I had written: "*my favorite line."

CLARITY

Even though unanswered questions abounded in my mind, I knew by the end of my Retreat Triduum what my next step had to be. Even knowing that Francis had decided to remain in the priesthood, by then, I could not be shaken from that conviction. What would happen now? I could not know. Which one of various possibilities would be realized? I was in the dark here, too.

But, as I sat in the convent parlor awaiting the entry of the "Provincial" (my regional superior) to apprise her of my decision, its light was strong and steady. I felt as certain of its goodness as I might standing before the judgment seat of God. Though outdated imagery for me now as I write this, and maybe even then, it nevertheless worked: I knew with a kind of empowering certainty that were I to die, my new resolve would be upheld as a decision of integrity. I felt euphoric. It was my own decision, arrived at through my own soul. It was not Francis' decision for me. He would not have thought of swaying me in any way. It was instead – a decision made because of him, yes, but – a decision initiated by many reasons that converged for me.

WHY DID I LEAVE THE CONVENT?

Looking back, in writing this story about my own exodus (the word Francis used later in describing his departure), I came upon a truth only time and distance can unveil. The finding, however, is enclosed in a clue, something I said. Sheer repetition preserved it. When anyone asked me, after I left the convent, why I had done so, I found myself repeating the same story. Using the word "convergence," I would tick off point by point, in going through my list: this, that, this and this, I'd say, explaining each one.

My list included Pope Paul VI's encyclical Humanae Vitae, issued in 1968, which prohibited all forms of birth control. His unilateral decision shocked the Catholic world, including me, enough to be added to my "convergence" list. The revitalizing Vatican II Council had established a principle of "collegiality" and "subsidiarity" to promote proper collaboration between clergy and laity. But here was the pope violating that principle by rejecting a majority report in favor of a minority report. One cardinal called it a "Galileo affair," and author Allienne Beck – "an exploding supernova fireball." I told friends, "My church delusions went right down the drain after that. It demythologized my thinking."

The expression "convergence of many factors" was an apt one to convey the complex process involved in deciding to change the course of my life. Since the doors of liberation in my thinking opened widest with my first summer of study at Providence College in 1966, I repeatedly told those who inquired that it had taken me four years to come to this.

20

The clue locked in my memory to which I refer, however, is something other than this birth-control encyclical "convergence factor." No, the clue embedded in my words, which was the most notable item on my "Why I Left" list, was this admission: "I discovered I was a woman in love."

CHAPTER NOTE

The "convergence" expression I consistently used from 1969 onwards, (which reached me through the years, thanks to memory) became, as I wrote this chapter, the key that unlocked the door to my current discovery: Although I had originally planned the title of this chapter to read "The Third-Way," I now realize that my journey (and Francis', too, I dare conclude) took us, not only from celibacy into marriage, but, from celibacy *through* the third-way, before it led us into marriage. I have therefore entitled this chapter more accurately – "*Through* the Third-Way."

At that moment of leave-taking and setting out onto a newly chosen path, however, in addition to the buoyancy of grace which brought joy supporting my transition – all I had to go by was trust. Trust that I would again be carried through new future challenges. In one of my letters to Francis, I had written, "The awe, joy, and awareness of having freely and deliberately opened a door to you as my friend, reigns over the half-formed fear, or sense of insecurity we all live with, or, more precisely, an awareness of risk. Risk is a good, in any case." I took the risk and discovered it was indeed – *a good*.

My responding to a call to leave the convent, anticipated by little more than a year the thinking behind an article published in *NCR* by Reverend Anthony T. Padovano, at the time, a priest, theologian, and seminary professor. (He also later left the clerical priesthood, and it was he who was instrumental in founding CORPUS.) To paraphrase his view: One who is called *into* religious life might just as well be called *out* of that priesthood or convent. Father Padovano's conclusion that what matters most is "fidelity to the Spirit" mirrored my own greatest desire. More than anything, I wanted then as now, to be faithful to Spirit. Like Mary (portrayed in Francis' Christmas card replicating the Annunciation) who responded to the angel with a "yes" – "Ecce ancilla Domini" (Behold the handmaid of the Lord), this little Mary that I was, Sister Maureen, also said, "Yes!"

CHAPTER TWO
Underground

Two things stand out about my departure from the convent: the palpable attraction between Francis and me as I stood before him at the rectory door saying goodbye; and the realization – first intuited in my final meeting with my superior – I was saving my life!

It's strange to admit that in this moment of such emotion, I don't remember who took me away; it had to be my parents who picked me up on the day of my farewell.

The drive south to where my parents still lived took over two hours. Once we left the turnpike, I relaxed at the sight of the one-lane roads. Their curves rose and descended toward Springvale, the valley of my hometown where I was born. My parents' two businesses at the center of the town square stood side by side below their upstairs apartment. As a child, with our Spitz dog "Tiny" next to me, I would lie prone on the kitchen floor, my face turned so one ear could get closer to catch the sounds of conversation below in Marie's Beauty Salon where both my mother, Marie, and my father, Joe, worked.

Because the Order of Saint Ursula I had entered was semi-cloistered, this was the first time in fifteen and a half years that I was reentering my parents' home. There was much to get done. Clothing came first, as I had nothing to wear but simple black and white religious garb. So my mother and I traveled to Boston by train to choose a wardrobe for me, as we had chosen clothing for her Mademoiselle's Fashion Shop during my high school years.

I was ready to step into my new life, with my shoulder-length naturally curly hair newly styled, no longer hidden under a veil, and a wardrobe suiting me. I had left my sisters in the convent and my students in the classroom in Waterville, midyear, without saying goodbye.

AUGUSTA

Years later at a yoga weekend workshop in Cambridge, Massachusetts, when a handful of us walked to Porter Square for lunch at Masao's Kitchen, I noticed that a young woman among us looked familiar. Once seated at table, suddenly recognizing each other, we simultaneously burst into tears. "We didn't know where you went!" Roxann cried out. "Oh, I'm so sorry," I was quick to answer. "I wasn't allowed to tell you why I was disappearing between semesters." By then I could confess that the *where* I had decided to go to live and work was Augusta, and mainly because of Francis.

Augusta, the state capital, was not only a half-hour's drive from where Francis was still serving in the parish, it also offered job opportunities. I was poised to explore those now and was ready to look for housing.

Some memories of my outer world during the two years when Francis' and my relationship had to go underground, return slowly, because my inner world was so large then. What stands out about the earliest days is driving my parents' Buick between Springvale and Augusta. I found comfort during those back and forth trips fixing my attention on the horizon toward which the car and I were advancing.

Though I hadn't been aware of Jack Kerouac's novel *On The Road*, published thirteen years earlier, I had the distinct sense of being *on the road* in some way myself – my own road, moving away from a former life and advancing toward my new life. Because I was moving more from *within* than from *without*, the looming horizon's steadiness and the turnpike's single-mindedness, gave physical expression to my inner exodus.

JOB AND APARTMENT

When I wasn't taking state exams preliminary to looking for a job in Augusta, I stayed overnight at the home of a sympathetic couple in Waterville who knew of Francis' and my continuing connection. The job I was looking for would have to be different from teaching, my main profession for the past ten years, because it was halfway through the school year. Luckily there were openings at the Department of Human Health and Services (DHHS) in the Disability Unit.

In addition to the job I acquired, doing secretarial work, it was fortunate I also found a miniscule third-floor attic apartment close to the DHHS brick building. It took five minutes to walk down the hill past the Lithgow Library to reach it. Not only that, I moved into the apartment on the same day Mr. Hathaway's letter arrived giving me instructions for my first day of work.

The apartment, with separate access at the side of a handsome old home, was literally an attic space at the head of winding stairs. A large closet door faced the entryway which itself, on its left side, functioned as a dining room, large enough for only a small table and two chairs. To the right was a small oblong bathroom with barely enough room for the toilet, tub, and sink. Next to it, squeezed into a similar space was a kitchen with a small refrigerator, cabinets and sink, but no stove. Instead, on the counter, a two-sided hot plate and a separate boxy oven built for long-term use, was all I had with which to cook meals.

To the left of this compact assemblage of necessary rooms, a long, wide room with a low ceiling served as bedroom and office. The only furniture here was a single-bed mattress on the floor and a small desk and chair. At the end of this cavernous space, one small window looked out on a large maple tree at this third-floor height and onto Elm Street below. I also kept in this room a record player and LP records given me by Francis. Playing his favorite Brahms, Beethoven, and Mahler records brought me much consolation and support in between his visits. But that is getting ahead of my story.

GETTING SETTLED

With job and apartment secured, I opened a bank account and a box at the post office. I also found the church where I'd go for Sunday mass. Having met some of my neighbors, too, I could now settle in. One neighbor I visited regularly was an elderly woman at the end of Elm Street whom I called Aunt Edie.

After work I also enjoyed spending time in the library down the street. Besides keeping up with the news, I was curious to look for new recipes to add to those I had cooked at home with my parents. I still use one of the two I found, for guests who aren't vegetarian – an especially tasty Chicken Adobo recipe from the Philippines. Another recipe I tried, fascinated me; it had been a favored food among Ashkenazi Jews. Called by a Yiddish name, *grieven*, it consists of scraps of chicken skin baked until they're crisp. It was good to be doing my own cooking instead of relying on menus chosen by the convent cook.

Secretarial work at the DHHS perfectly fit my unique circumstances. With Mr. Hathaway's ready approval and other office workers' relaxed acceptance, I would get all my work done and then use the extra time to type my thesis required for the Religious Studies MA degree I was pursuing. With only one season left to complete my five summers of study at Providence College, I was determined not to let it slip by, even if I'd be attending, not as a nun now, but as a secular.

For books, Dr. Thomas Longstaff, archeologist and Colby College professor of religious studies, let me borrow some of his own and arranged for me to get all I needed from the Bangor Theological Library north of Augusta. I looked forward to getting those packages in the mail. The thesis topic I had chosen contrasted the "just-war" theory with the non-violent approach of Jesus. This project gave my life a helpful focus. In fact, just as my paying job provided unexpected extra time to type my thesis, I also found it fulfilling work.

Besides Aunt Edie, I made friends with a couple who lived nearby. I met them during my daily walk to the cemetery at the top end of Winthrop Street's steep hill. In exploring other streets in my own neighborhood, I also came upon a large white mansion that I knew well. In 1953, seventeen years earlier, I had come to this St. Paul's Retreat House for a weekend retreat with my high school senior class. By the end of that weekend I had come to the decision to enter the convent. Upon returning home, I returned my engagement ring to my boyfriend.

I had no confidants in Augusta, but at this juncture in my life I had little inclination and time to seek even women friends, since my relationship with Francis already consumed my desire and extra time.

SUPPORTIVE COUNSELOR

I did, though, come upon an unexpected ally. The priest, theologian, and seminary professor, Father Anthony T. Padovano, to whom I had written my gratitude for his article in a 1971 issue of *NCR*, responded to my letter with encouragement. In him I found a friend I could trust, a counselor, and even the confidant with whom I shared Francis' concerns and mine.

He was still in the priesthood at the time, and I, one who had left her Order. His article had been targeted to encourage precisely people like me.

The approval he gave me in our correspondence had, therefore, in my eyes, all the more authority. Fresh out of the convent, I still respected authority, that is, *genuine* authority that discerns and judges wisely, rather than authority that only adheres rigidly to rules. I entrusted Father Padovano with the more personal details of Francis' and my relationship.

LOVE LETTERS

I got the first of forty-three extant letters Francis wrote me within three days of my leaving the convent. He joked that getting sick with a temperature enabled him to write me four letters within nine days. At first shy, their tone warmed considerably with each letter. By the third one, I had become the "dear one," and in the fourth, he addressed me with "Hi little cherished one." Francis' love letters captivated me with their tenderness and creativity. I delighted in the names he gave me and those he used for himself in penning the salutation and complimentary closing parts of his letters. For example: "Take care Little Red Riding Hood," "Hello Alice in Wonderland!" "Cheerio dear one." "Until the next time, I am your unorthodox, renegade human friend," and, in his sixth letter, on January 31: "Closed with a kiss we haven't had yet."

Francis reiterated in his second letter what he had told me in person after I brought it up again in writing – that he would probably be a "transitional person" for me. "Yes, I guess that is one of the ideas in my mind," he wrote. "In my judgment you have a great deal to offer as a person, and you really need more in your life than I can promise you, given the ambiguities in the clerical profession." He realized I might not like hearing this. "Actually," he explained, "neither of us can really know now (except you by feminine intuition – and I believe in it) but we can only gradually experience it by patience and sensitivity – whether it is possible or advisable for you to fashion your life and your style of living on a necessarily tenuous relationship with me. It even remains to be demonstrated," he wrote, "whether in fact, such a fragile, tenuous shared-existence is sufficient to sustain you in depth and growth. OK? That's just a tiny inkling of my thought about you and the future."

All but a few of my letters still exist, but my prompt response commenting on Francis' idea of being for me just "a transitional person" pleased him. "Thanks for your very balanced and understanding response to my serious comments in one of my letters," he wrote. "Do you know how I have been describing to myself the present and future of your relationship with me? I say to myself 'I am preparing a place in my life for her'– and to me that is the warmest, most intimate and tender reality that is being expressed by a few simple words. It kind of leaves me breathless!"

When I asked Francis what he meant by calling himself "unorthodox" and "renegade," he interpreted it like this: "Maybe I just like to scourge myself. I guess I like to think it is part of me, just one of the qualities which makes me who I am. So I express my uniqueness in a kind of offbeat, free-wheeling way in relating especially to chosen, intimate, special people like you."

JOURNALS AND MARRIAGE ENCOUNTER NOTEBOOKS

Since Novitiate days, when a nun is in training, I had been keeping journals. Francis also kept one. After I left the convent, living alone in an attic apartment in Augusta, I needed to write my reflections more than ever. It was journal writing along with prayer that got me through the crucible of Francis' and my "underground" period, made challenging by alternating reunions and separations. It was a time of great romance, because secrecy enhances romance. But there was agony along with the ecstasy.

The ecstasy came first. Francis' and my first unforgettable meeting took place on February 2, two weeks after I had left the convent. Francis, having removed his priest's collar and dressed like any other man, had booked one room for both of us at the Wishing Well Motel in Winthrop, a nearby village. It was the first time we had lain together, the first time so physically close. But we were chaste as quiet spoons lying next to each other. In his personal journal, Francis had characterized it as "Wishing Well's tenderly trusting exploration."

Six years later during our Marriage Encounter Weekend at the Franciscan Monastery in Kennebunk Maine, Francis brought it up again. The method used at these weekends to get couples dialoguing in a deep way was to give each person a notebook in which each would answer given questions. In answer to the question: "What are the qualities which most attracted me to you?" he had written: "At Wishing Well, I recall being impressed with your total trust, that it was right and good for us to be intimate (at least to some degree). Simply that you had an absolute and unquestioning trust in my judgment in giving yourself to me in our first really physical encounter. Your sense that you were right for me, and I was right for you, had all the markings of being both altogether reckless and yet thoroughly responsible."

FIRST MORATORIUM

A shock awaited me, however, when I read Francis' letter written four days after our intimate night. It must be told in his own words:

Sacred Heart Church
February 6, 1970

Dear Elaine:
I was a little more than mildly concerned at some of the implications in your most recent letters. I also felt really guilty that I had misled you some way – but I assure you it was unintentional.
I am going to give you a practical example to try to point out to

you what I mean. Here goes: if Pope Paul (God save us) came out to-morrow and said that priests could marry, I can realistically envision waiting a minimum of a year and a maximum of two years before marrying you, thus giving you time to adjust after 15 years in the convent and time for our relationship to mature and mellow. Alas, we both know this is a condition contrary to fact.

So I am repeating what I told you before – I have no definite nor indefinite plans to leave the priesthood – thus I will not be free to marry anyone.

All you can expect from me is an underground relationship. I feel guilty because, being a man, I know it is my role to really advise you to find your own place, but I haven't come to this yet – I really mean it – but I know that unless I end it, you will go hoping in vain.

You have to follow your head, Elaine, as well as your heart. The fact that you are now entertaining the idea of children (which is marvelous and perfectly wonderful) could indicate to you that I am not the person who can fill the role you are looking for. We talk about honesty. Let's really look at honest facts. Sure it's romantic – we can be tender and sensitive with each other. Where is it leading for you?

Please do not decide to ignore these honest facts under the illusion that you are giving a sacrificial love in return for some vague illusive return from me. You deserve a loving husband and children of your own – not some kind of shadowy vague tenuous unreality. Don't undersell yourself or delude yourself. See the contrast between the two.

Please remember that if it became known in Waterville of even a casual relationship that I was having with you, my effectiveness in my profession could be dead. That's simply the way it is.

You know me well enough to know that it pains me to point these things out to you. At the same time I am aware that the female psyche is less cerebral and more intuitive when it comes to these judgments. I could have wished it were otherwise.

Another thing, little one: you must jealously guard yourself in Augusta. Unless I miss my guess – any tourist home would take a dim view of a single girl having a man come to her room, and you would have an unsavory reputation overnight.

There are a lot of things one doesn't reflect on in 15 years of convent life. But you knew you would have to learn new ropes – that's why I dare to point these things out to you.

I am –your bitchy friend,
companion and counselor,
Frank

I was in pain, too. He was calling for a moratorium. Heedless of the snowstorm a few days later, I went out into the night to walk in the dark. Alone in the middle of an empty street, I wept aloud in the howling wind.

Fortunately for both of us, this suspension of our relationship lasted less than a month. But not knowing the outcome of a harrowing period at its beginning, one must endure a painful decision as if it were permanent.

It was Francis who initiated its end. Again, no summary can replace his own words:

March 5, 1970

Dear Elaine:
I know Fr. Joe Brannigan is meeting with you tonight and that I will be talking with him tomorrow about us, for the last time before he goes west.

By reflection, analyzing and quiet time, plus my talks with Joe about myself and you, I have been able to clarify some of my needs and clear up some of the uncertainty. My instincts tell me that possibly not much will be accomplished by extending our time of separation, unless you now wish to do so for your own reasons.

But before I arrange to see you — (sometime in the next two weeks) I wanted you to have my thoughts on the only possible premise for me to build a relationship with you. Premises are always subject to alteration, but only by mutual agreement. I am saying this about premises because I sense that you do evolve from one premise to another very rapidly, and this is one of the aspects that threatens me and shakes me up! Here goes:

1) From my viewpoint — as a basic premise, we will begin a relationship to see if we would be able to build compatibility with each other — to see if we could make a good couple should priests be allowed to marry.

For example: If this works out well, and a distant diocese should be the first to assign married priests — I could see our pulling up roots and building a life together in such a distant diocese — as a married priest.

One factor about us, now and in the foreseeable future, could bring me tension and unhappiness — if you, or our relationship, became a threat to my present lifestyle as a functioning priest.

2) From the viewpoint of your expectations — if your basic thrust and deepest desires take concrete form in the explicit hope of marriage and children within some definite time span, say two to five years — if that represents your concrete expectations now — then we leave each other now in all fairness to both of us.

a) You to pursue your goal in a certain manner

b) Me to follow my own, wherever it may lead.

I know that there are many imponderables and many vexing questions which we would have to work out mutually, should all signals be go — but these can be attacked together, as long as we both realize the

33

premises I have outlined, and the expectations each of us have.

    I don't expect you to write or call me in answer to this letter; in fact I ask that you do not do so. I will be calling you within two weeks. That will give you time to reflect on the contents of my letter; you could even write down your thoughts if you like, so that we can better come to an understanding of each other, and thus share them when I see you.

    I have expressed myself and my inner thoughts as clearly as possible in their relation to you. I am trying to be as honest and direct with you as I can. I believe you are a person I could treasure – I respect you and care for you deeply; all the more reason why I believe it is important now for both of us to put labels on what we expect of each other and our relationship.

    If one of us knows now that he cannot fulfill the expectations of the other – now is the time to face it squarely and leave each other free to go separately. Even such a short separation as two weeks has helped me to view us from a distance, and see the possibility of an honest mutual decision and permanent separation. I have suffered my own kind of anguish during these two weeks, not the least of which was my thoughts about you and how you were doing.

    Until later,
    your man child,
    F.

I latched onto Francis' mentioning I could write down my thoughts if I'd like. I certainly wanted to, and so I wrote him the following response:

Augusta, Maine
Sunday, March 8, 1970 – 9:15 P.M.

Dear Frank,

I have been thinking for two days, so these thoughts do not come from the spur of the moment:

I awoke yesterday with the realization that my expectation is really exactly what you described as your expectation. If you look back, Frank, I think you will agree, that although I have envisaged marriage, I have never done so outside the context of your priestly ministry.

I do accept your premises. But I want to say much more than simply that I do.

1) About your expectations: I perfectly understand, Frank, how you feel about not leaving the priesthood. You may have felt that my expectations urged you to leave – but if you did, it was no more than your feeling (vaguely) threatened, because not only have I never asked you to leave, but I have never, even in my own mind and heart, desired that you do so. I have felt the way you felt about my decision: desiring to leave you free, wanting you to follow your own inner need. As a matter of fact, I like to see you as a priest. I can see that the church needs more than ever priests like you. If you think of what I've told you, Frank – about being willing to wait years; about our perhaps getting married "in our old age" – and the very night you left, I told you that you needn't leave the priesthood for me – you will realize that I, on my part, have not given you any pressure to leave.

2) My expectations: Perhaps your having felt threatened in that way resulted from my seeing – and hearing me say – that I want to be your wife. I admit that I want to. I can't change that desire, because I love you. But my desire for marriage with you is NOT tied to a definite time span.

35

It's true that at one point I told Joe that I could wait two to even five years. But you have to understand what I meant by this. I meant that I could wait that long (with you, but not separated from you) for the uncertainty to get cleared up. That's quite a different thing from saying that I expect marriage within that time frame.

But there is a new element in my awareness that I want to explain. It doesn't change the fact that I accept your premise (I do not have an expectation different from yours), but it is a new realization. I don't need to tell you this, but I keep nothing from you.

Before our two days together in New Hampshire, I could envisage the possibility of remaining single all my life. I know – and still believe – that I could be happy just loving you, unmarried.

But, realizing now how important sex is in our relationship, I see that, although I do find justification for an underground relationship for an indefinite number of years, I could not justify for myself such a relationship for life. If there were no sexual intimacy in it, that would be impossible, superhuman.

None of this affects what you described as your expectation, namely 1) that we ascertain "if we would make a good couple should priests be allowed to marry," and 2) that your present life style as a functioning priest be not threatened.

You said, Frank, that my evolving rapidly from one premise to another threatens you. I hope that, as you understand me better, you will see that this trait of mine is not as threatening as it may seem.

First of all, I don't expect that everything I intuit is ripe for action. I have been very free telling you everything that's on my mind, but I'm aware that my intuitions are only initial, undeveloped probing. I really can wait – and I want to give them time to mature. In a sense my opening my mind so fully to you has been a kind of trustful surrender, a kind of submission of my ideas to you with the expectation that you will comple-

ment me, and them, by your own pondering and testing of their validity.

Frank, dear, I believe that what I am saying is really true. Is this not proven by the fact that I willingly cooperated with your decision to call a moratorium on our relationship? Did you find me reluctant to wait upon your need for it?

In fact, I accepted it positively, seeking to profit from it myself. Painful as it was, it added depth to our relationship; it enriched it. Somehow I grew through it, Frank.

So you see, although I may seem to leap ahead, those leaps are taken only imaginatively at first. I would not actually go ahead without you. In fact, my darling, I sincerely believe (just as I physically adjusted to your changing sleeping positions (smiley face) that love will so attune me to you – in your whole person – that, while remaining myself – I will just sense by some sensitive sixth sense, how to keep in step with you.

The key to meeting the "vexing questions" as you so perceptively observed, lies in our working them out together. Evolution is another key, I think. I agree with what you said – that where premises may be subject to alteration, they will become so, only by mutual agreement.

I have been thinking about your idea of our seeing if we would be able to "build compatibility with each other." It seems clear to me that we are sexually compatible. During our separation, I found solace and pleasure in reading, study, and music. I realized that we've hardly begun to share our interests. We've had so little time together, and then we couldn't get enough of love-making – so there are whole areas yet to be shared and discovered about each other and our interests.

When I saw The New Yorker in the library last week, it made me "nostalgic." (Smiley face.) I thought of how we could mutually enrich one another – with you telling me about what you found to your liking, and I, sharing some of Gandhi's insights I'm discovering in writing my thesis. Here's my estimate or my guess, about our undertaking: I will like you, *as well as love you, which of course, I already do!*

Call soon, dear! I'm ready now to end our moratorium!

My experience seems to have paralleled yours in some ways. For me, the moratorium put objectivity and perspective in our relationship. Without a lessening of my love for you, I nevertheless, like you, could see "the possibility of an honest, mutual decision of permanent separation."

I prayed, spontaneously, and very earnestly. At first, I prayed that we would not become permanently separated. But then, realizing how finite and fallible human understanding is, I asked God to give us light, wisdom and strength to make the right, the true and the good decision.

The moratorium went deep. It was real. "ANGUISH" as you said, and to me, real fasting and a kind of inner purification and chastening. But then, by the second week – it was peace in real abandonment to God's own wise will.

So, my love, having the ability to choose otherwise right now, I choose to return to you, having the same expectation you have.

I'm actually happy about having had that difficult suspension of communication between us. It proves to me that the foundation we're going to try to build on, is solid: that we are coming together, not by reason of having been emotionally swept off our feet, nor by my stubbornly clinging to you. I even feel that it is not by my own choice alone, nor yours alone, that we are about to return to each other. Instead, I firmly believe our reunion has been provided by our Provident God. It is the answer to my honestly questioning prayer of abandonment.

Now I'll have to use mental telepathy on you to call me soon, because I'm so eager to see you, my love.

Your Elaine

Francis' letters and mine demonstrate how, through our process of discernment while apart, followed by our "dialogue," we came to new self-understandings. Now, however, we had to grapple with what he called "vexing questions."

What we each desired could not be joined, priesthood and marriage, and all because of man-made rules. We knew that St. Peter, one of Jesus' first apostles, had had a mother-in-law. And we knew that the Catholic Church of the East, in "the *Eastern* rite" from the beginning, had had a tradition of accepting married men into the priesthood. But since recent debate at the Vatican remained unsettled (whether or not to change this *Roman* celibacy discipline), we were in a sense, kept in midair until its resolution. Love, however, (and knowledge) found a way to deal with the uncertainties we faced, because, as I wrote: "love inherently has authority over law."

UNDERGROUND MARRIAGE

Because of our background as students of theology, Francis and I knew what constitutes marriage. It is not something bestowed through a sacrament by church clergy; rather, it consists of the exchange of vows between two people committing themselves to one another. St. Thomas Aquinas, considered the Church's greatest theologian and philosopher, said that marriage is primarily instituted by what he called the "first cause" of mutual consent between two people, which is then sealed by the "final cause of intercourse."

A 2012 *New York Review of Books* article, "The Myth About Marriage," gives supporting evidence now for our general impression then. In it, Garry Wills quotes scholars who declare that until the eleventh or thirteenth centuries "there was no such thing as a Christian wedding ceremony in the Latin church, and throughout the Middle Ages there was no single church ritual for solemnizing marriage between Christians.'"

Unequivocally aware that priesthood and marriage are not *intrinsically* incompatible, Francis and I privately took our vows of marriage, pledging ourselves to each other. We referred to ourselves as husband and wife, adding the word *underground* to our new self-chosen titles. When I wrote to Father Anthony about this, he picked up on our language. For example, in his April 5 response to my first letter, he wrote: "I do hope that the joy and consolation of your marriage and the grace and peace of your husband's ministry may support the two of you so that you will continue to give your lives and your love to a world that has so desperate a need for life and for love." It is interesting to note he did not add the word "underground" as we had.

Francis listed in his Journal the five or so places where we spent time together during our two-year "underground" period. When out of town, we were naturally more at ease and felt freer in public because of anonymity.

One of those places was a lake cottage owned by the "sympathetic Waterville couple." As educated church leaders in our parish and diocese, they understood that our predicament was created by church laws, actively being debated at the Vatican; it was *not* God-ordained.

By the end of our first holiday at a hotel in North Conway, New Hampshire, in late April, my joy was buoyant. By the end of the first evening, I told Francis I could now sing my "Nunc Dimittis." That is like saying, as the prophet Simeon did when he saw Jesus in Mary's arms – Jesus, for whom he had waited a long time – "I'm ready to die now."

That weekend was the first time I had drunk hard liquor. In the convent, on Holy Thursday, we nuns would sip on a small glass of wine. But this was a Manhattan. Because it tasted good, and unaware of the effects of liquor (even if I was not rapidly downing it), Francis used the opportunity to teach me how to drink liquor. "Very slowly," he advised. I admit the Manhattan likely added to my great joy, but not to the extent I would have sung a Nunc Dimittis over *that*, not even if it was a first drink. No. My Nunc Dimittis was about losing my virginity.

Once in my apartment by Sunday night, I wrote: "Re-discovery of myself in affinity with F. Such fulfillment that to have reached even this beginning, a beginning of such ecstasy, is enough meaning for my life. Ready to sing my Nunc Dimittis if necessary, but I want, more than ever, to live!"

While at work in the office the next morning, I was grateful a typewriter sat before me instead of students. Experiencing a sexual relationship for the first time in my life at age thirty-four, how could I possibly concentrate on class preparation and engagement with students when my mind was absorbed in ensuing and future days with what my journal jottings expressed: "One's own soul in another . . . merging of subjective worlds . . . *Deep* things happening to me. Intimacy being established – what my whole life's desire has been driving toward, etc. . . . I'm next closest to being him. Surrender to absorbing wonder of richness of our love. Endless ecstasy – never reach the end of it. Love – bottomless source, ever refreshing spring."

JOB HUNTING – PARENTS' VISIT

In spite of, or along with, my preoccupation with "us," I was tending to a lot of practical things, including looking specifically for a teaching position in the area. I knew that by autumn I would want to get back into the classroom where I belonged. An inquiry at Gardiner Area High School, about seven miles from Augusta, led to two interviews with the Superintendent in May. My contract assigned me to teach high school English to juniors for their 1970-71 school year.

Sometime that spring I had two visits. Two sisters from Mount Merici Convent came to see me, younger nuns about my age. I was grateful for this kindness, even if the visit only strengthened me in my decision. "Life everywhere, of course, is somehow confined," I wrote in my journal. "But I have room to move now. I am free to be myself and to follow my own call. The rule-bound nature of convent living, for me, blocked off natural responses to life."

The second was a visit from my parents. Stepping off the top of the winding stairs into my attic apartment, they entered the miniscule dining room in which Francis and I ate when he could visit me. I showed my parents around the tiny apartment. When I opened the closet door, inviting them to notice its spaciousness, my mother spotted a rust-colored sweater I had not expected she would see. Its ample size clearly signaled it was a man's ski sweater. I have forgotten the wording of both her question and my response. But it was decidedly an awkward moment.

UNDERGROUND HONEYMOON

With my master's thesis completed on June 9, I made plans to return to Providence College for my last summer session. But not before Francis and I took, in mid-June, what we called our honeymoon. We spent an entire week in Truro, Massachusetts, a town two hours from Boston near Cape Cod in an area known as the Outer Cape. There, Francis wrote, we "reveled in sand dunes" and, at another stop en route back home, at Wingaersheek Beach and Bass Rocks in Gloucester, we "jogged, alive!"

Our life-long love of cooking and especially collaborating in the kitchen took its roots that week. We used the Chicken Adobo recipe I had shared with Francis. For that reason, in addition to walking in the dunes and by the ocean, we spent a good bit of time in our cabin. A good bit of time also doing what honeymooners do, on this our *real* and first of two honeymoons. Underground or not, we were husband and wife. I wrote: "Such ecstasy! Only half-living before."

Less than a month later, writing from Sebago Lake where Francis had spent a week with two priest friends before opening the girls' camp which he directed, he wrote: "By the way, I used that chicken recipe you gave me with mixed success. First time, I boiled it, and then it got too black – 2nd time I baked it, but it was too white and the flavor wasn't there. You and I together did a better job when we used the recipe in Truro, Cape Cod. Don't you think that's another indication that we fuse wondrously with each other when we are together? But singly and apart, we don't do nearly as well."

SUMMER SCHOOL IN RHODE ISLAND

I was at Providence College when I got that letter. This would be the last of my five summer-school sessions there. I had arranged to carpool with the same two nuns from Maine. Anticipating not seeing each other for several weeks, our longest separation yet, Francis and I had spent the night together in my apartment. To make the bed wider, we'd pulled up alongside my single mattress on the floor an additional mattress. When the nuns picked me up the next morning (of course, by then he had gone), I was hoping they wouldn't notice I had gotten very little sleep the night before.

Going to Providence College as a secular woman surrounded mostly by nuns dramatized what major changes my life had undergone. Francis had initiated visiting me in the convent in the autumn of 1969. Yet now, one year later, we referred to each other as husband and wife. It's there in the love letters that went back and forth from Maine to Rhode Island. In his July 14, 1970 letter, Francis signed off: "From your lover husband now and forever." One year earlier I had been in platonic style third-way mode. Now, instead, having gone *through* the third-way, we were en route toward publicized marriage. We did not, of course, know at this time *how* that could happen. We only knew we had *made* it happen in our underground way.

My summer studies at this college helped illuminate my own earlier and blessedly short-lived, black and white mind. They helped me – even before the liberating Vatican II Council – to journey along the path of valuing the good in all traditions, East and West. I had come to the right place.

AFTERMATH – TALK WITH FATHER TOM

I do not recall talking with one of the priests, a Father Tom. But Francis' and my letters indicate I had confided in him. Father Tom told me I was fooling myself, that I should leave Francis alone because I was interfering with his priesthood. Before Francis realized I was not *seriously* bothered by this priest's opinion, but was only reporting it, he was somewhat shaken, even if he admitted: "I am glad that you are putting yourself in these testing situations, because it accomplishes the goal of my being more explicit with you in these basic areas which are so essential to both of us."

In the process, Francis wrote some interesting things, for example: "I have never sought a moral evaluation of our union from anyone but you. Naturally your deep approval would be necessary. It was not in any sense a moral judgment that I sought from Joe – only the patient ear of a friend when you and I ended our "moratorium." And this, too: "Since I cannot foresee that I will ever live a celibate life again, if you leave me for the noble motive that you are a threat to my priesthood, then inevitably it will be only a matter of time and circumstances until someone else chooses to share herself with me. I do know that you will understand the spirit in which I wrote that last sentence. I choose and want your love – yourself – you – only you, but if you leave me to go it by myself again, I think the future would be predictably the way I have described it."

Taken together, my report and our dialoguing about it in our letters only solidified our union. It also led me to expand my reading.

SUITABLE READINGS

In previous summers, after completing my assignments, I would go to a certain empty classroom which I called my reading sanctuary, to read books on the Quest for the Historical Jesus. But during that fifth summer as an "underground wife," my free-time reading matched my new station in life. I was reading, for example, not only the *New Yorker* and *Psychology Today*, but also Marc Oraison's *Psychology of Human Sex*, the Dominican theologian, Edward Schillebeeckx's *Marriage Human Reality and Saving Mystery*, some German papers on the *Ethics of Sex*, and articles in *NCR* by Sidney Callahan and Rosemary Haughton.

A particular article, "Why Marriage and the Sexual Encounter Are Salvific," so impressed me, I took notes from it, for example, on "the importance of a ritualizing ceremony to signify commitment" because it claimed "sex is the most intimate possible human encounter, the one that demands of its nature, the most." Francis was open to my idea of creating such a "ritualizing ceremony," a simple one. "I think the ritual for us is a splendid idea. I can see what you mean," he wrote. "We can compare each our own." We did that at the end of the summer. During our private ritual, I gave Francis my nun's ring.

WHAT STOOD OUT

Since in varied ways, my last summer at Providence College was productive for both of us, it may sound surprising for me to affirm, in hindsight, that what I remember first about that summer, what made the deepest impression on me, both then and now, is Francis' love letters. He wrote the following from summer camp at a time when his mother was with him for a week: "I have really looked forward to sharing myself with you for these moments. Of course I share myself with you many times during the day. You would think it would be a distraction to be talking to someone and thinking of you, but it really isn't. It just sort of adds a pleasurable dimension to the person with whom I am communicating."

This next expression Francis used in his letter of July 15 continues to astonish me: "You are in my central core, and I am in yours." It inspired more than a few poems that came to me after Francis died, years later.

But the whole passage deserves pondering: "I was thinking this afternoon what our physical separation means. A lot of things, I suppose. My inner life is enriched now and every day by the simple reflection that you are very much a part of me. Today I felt no pain from physical separation – just a quiet confidence that you are in my central core and I am in yours. That's really a profound experience of unity don't you think? And then, when we once again face each other – we will once again share physically with each other what the experience of separation has added to our united selves."

Francis' words, in affirming that physical separation is no obstacle to the union of lovers, console me now as a widow. They go beyond life and death in professing that the experience of separation even "adds" something to the lovers' "united selves."

I was scheduled to return from Providence on July 31, accompanied by the same nuns with whom I had traveled from Augusta. Francis was spending the summer at Camp Pesquasawasis as he had done since 1959 when appointed director and chaplain of this diocesan camp for girls. But he didn't waste a moment to rejoin me on the day of my homecoming. Just as we had used a little stratagem when I left for summer school in June, we did the same for my late afternoon arrival. One of his letters discusses our plan. As before, with his accustomed generosity, in anticipation of his joining me that weekend, Francis had sent me some money for groceries. Our arrangement worked. When my guests left, I signaled him by a wave of the hand from my window, that he could come up to my apartment now.

CAMP PESQUASAWASIS

After Francis' brief visit in Augusta, he returned to Camp Pesquasawasis in Danville where he was committed to stay until the end of the month. Because this was the last of his twelve summers there – the diocese was planning to sell the camp – he had to clear out of his cabin. Instead of completing this project on his own, he made it an opportunity for both of us.

I was entering into Francis' summer sanctuary for the first time, only to join him in taking leave of it. To be at his side at a time like this, closing the door on an important part of his life – I *felt*, indeed, like his wife.

Francis reveals in the autobiographical piece posted on the **CORPUS** website that the summers he spent doing this work had provided him "with a more casual environment than the rigid and role-bound atmosphere of rectory life." As a result, every fall when he had had to return to the parish setting, he admitted experiencing "a subtle but palpable feeling of depression."

We thrived being together, whether we were packing or swimming, or walking around the various cabins, with Francis pointing out the community sites. In the evenings, listening to some of his records, I learned something new about him. I witnessed close up what music meant to him. Lying on our backs on a blanket in front of the fireplace, we were transported by Mahler's *Resurrection Symphony* and energized by Handel's *Messiah*. I experienced for the first of many times, Francis' animated way of singing along in sync with the music. Its rhythm, beat, and melody resonated in the cabin.

In packing up, Francis selected more records to give me. Once returned to town, it wasn't long before I made a point of listening to the Bach cantatas and Beethoven and Brahms symphonies, and other pieces by his favorite composers. From the beginning of our relationship, although I had taken piano lessons for five years in high school, played some classical pieces, and was even the pianist for our high school glee club, when it came to classical music, Francis was my teacher.

Like all departures, it was a little sad for him to leave Camp Pesky, and for me now to remember what this place had meant to him. But as some doors closed, others opened, for both Francis and me.

MORE TRANSITIONS

With summer school over, I was now preparing to teach at Gardiner Area High School near Augusta. Francis, on the other hand, had not only moved out of Camp Pesquasawasis, but because he was reassigned to be the Catholic chaplain at Maine Medical Center and Mercy Hospital in Portland, he had recently vacated the rectory in Waterville, and was now unpacking in his new apartment.

Francis wrote me his thanks for the piece of African fabric I had given him to use as backdrop for the large crucifix of the resurrected Christ he had bought in Boston. He was very proud of this stunning cross. Made of dark teakwood, its 2 ¼"-thick cross beams stretch three-feet long both ways – as tall as they are wide. These are simply adorned with dark red-orange and brown contiguous rectangles, creating their own cruciform inlaid design within the beams. A bronze corpus of the resurrected Christ stands erect and serene, palms opened. We later hung it on our living-room wall.

Wanting to live closer to Francis in Portland, I knew my new job in Gardiner would be limited to a one-year commitment. My plan was to start looking for a second teaching job farther south, in January of '71. Even so, I was ready to give my new students in Gardiner my fullest attention.

In Portland, Francis was making adjustments of his own as the Catholic chaplain at both major hospitals in Portland. This full-time job included ministering to people in crisis coming through the emergency room. In doing pastoral care in nursing homes as well, he was learning how to respond to the aging and dying. Being naturally a good listener, Francis considered this work "one of the most interesting jobs [he] had as a priest."

With both of us in new jobs now, we were busy enough. But when I didn't hear from Francis for two weeks, I complained, while teasing him about my complaining: "You have to put up with my complaints," I wrote, "but I have to put up with my feelings. I wish I were super human." His response in an October 30 letter made my "disappointment" worthwhile, not because he admitted, "It was insensitive of me and an indication of human imperfection," but because he went on to say things that helped me: "I guess I accept the fact of our separation. If I try to measure the amount I miss being with you," he wrote, "it would be counterproductive. My balance and metabolism could be thrown off and I might be running to the doctor . . ." And especially these words: "I really do feel you with me, in your presence, when we are separated . . . because you fill my life also while we are apart."

In spite of not hearing from Francis for two weeks, once settled in his job, his visits were otherwise quite regular, facilitated by his new setup, living in his own apartment instead of in a rectory with a pastor overseeing him. His schedule was also his own to arrange. Weekend after weekend, he would bring me a good-sized cut of prime rib roast that it was a treat to cook together, and with good results, even in my Augusta garret. The roast's leftovers lasted me a week.

RELOCATION – APARTMENT AND JOB

Before we knew it, the New Year had arrived. After some research and finding an opening at Thornton Academy, a high school where I wanted to teach the next autumn, I applied for the position of English teacher and in May was offered the job.

When I got word that my father was admitted to Mercy Hospital, the Catholic hospital in Portland, I traveled there to visit him. It turned out to be less serious than my mother and I had feared; a lump was removed from under his tongue. But two interesting things happened.

Sitting upright in his hospital bed, Dad told me with obvious pleasure that a tall, dark-haired priest had brought him communion. I certainly knew who that was, since Francis visited the sick at both hospitals, but I encouraged Dad to say a bit more about it. When I told Francis that he and my father had met, he was as tickled about it as I.

The other happening was a welcomed, serendipitous thing. While Dad was undergoing surgery, I got the idea, why not look for an apartment now? Although I was told when I inquired that in this college town it would be difficult to find one in the location I wanted (near Francis' apartment on 41 Winter Street), I found, in fact, exactly what I wanted and within an hour and a half. This would allow me, during the month remaining before my final move out of Augusta to Portland, to begin shopping for and moving a few pieces of furniture into my new apartment. I would slowly work on what needed doing there, and then drive back to Augusta where I was still living.

The weekend of Francis' last rendezvous with me in Augusta was more satisfying than regretful – just a touch nostalgic instead, since this was where our love laid its foundation. The ground had been broken in Waterville, but our first dwelling, underground or not, was in Augusta. We took a long walk up the steep hill, the one we had frequented on weekend evenings because of its privacy, and together said goodbye to this small city that had kept our secret. Seven days later, on June 18, 1971, I moved out of the apartment, not to return until I revisited it, forty-one years later.

UNDERGROUND IN PORTLAND

Leaving one Historic District in Augusta, I found a home in another, in Maine's largest city, Portland. It was first settled in 1633, but the Somerset building where I found an apartment, built in 1895, also had the feel of history about it which made it charming. Living at the rear of the building and on the top sixth floor provided a view from that height that included both Deering Oaks Park down High Street and, to its right, a little farther, the Back Cove of Portland Harbor. Two things especially pleased me: the Portland Public Library was located next door in the handsome historic Baxter Building, and Portland, as a peninsula city, gave Francis and me opportunities to walk and jog on Baxter Boulevard overlooking Casco Bay.

Within three weeks in late May and early June, it took four back-and-forth trips from Augusta to Portland, with my Volkswagen Bug crammed with my belongings, to complete the relocation. On one of those trips, the Bug carried ten cement blocks, forty-two bricks, and six raw pine boards. I used them (it was my mother's idea) to create a bookcase dividing the bedroom side of the large room from the living and dining room sides. A small kitchen and bathroom and the living room couch were on the Congress Street side of the apartment, close to the door which in turn was near the elevator or stairs. It was strategically perfect for Francis who could enter the building from the rear stairs.

My parents arrived the day after I spent my first night at 633 Congress Street. Dad put up the blinds for me. During Francis' and my married years, whenever I came up with a creative way to do something, especially something concrete – nuts and bolts kinds of things – Francis would tease me: "You just did a Josephat," (my father's actual given name). Although Dad had no formal carpentry training, he had a special gift for improvising. After that, Mom, Dad, and I went to Wells Beach together for a swim, not far from their home in Springvale.

My parents were pleased with my move. Instead of having to spend over two hours on the road to visit me in Augusta, their drive to Portland now took only thirty-five minutes. Moreover, because I now taught in Saco, roughly halfway between Portland and Springvale, I was able to visit them more frequently.

SUMMER SCHOOL

Electives were the in-thing in some high schools in those days. Assigned as a teacher of three English composition classes, and wanting to do a good

51

job of it, I decided to go to the University of Maine in Farmington for summer courses in writing. The session was six-weeks long. I'd leave Portland on Monday mornings and make the two-hour return trip home after lunch on Fridays. That way, Francis and I had weekends together. With both of us living in Portland now, he was freed from his commitment to a weekly roundtrip drive north to which he'd been faithful over the past nine months. On top of that, we were now blessed with daily local telephone conversations.

For my summer-school writing course, I chose a topic of personal concern for us: the issue of optional celibacy. Good resources were readily available at three libraries; the University of Maine Library in Farmington, the Portland Public Library at my doorstep, and the University of Maine (USM) Library also in Portland. The last carried the daily French newspaper, *Le Monde*. This newspaper allowed me to follow the current celibacy debate in Europe.

My assignment paper, "The Celibacy Crisis Is Not New in History," mailed to the *Church World*, was published in their August 20, 1971 issue. I made clear in the article that only in 1139, the early twelfth century, and only in the western rite's Roman Catholic Church, had the law of celibacy been imposed upon its priests. And that was partly due to disputes over inheritance and church property. Prior to the eleventh century, thirty-nine popes were married. One sidebar asks: "Is the clerical celibacy law a matter of changeable Church discipline?" to which another on the facing page responds: "There are no theological obstacles to a married clergy."

OUT OF TOWN JAUNTS

A week later, before the start of school, Francis and I went on a short vacation. We stayed again, as we had fourteen months earlier, for our honeymoon, at the Wingaersheek Beach and Bass Rocks. We did some cooking together again, even taking the time to make the authentic spaghetti

sauce recipe my parents had gotten from an Italian woman. With its selected spices, it has to simmer for six hours. The aroma filled our cabin.

Two months later our "sympathetic couple" friends gave us the use of
their lake cottage for Columbus Day weekend. We went skinny-dipping
in one of Maine's Belgrade Lakes, a proper thing to do on a warm Indian-
summer day. Then in mid-October, once Francis' Hospital Chaplain's
Conference was over, I flew to Washington, DC, to meet him. We enjoyed
a sightseeing weekend there together.

THE VATICAN SYNOD

These autumn interludes and my delight teaching English at Thornton Academy were offset by two events that would soon seriously challenge
Francis and me. The celibacy debate was intensifying.

The web is rife with many of these old articles that reflected and added
to the heat. In September, *Church World* called for "An Open Forum on
Why Priests Should Be Allowed to Marry. The United Kingdom's *Catholic
Herald* spotlighted a front page piece on October 15: "Two Cardinals in
Synod Call to Change Celibacy Law." And *America*, the national Catholic
Weekly magazine, published by the Jesuits, headlined: "Hopes and Expec-
tations for the 1971 Synod."

In late November I turned to Father Anthony, referring to an article
in *America*. "I trust," I wrote, "that the Synod did not 'dash' your 'expectations' as they did Gary MacEoin's, and I pray," I added, "that you do not
share Father Andrew Greeley's pessimism. I could have cried when I read
MacEoin's concluding paragraph."

My letter went on trying to express a kind of bravado, saying: "Francis
and I maintain a paradoxical stance. Whereas we follow Church developments with keen interest, we are not depending on an immediate change
for our happiness." I joked about using a pen name. When leaving home-

cooked food for Francis at the Mercy Hospital Interfaith Office, such as spaghetti sauce and meatballs, I would mark the package: "From Eric Gill."

That's all it was, nonetheless – bravado. My journal entry of the next day reveals I was feeling considerable anxiety. I gave myself a pep talk: "Remember concern for a job? Remember the lesson learned? That the unknown, the frightful, unknown periods, are precisely the times of grace when faith and trust are proven? Rejoice in this call to trust!"

That did help, but it was short-lived because the next day, I wrote at length, struggling not just with anxiety, but with the pain of our physical separation, even though we lived now only one block away from each other. My pain almost prefigured what would happen next. Francis' world and mine was about to fall apart.

REPORT TO THE BISHOP

Francis gave me shattering news on December 8, 1971. A priest who knew about our relationship had reported him to the bishop. As a result, he was called to Bishop Peter Gerety's office at the Diocesan Chancery. As the word "chancery" connotes, it was like being called to court.

Because a young friend of ours, Thomas Ambrose, did a "Life Story Interview" with Francis in 1999, we have it in Francis' own words what it was like for him. To his interviewer, Francis related what happened during this showdown with the bishop: "Put on the spot, on the spur of the moment, looking at your authority figure," Francis told Thomas, "the Church is very authoritarian, so I said to him 'I'll break it off.' That's what I told him. Then I came back, and with Elaine, it was terrible breaking off this relationship. It didn't take long; this was December 8, 1971, and so we agreed that we would part."

SECOND MORATORIUM

It was indeed "terrible" for me. I turned to my journal to express my sense of loss, "mourning like death," I called it. I used even stronger language after telling another priest who knew about us what had happened. Because he called our situation "unreal, a make-believe marriage," and made other disillusioning comments, I was left more downhearted than ever, and even bitter. I wrote, as if addressing Francis, but only in my journal: "I put my trust in our way. But I was deceived. If you're ready to leave me to save face, forget me. I gave myself fully, but you're not fully my husband." This note I wrote was one I did not mail him.

Francis' account to Thomas continued. Although it was twenty-eight years later that Francis confided these words to him, they plainly revealed, even then in 1999, in the mere telling of it – that he was in as much shock as I: "I was still the Chaplain at Maine Medical Center," he related to Thomas. "I went through my work, and they even had a Christmas party. I played some kind of a part at that party, but it was as though my head . . . my body, was a separate part from my head. I was numb from December 8 on."

Francis went on talking: "I realized: 'My God, if I end everything, and go back to being a Roman Catholic Priest, projecting the image of being celibate, because there'll probably be other women, if I lose Elaine – I'll have to ask: Which is the real me? I have to end this duality!' So I went to see a priest for counseling. He was an Episcopal priest working at the hospital. I went to see him and he said, 'Well it's simple. You have to decide whether you are a celibate, or whether you are not. You have to decide. You have to make a decision. Are you, or are you not? If you *are* a celibate, OK, fine, stick with what you are doing. If you're not a celibate, go in the other direction.'"

WISE INPUT

Meanwhile, I had Father Anthony to turn to. Given his telephone number at the Darlington Seminary in New Jersey where he was teaching, I called him there to discuss Francis' crisis and mine. Father Anthony's advice was compassionate, supportive, constructive as always – and frank. Understanding the constraints in our not being public and open "it *could* be a blessing if it leads Francis to make a decision to leave," he said. On the other hand, Francis could also resort to transferring his priesthood to the Eastern rite which would allow him to marry. Anthony even gave me the name and telephone number of the Archimandrite, an abbot of the Eastern Orthodox Church, whom we could telephone to set this process in motion. Or – this turn of events could, (Father Anthony saved this for last) – it *could* mark the end of Francis' and my relationship.

He also clarified for me how Francis' bishop, Peter Gerety, had been put in a difficult situation. "Even if he were sympathetic," Father Anthony explained, "since he's been given someone's testimony as well as names, he's in a juridical bind." He also commiserated with us: "It's delicate because there's so much between you and Francis." Then, expressing further willingness to help, he gave me his home telephone number and asked me to assure Francis of his prayers.

CHRISTMAS VACATION CONVERSION

I was still beside myself with grief. I had stopped taking birth-control pills. Unable to think straight in spite of Father Anthony's help, since Francis' mind was also too much in turmoil to consider transferring to the Eastern Rite, all I could do, was think of getting away.

I would go to Boston during Christmas school vacation, and I'd look for a teaching job there for the following year. My friend's friend in Boston would be away for the holidays, so we arranged for me to stay at her apartment. She also relayed information about a Church holiday party, so I planned on going to that.

I didn't get anywhere with the job-hunting task I had unrealistically set up for myself. After all, the school vacation time was short. In my depressed state, and crying a lot, I came down with a bad cold. So I headed my VW Bug back home to my Portland apartment on New Year's Day.

In the meantime, Francis had driven to Beverly, Massachusetts, to spend Christmas with his Aunt Irene. Consequently, we were both separated by only a few miles, as if we were meant to travel side by side. Before we parted, Francis had told me he was really "haunted" that he might be writing off "the most beautiful event" of his life. Yet he felt he had to do what he called his "experiment." He needed time to rethink everything. Before leaving for Boston I wrote Francis a short note: "It takes courage to launch into your 'experiment'. I respect that in you. And you know how I'm hoping it will turn out, don't you? Never forget that. Love, Elaine."

IN FRANCIS' OWN WORDS

Nothing better describes the depth of Francis' soul searching during the next ten days than his own narrative recorded by Thomas. One can feel the wonder of it in the tone of his breathless words which lapse into present tense, colloquial talk:

"I came back to Portland right after Christmas, and whatever powers were moving, I don't know, but right around December 30, it . . . just the turmoil in my own soul and mind . . . increased, and I remember saying to myself, I remember asking the question to myself – 'What would I do? What would I work at?' So then, as soon as I said 'What would I work at?' I realized that I *had* to leave!

"So it was New Year's Eve, and I was dying to have somebody to talk to about it. So there was this priest in South Portland who was a friend that I had been talking to. I just went to him as soon as I could and bounced it off him. He says: 'Of course, of course!'

"So January 2 right away, I called Elaine. I says, 'Oh we're going to be together permanently!' What happened was, she went down to Massachusetts, 'cause she was trying to make new connections, she was down in Boston, and I just, when I talked to her I said 'When you were down in Boston, you know, did anything happen down there, to affect our relationship?' She said 'no,' I said 'well,' I said – 'I'm leaving! I'm free, you know, I'm leaving, I'm free!'

"I went over to see her in her apartment. She had this heavy cold, but she was just overjoyed. Then, right away, I made an appointment with the bishop, the head honcho. I had already seen a Jesuit confessor at Cheverus, and he said 'You're out.' Interestingly enough, I felt tremendous. I felt it was like the exodus. I really felt it was the exodus. Yeah!"

GET SET . . . GROW

In this account to Thomas, Francis stopped short of what happened next. I must tell the rest of the story.

As Francis walked into my apartment, he waved a single sheet in the air, and then thrust it into my hand. It was an ad in a magazine whose page he had torn out, he explained, while waiting in the rectory parlor to talk with his priest friend, Father Mike McGarrigle, about his decision to leave.

Above a colored photo of orchids and gladiolas, the caption reads: "on your mark, get set . . . grow!" Francis had written at the top of the page: "Whoopee! January 2, 1972."

I framed it. It has hung on our bedroom wall ever since, declaring the theme of his life and mine.

In 1978, six years after we were married, Francis brought me a bottle of wine on December 8. The note he wrote me expresses a ritual we reenacted in one form or another thereafter: "My beloved, I have selected this bottle of French Bordeaux to begin our celebration of the December 8 to December 31, 1971 – events which we remember with awe and dread. We celebrate with joy that the Lord saw us through that desert and into the liberated life we now enjoy together."

CHAPTER THREE
From Exodus to Avalon

After our two years of living "underground," now together, now apart, Francis' and my uncertain future appeared full of promising light, in spite of certain immediate concerns. Those felt now like mere passing shadows.

How would Francis' mother react? Would the Vatican give him a dispensation from the clerical priesthood enabling us to be married in the Catholic Church? And what would he do for work?

Now "permanently together," as he had declared when announcing his breakthrough decision, we faced these questions with confidence, as fiancées in the public eye.

We began by telling my parents. I was their only child. They rejoiced, for now they would have a son-in-law. My father was quick to tell the "tall dark-haired priest" who had given him communion at Mercy Hospital – "I have some Irish friends, too!" Now dad would have a buddy to accompany him while driving from Springvale to Rochester, New Hampshire, for his periodic visit to the liquor store. My mother, a hair-stylist like my father, offered to cut Francis' hair, "a new hair cut for a new life," she called it. Looking even more handsome after that, Francis made her his barber from then on. Mom and Dad were in our inner circle now.

WEDDING ANNOUNCEMENT

Writing to family and friends came next. We announced we would marry in the Catholic Church when the dispensation from Rome arrived. The return letter Francis looked for most was the one from his mother. She did not disappoint, putting him and me instantly at ease: "You are very happy and we are all very happy for you," she began. "Yours was a big decision, and you reacted truthfully and honestly, so you will have no regrets." She understood. "You and Elaine both gave a number of years in the service of the church and I am sure are the better for that. So rest assured you will both always be in our thoughts and prayers. We are behind you 100 percent." Why did we worry at all?

Francis' new haircut.

Francis' siblings were equally magnanimous. His brother Lou wrote: "I commend you for having the courage of your convictions after much thought and perhaps considerable agony." Paul McGillicuddy, now one hundred-years old at this writing, the elder cousin who had given Francis a job working in his furniture story in Houlton Maine until he entered college, congratulated him. Helen, the housekeeper at the Waterville rectory whom Francis called "my girl Helen," wrote she was very happy for him because, she said, "You were like a son to me, and I felt very close to you." She also confided: "They had it around that you were married quite some time ago. But I really didn't believe it."

For my part I was heartened by letters from the two Ursuline nuns I most esteemed. One was my college English professor, Mother Irene Mahoney, now, as I write, in her 90's. This congratulatory letter of hers, only two years after I myself left the convent, sealed our friendship. The other I revered was Mother Amadeus McKevitt who had been both my Juniorate mistress and then my superior. In this letter, she called Francis and me "pioneers." [1]

Another letter that especially cheered us came from Father Raymond Picard, the priest in Waterville to whom I had confessed four years earlier that I was struggling with my attraction to Francis. "I had a funny intuition," he wrote, adding, "Marriage is not a second-rate vocation. Christ had something to do with bringing you two together."

Recipients of our own letter could spread the word near and far, to some extent, but the *Church World's* feature article on Francis' leaving the clerical priesthood reached a still wider audience. Its editor, Henry Gosselin, told us that letters to the editor were, as he put it, "three to one in favor." Shortly afterwards Francis and I were invited to Henry's home in Harpswell to sail with him in the Gulf of Maine. This jaunt occasioned a follow-up article. As editor, Henry wanted to continue the discussion on the important issue of optional celibacy.

FRANCIS VISITS HIS MOTHER

It was time now for Francis to visit his mother in person. After my parents, it was she he wanted to meet next, face to face. He would drive alone to her home in Saint John, New Brunswick, but stop en route back to stay overnight at his sister, Jo's home, in Houlton. After Francis became an

---

[1] Before Vatican II after which all Ursulines were called Sister – only novices and postulants were called Sister, while fully professed Ursulines who had pronounced their final vows, were called Mother.

American citizen, she and her husband Lou Curry had given him hospitality while he worked for his elder cousin, Paul. Weeks of stress in coming to his decision had taken their toll on him. After climbing the stairs to go to the bathroom, Francis fainted near it onto the hallway floor. Jo and her husband Lou immediately telephoned Dr. John B. Madigan whom Francis knew. When Dr. Madigan heard Francis' story, he said: "No wonder!"

Four years later during our Marriage Encounter weekend, Francis chose to write about this unforgettable experience. To the question: "What is your reason for wanting to go on living?" he wrote: "When I passed out from sheer mental exhaustion en route to see my mother, I wondered if the Lord was taking me to himself. My predominant thought was 'Lord, don't take me now, not when I am on the threshold of experiencing the destiny toward which my life has been urging me!' Even now," he wrote, recalling that episode four years later, "I am overwhelmed recalling that moment. Now that I am savoring it, I want to go on living – though I entrust my life to the Lord's care, for whatever length of time is allotted to me."

The next day, Francis was back on the road to see his mother in Saint John. He was eager to tell me when he returned that he could not have hoped for a better response from her. She volunteered, "I always thought – if a priest would leave to get married – it would be good if he married a former nun."

DISPENSATION

Francis requested a dispensation from the priesthood to be married in the Catholic Church. There was a veritable flurry of letters between the church hierarchy and us, usually detouring through our intermediary, Monsignor Raymond Begin. Bishop Gerety had written Francis on January 10 notifying him that this monsignor, a canon lawyer for the diocese of Portland, would be handling his case. Francis was pleased because he knew well this Monsignor whom he called by his first name. On March 10, Monsignor Begin wrote an official letter (with a personal PS) telling Francis his case had been mailed to Rome.

With no news yet by May 29, I wrote to the Vatican myself on Francis' behalf, asking Cardinal Seper, in essence – "Why no word yet? It's been over two months." (I had enclosed Henry's *Church World* article in that letter.) Then on June 27, I wrote again, this time to Cardinal Villot explaining that the lack of response from Rome (it had been four months) meant our marriage license application of April 21 had expired, and that we would therefore have to reapply with the city for a marriage license. Two weeks later Francis got a letter from the Vatican's Secretariat of State confirming receipt of his request.

July 28 was the day on which Francis' Decree of Laicization from the Sacred Congregation of the Faith arrived. This decree, or enactment, stamped with the Vatican's seal, was written in Latin. Now it was official: Francis could marry me in the church.

Curiously, we found this letter in our mail slot only after returning from the wedding of a priest friend who had chosen not to seek a dispensation. He and his bride-to-be had made this decision for reasons of their own. If we had done the same, although we wouldn't have had to wait, we would not have been able to be married in the Church. Now, however, our period of waiting had ended. With this piece of paper, we could now proceed with our own wedding.

We knew, nevertheless, it was not my having importuned Rome that had made the Vatican act. Upon hearing that Monsignor Begin was going to Rome, Francis had asked him to look into his case. He did so in a specific way. When returned to the states, he reported back to Francis. While in the Vatican office that handles requests by priests to be freed from ecclesiastical control, he had gone through the files, found, and pulled out Francis' case, and suggested to the Vatican official there, that it be given attention. This had the effect of putting Francis' case at the top of the pile. When

Francis heard this story, he went out and bought the good Monsignor a bottle of scotch.

Francis later wrote to Bishop Gerety and thanked him for his substantial part in making possible our marriage in the Catholic Church. "I experienced nothing but warmth and respect," he said, noting that the people who interacted with him were "respectful of the honesty and agony which went into my decision." In his congratulatory letter, Bishop Gerety's reply was just as warm. "I saw Elaine on TV," he said. "She did a good job presenting the Catholic position on war and peace. Furthermore, she was the best-looking member of the panel."

JOB AND PICNICS

After spending some time in the winter looking for a job, Francis applied for two in April that suited him. In May, both agencies offered him a full-time job. He accepted the one in Portland, a position as associate director of Huckleberry House, also known as Little Brothers. It was a live-in house for boys who were in danger of getting in trouble with the law. A couple had been hired to live with them *loco parentis*. When we heard that the second job as a social worker was offered to Francis' and my friend, Joe Brannigan, we applauded. Joe had left the priesthood and married Claire only months before Francis left and married me.

Francis liked this job even if it turned out to be a temporary one. Later he was hired by the Portland Housing Authority (PHA) as a supervisor of social workers for older people living in low-income housing. This one would last until his retirement 23 years later. "I so enjoyed this work which I experienced as pastoral," Francis wrote, "that I did not miss presiding at the liturgy."

That summer we met my parents for swimming and cookout suppers at Crescent Beach State Park in Cape Elizabeth. Picnic tables were set up there in several nooks under the trees near the beach sand.

Because we invariably arrived in good time to claim the same spot, Dad liked to joke, "This is our private lot." Joe and Claire joined us often for these picnics. After seeing Francis getting an outdoor haircut from my mother, Joe agreed to let her do the same for him, so he donned the same salon barbershop cape. While steaks were slowly grilling, we younger couples frolicked in the Atlantic Ocean.

Francis' and my wedding was fast approaching.

All this time, Francis was living with me in my Portland apartment. But when the bans of marriage were announced in the Portland Evening Express on August 5, the place of his residence read – 70 Forest Avenue. That was the YMCA's address, just two streets away. Francis paid for a room he never occupied, "for propriety's sake," we said.

THE WEDDING

We were married on August 13, 1972, the same day as my mother's 59th birthday. Although unused to Vatican delays on a personal level, I should have known better than to ask my mother to make my wedding dress for a possible late winter wedding. That long sleeved white dress befitted a colder season, but not a summer wedding. Although it cheered me later to wear it, I bought and wore instead, a cooler, off-white, soft linen dress for our wedding day. A few embroidered blue flowers adorned the front of its sleeveless bodice. The tall ruffle at the bottom third of its full-length skirt added elegance. Instead of wearing a corsage, I wore a headband of rosebuds. Francis for his part, wore a light-blue suit with a red tie and red boutonniere.

Only hours before our wedding, Francis and I held a short singing rehearsal in our apartment for my parents and for my aunt, my mother's sister, Mother Edwarda, once my Ursuline superior in Waterville (the town that had brought us together). Seated in a circle in our small living room, we

sang from the booklet I had prepared as a handout for those who
came to our wedding. The opening hymn was taken from the
musical *Fiddler on the Roof* which
had made an impression on
Francis and me: "May the Lord
protect and defend you . . ."

We drove in separate cars to
Holy Cross Church in South
Portland where Francis' friend,

En route to their wedding...

Father Richard Murray, officiated at our wedding. My parents brought my
aunt in their car, while Francis and I were chauffeured by Joe and Claire.
While we sat in the back seat, smiling at each other, Claire occasionally
turned around to snap photos. Francis had in his pocket our pair of custom-
made rings. They were simple, matching wide bands, but the local high
school teacher who had hand-crafted them had beaten the gold. The rings
looked lustrous.

As we pronounced our vows and slipped our wedding rings around
each other's ring finger, I saw in Francis'
face some of the reverence and wonder we
felt in listening to our favorite love song,
"The First Time Ever I Saw Your Face."
Eyes brimming, our joy knew no bounds.

Our small wedding party then gathered at the Roma Cafe. Including my parents, my aunt, the celebrant, and Francis
and me, we numbered fifteen people. Fr.
Leopold Nicknair, my Colby College
campus-minister partner, had come.

in a breezy car.

Henry Gosselin was our best man. Besides us newlyweds and my parents, three other couples were present, two colleagues from Thornton Academy, Joe and Claire, and Mike and Margaret Nobel. I had written an article for the *Church World* about Mike and Margaret's founding of The Maine Peace Center out

At Roma Café with Elaine's parents.

of which grew The Maine Freeze Campaign and the current Peace Action Maine. Peggy Elkus, a graduate of Colby College was also present. Francis and I had met her there as nun and priest members of CALCAV.

Once an old brownstone mansion, this Italian restaurant at 769 Congress Street now served meals in several of its small rooms, three of them at the head of the winding staircase. We were ushered, though, into two adjoining rooms on the first floor. Huge windows looking out onto the street were partially covered by pale, grayish purple curtains adding a subtle touch of color to the room. The lighting created a soft atmosphere, perfect for a small wedding party.

Francis had bought a special bottle of aged Chivas Regal Scotch whisky to serve our guests. Its splendid silvery metal box has been my sewing box ever since. Our guests were happy, my parents looked radiant, and Francis and I, dancing cheek to cheek at the meal's end, were in bliss.

On our wedding night, we didn't drive

Cutting the cake.

far, just sixteen miles out of Portland to a small motel in Windham called Suburban Pines. The next morning we drove north to visit each of Francis' siblings and their families in Millinockett and Houlton, Maine, and then, his mother and sister and family in Saint John. We stayed a few days in Quebec City before visiting Francis' fourth and fifth siblings and their families in Montreal and Ontario. En route home, we made a stop at Niagara Falls.

Dancing at their wedding reception.

HOME ON AVALON ROAD

Two months later Francis and I found and bought a house on Avalon Road. "It has only one floor, you know," the real estate agent pointed out, "so it's a good starter home, or a good place to retire." But the moment we walked through the entryway into the living room, we knew this bungalow had our name on it. No waiting until retirement for us! This was the house we chose, located in a modest neighborhood on a street without sidewalks and few houses, where in springtime, choruses of peepers emanate from vernal pools.

After our exodus from a life of celibacy, it was fitting that Francis and I began our new life together on Avalon Road. In the Arthurian legend, Avalon was an island paradise in the western seas to which King Arthur went at his death. This sweet home was made our paradise for thirty-eight years by our living in it together. Then, encircled with fruit trees, grape vines, and berries, it became (as edible landscape) our permaculture eden. When the time came then, for Francis' death – he did indeed die in a kind of paradise.

Chapter Four
Family Affairs

A s a child, I had asked my parents every Christmas, "Could I have a baby sister, or a baby brother?" But it was never meant to be; I remained an only child. Now the question arose – would I be childless also? I was thirty-seven, and at forty-five, Francis was my senior by eight years. On his part, he could not see himself, as an older man, having a teenager. As for me, I was ambivalent.

In the early seventies it seemed rare for older women to have children. The possibility of a difficult pregnancy, but especially abnormalities in the fetus, concerned me. There were no studies readily available to us at the time, and no research on the Internet to assure us.

What caused my own ambivalence was awareness that if something would go wrong with the pregnancy, I would not have been able to have an abortion – not because I am a Catholic, but simply because I personally could not do that. I say this without, in the least, judging women who choose to do so.

My choice to honor Francis' needs, once I saw his anxiety over this issue, was based, nonetheless, not so much on my ambivalence, nor on the general tendency of women in the early seventies to put aside their own

desires and defer to their husbands. No –
deeply in love with Francis – my choice
was based on love.

Looking back, I would say our joint
decision not to have a baby was colored
partly by the times and partly by our ages.
The thought arose later, at various times
over the years, that I might have preferred
having children, because there was indeed
a loss involved in not having children of
our own. We both acknowledged that. But
even at those moments when looking back

Elaine and Francis at home.

at our decision, I remained ambivalent for
yet another reason: The fact it had not happened led me to conclude it was
not meant for us. Francis and I also saw, because of this – because of what
did not happen – our relationship and our lives vis-à-vis the community
would (and they did) take on a different character. Hearing it said, "Children
are like mountains; they belong to everyone," we decided to live our lives in
a way to benefit the next generation.

ADOPTION ATTEMPT

Francis was open, however, to the idea of our adopting an older child.
After spending two preparatory years as members of Families for Adoptable
Children (and also playing an active role in that organization), we discovered that at our age, we could not have adopted a baby anyway. Only older
children were given to older couples. Their policy seemed to corroborate
our decision not to have a baby.

We entered into the process, then, of adopting a ten-year-old boy
called Donny. After a gradual period of visiting him at Sweetser Home for

Children in Saco and bringing him to our home for weekends, the day finally arrived when he could move in with us. I could now call him our son, I thought, but the day we picked him up, the director warned us that Donny's moving in was only for a trial period during these last six months of 1976. "I've seen cases like this," he confided, "where it doesn't work out." We knew that Donny had already been adopted and then "unadopted," as they put it. He had been given back to the state. But this was the first time we were told he suffered from encopretic, eneuretic behavior. (Involuntary defecation and bed wetting.)

Donny's summer with us started out well. He liked Eastern Promenade overlooking Casco Bay where we took him for picnics. He came with us also on a week's vacation at the beach with my parents and to a McGillicuddy-Dever wedding in New Brunswick, Canada. My parents enjoyed having a grandchild for the time it lasted.

With the arrival of the school year, however, challenges also arrived. Donny, now enrolled at a nearby elementary school, refused to go to school some mornings. That caused problems. Francis stayed home with Donny on his "sick" days, since his schedule at the housing authority was more flexible than mine. Objects then started disappearing from our home. We discovered that Donny stole and sold a few things, such as a teakwood tray, to someone in the neighborhood. He also bashed in the lattice work at a side entrance porch and cut up the workbench in the cellar.

Francis and I took turns getting depressed. I had never seen him like this. Nor had I ever had my buttons pushed the way Donny knew how to. "We've joined the human race," I told a friend. "No," he said, "ordinary family life is not like this." I was relieved, though concerned, to hear our friend add, "you're dealing with a disturbed child. He needs counseling."

COUNSELING

With the Sweetser director's encouragement, we enrolled Donny and ourselves in a program offered at the Portland Community Counseling Center. While Donny was getting individualized testing and counseling, we were introduced by the counselors to Genograms. This method was intended to help us counselees identify and better understand the dynamics in our own family relationships for three generations. With other individuals in our group standing silently to represent our family members, each of us in turn would tell his or story. What Francis and I picked up from Genograms, would serve us personally, for life.

Both the Counseling Center and the Sweetser agency concluded overall that Donny should have been placed in a home with siblings. They surmised, "Your being so good to him likely triggered something rebellious in Donny."

By prior arrangement, Donny gradually made an amicable transition to another family. After he left, we subscribed for him to a children's *Nature* magazine thinking its monthly appearance would signal our concern for him and for his welfare. He and we corresponded periodically. Even his new mother wrote once to tell us he had gotten baptized. We were glad to learn he was happy in his larger family. But nothing, it seemed, could take away Donny's disturbance. He committed suicide at age fifteen.

Francis and I were advised not to attempt adoption again. It would have been on the rebound, we were told. Some months later we got a kitten we called by the biblical name, Jezebel. When Francis arrived home, Jezebel would throw herself at his feet, paws in the air. While I sat at my desk working, she would sit at the edge of a bookcase shelf to my right, above my head, watching me. In the bathroom where her litter box was kept under the sink, Jezebel would slide the shower door from one side to another with her paw.

But we had to give her up because of Francis' allergies. The loss of Jezebel was like the loss of a baby, a second time. In my sadness, using the best of many photos I had taken illustrating her playfulness and endearing ways, I wrote our Jezebel story in an album. When friends lost pets of their own, I would invite them to read my Jezebel book. One friend urged me to make it into a children's book, for it moved readers to tears.

MARRIAGE ENCOUNTER

Francis was not averse to learning from modes that can shed a little light around the corners of the human heart. Besides having recently utilized the Genogram instrument, we would also benefit from two models of human personality – the Jungian-based Myers-Briggs Type Indicator and the Enneagram, originally taught by secret oral tradition. But it was from our Marriage Encounter weekends later this same year that we acquired a practice which served us equally well. In a sense, it shaped us. We began using our Marriage Encounter notebooks in 1976, four years after we were married.

Since many people can express and reveal more of themselves through writing, this approach of initiating discussion with preliminary writing seemed to us sound. We were given a means for the honest expression of even deep feelings. A case in point was the baby question we had recently faced just before giving Jezebel away to friends. The timing was perfect. Francis took the opportunity to bring it up.

"I felt very vulnerable about the possibility of our having a baby," he wrote. "In a sense, you were in a position of power over me, but you resolved the question without making me feel any less a man, any less strong, etc. than if I had had the courage, if that's the right word, to leave our lives open to a child."

Francis was thanking me because, he wrote: "I experienced your love and your unlimited consideration. You could see that I was falling apart from the stress." I knew the baby question had caused him stress, but I hadn't realized how much. I was grateful indeed I had put his feelings over mine in such a sensitive matter.

MORE FROM OUR NOTEBOOKS

During the leisure of the weekend, we had looked deeply into ourselves and our shared life. Examining my mild extroversion and his introversion, I told Francis I was excited about the possibility of learning a new tool of communication because "it might help me to talk less, or somehow let you emerge more with your feelings. I jump in so quickly," I ventured, "with my own reactions and feelings that I think sometimes I rob myself of hearing more of yours." No! I didn't want to do that, I repeated.

Questions about what we liked and disliked about ourselves elicited in part, this from Francis: "I like the knowledge I have achieved about myself. It came through considerable suffering. I like my tranquility, evenness of temperament and patience, but I dislike a certain lethargy in my temperament." And I wrote this about myself: "I like my enthusiasm for life. It makes me joyful."

We both commented on what I told Francis I sometimes found frustrating about myself, "being too meticulous, even a perfectionist." He said, gently, "Your need for order, whether it is to some degree a compulsion or not, I do accept as part of you. The only time I do feel it necessary to moderate this – and this is rarely – is when you seem in danger of playing yourself out, or overdoing it. But you have made much progress in this, as you know."

I acknowledged that "feeling compelled to take the initiative, solve the problem, do the work" led to my inability to relax "until what needs to be done is done." (He knew this by now.) "That is so engrained in me," I confessed, "it's hard to eradicate." But "your support and example," I acknowledged, "has given me a kind of elasticity that helps me counteract that tendency."

It took years for me to grow more like him in this regard, because I was by nature an initiator. But Francis' example of having *had* to pace himself because of asthma, helped me. I called him "my Rock." I was delighted when to this question: "Do you see me as I really am?" Francis wrote: "I believe you do. I sense that you respect my sensitivity. You recognize the kind of delicate handling to which I respond."

By the end of the weekend, Francis and I agreed we were both open in sharing ourselves with one another. It was just a matter of difference in style. He tended to wait until he had worked things through, whereas I liked to involve him in my process of working things out.

We found the question asking us about our "defenses" helpful: I brought up my strong inner critic. Francis thought "the use of shyness" was his. "It's my style, anyway," he wrote, explaining "it's easier and safer not to expose oneself too much." Francis admitted: "I have an instinct to let others declare themselves before I emerge from my shyness." But then, noting that "confrontation is threatening and painful, and not always productive for me," he added that by waiting, "things often eventually evolve, and I achieve the same results without confrontation."

What Francis wrote next expresses well what our practice of writing through the years brought us: "I know realistically that our mutual faults, weaknesses, or imperfections, can in fact diminish wonderment. But," he elaborated, "I believe that recognizing this danger in itself protects our capacity for wonder."

Francis' response to a question about God's place in our marriage gave him, as he said, "the pleasure of adding a little Latin to our dialogue: *Vere, Deus*

At a former student's wedding.

est in hoc loco!" (Truly, God is in this place.) He then concurred – "we do have, as you put it, a mission of quiet witness to God's Love."

This was something we were aware of since our wedding. It was demonstrated by the fact that eight years later, on our twelfth wedding anniversary in 1983, Francis wrote this note accompanying a bouquet of flowers: "May the Lord deepen our love for each other so that it overflows on all we meet."

A WINDOW INTO OUR LIVES – ELDERS

Life on Avalon Road took on a meaningful, pleasant rhythm, even without the presence of an adopted child or a cat in our home. For pleasure, not just for duty, Francis and I regularly visited certain elders both at his Portland Housing Authority workplace and in our families.

Several at work called him *Father* McGillicuddy. That made him smile, but he did pastor them. One such person was an elderly woman whose only son had died. After Francis introduced me to Belle Pike, I also became her friend. Sitting in a rocking chair in her living room, I would

Francis in the dining room.

listen to her stories and in the summers, we would sit outside her apartment, admiring the few vegetables she had planted along her side of the building. Belle especially liked shopping in used clothing stores.

Aunt Irene in Beverley, Massachusetts, had a history with Francis. She had provided him with lodging during his days at Prep School in the Boston area before he went to Holy Cross College. Our visits often included overnight stays. I loved this spunky, outspoken aunt of his who took a shine to me as I did to her. After two hip surgeries in her nineties, she was eager to practice some simple therapeutic yoga poses I showed her. To facilitate that practice, I made up and left behind for her to follow – an 8.5 x 11 sheet with stick figures on it, headed with: "Yoga for Aunt Irene."

Aunt Irene asked me to be her nail cutter – to do what a manicurist and podiatrist would do. I would sit close to her, her hand in mine, as I clipped away while she kept talking with Francis and even a few other McGillicuddy family members present at the moment. Francis and I helped Aunt Irene, too, with spring planting of her miniscule garden around the house. Her bedroom was at the top of a spiral staircase, but she made it up there every night until the following incident. Since whoever had shoveled her driveway hadn't left it quite as she liked, even at 102-years old, she had gone outside with a shovel to tidy things up. The mailman had found her fallen in a snowbank. Aunt Irene agreed then to move to Girdler House. Meals were provided in this charming home for only twelve other seniors. Aunt Irene died there three years later, only two months short of her 105th birthday.

My own Aunt Aldea was another outspoken woman who delighted Francis. She received our monthly visits with eagerness in spite of her telling us, with perhaps shocking candor, after she became crippled, that "these aren't the golden years, they're the ____ years." My father's siblings, the Goulets, like my mother's, the Plantes and Provencals, were French. When relatives on both sides of my family came to my mother's funeral in 2000, observing them on this rare occasion when both families were with us, Francis noted it seemed to him the Goulets are earthy, while the Plantes are religious.

RECREATION

Something dramatic had happened to me the first time Francis took me skiing. When we disembarked from the ski lift and I saw the moguls on the descending mountain, I froze. So Francis summoned the ski-patrol rescue. They guided me down the

At a winter festival in Montreal.

mountain, while I sat in a toboggan holding my skis. Francis skied alongside us, assuring me I needn't feel embarrassed about my fear. It was all right to be afraid, he said.

In the summers, Francis and I drove to Tanglewood to hear the Boston Symphony Orchestra at their summer home in Lenox in the Berkshires Hills. Lucky for us and our budget, motel rooms were more reasonably priced then. Tanglewood was a soul feast for us. Francis and I either picnicked on the expansive Tanglewood lawn and then listened to the music from our lawn chairs, or we sat within The Shed where the sound was more clear and resonant. We purchased tickets for the music Shed for several concerts special to us, such as *Bach's St. Matthew's Passion*. That great oratorio directed by Boston Symphony's music director, Seiji Ozawa, captivated, even transported us.

Audubon outings were another warm-weather activity we found stimulating. One summer, during songbird mi-

Francis backpacking in Gulf Hagas.

grating season, we spent a weekend on Monhegan Island on a bird watch. Our master birder guide taught us how to flush out the birds by making a "whoosh" sound so we could watch the way they flew out of the trees and then see them more easily with our binoculars. I started keeping a bird-life list after that, assigning a 3 x 5 card for each bird. I would record the sighting of a bird's return whenever Francis or I spotted one. We spent another memorable weekend hiking in Maine's Grand Canyon, Gulf Hagas.

FAMILY GATHERINGS:
GOULETS AND PLANTES & PROVENCALS

My father, a Goulet, like my mother, a Plante, was one of fifteen children. (For a number of cultural reasons, large families were the norm for French Canadians.) This explains why, while growing up, I went to a lot of weddings. Older than most newlyweds, Francis and I still had such family affairs to celebrate. With both of my paternal grandparents gone by then, however, those visits to Lewiston relatives were limited to attendance at a

few funerals as well, though more weddings. The weddings or anniversaries were jolly affairs. Francis enjoyed being among my convivial Goulet relatives.

To help him understand where that *joie de vivre* came from, I gave him some information about the Goulets, emigrated from Quebec. Some worked in the Lewiston mills, but my paternal grandparents had also created their own business – selling ice from nearby Lard Pond. Weekends at *Memere* Azilda and *Pepere* Edouard's camp had made a big impres-

Elaine, age three, with her parents.

81

sion on me. There were enough family members to create two baseball teams. Going to Lard Pond felt like nothing but fun. We enjoyed the camaraderie, ate good French food, didn't mind using an outhouse and, while sitting on the wide front porch overlooking the pond, laughed at jokes and stories about my uncles' and cousins' pranks.

On other weekends in the summer, Francis and I had get-togethers at Mousam Lake with my mother's family members, the Plantes and the Provencals. We had more out-ings with them than with my Goulet relatives because they lived in or near Springvale where my parents lived. Francis and I would join Mom and Dad for a drive to Aunt Isabel's and Uncle Arthur's summer camp. My mother and I would sit with her half-sister on the wooden dou-ble-sided gliding chair under the

Elaine's mother made his shirt.

trees, while Dad and Francis chatted with Uncle Arthur and their son and daughter-in-law, Pat and Dell. Often we'd go for a swim before lunch.

Located five miles from my childhood home, this lake held special memories for me, for my parents also rented a camp for us to stay at that lake for a week, during many summers. Owned by Aunt Rachel, another member of the Provencal family, and her husband, Uncle Vic, it was lo-cated directly across the lake

Francis, age three, with his family.

within view of Aunt Isabel's and Uncle Arthur's camp. Francis, as a farm boy born near Skiff Lake, shared with me stories similar to mine about living in the wooded regions of his own childhood. So he could take in my wistful recalling of the sounds of waves lapping on the shore at night, and especially, the spellbinding calls of the loons.

Francis and I spent one week each summer with my parents. Quebec City was our choice for the first two summers, and for the other six, we rented the first floor part of a duplex at Wells Beach, fifteen miles from Springvale. We read, collected shells on the beach, swam in the ocean, walked along the large rock jetty and, being good cooks, each one of us partook of the dinner we had cooked together during a "happy hour." Then we sat outside to watch the sun gradually sinking toward the horizon over the clam flats.

McGILLICUDDY FAMILY GATHERINGS

Every year on the occasion of Canada's Thanksgiving on October 14, Francis and I were beckoned northward to Saint John, New Brunswick, to celebrate it with his widowed mother, Margaret. We made trips to visit all his siblings and their families, but because Francis' mother lived in her own small apartment in the same city as his elder sister, Mary, we visited them more often and enjoyed many meals with Mary, her husband, Jim Dever, and their five children. We watched the younger ones grow into adulthood, marry, and have children of their own.

Mary and Jim also owned a cottage a bit further north from their home. It was set on the banks of the Saint John River. Mary made a point of inviting us for a weekend every summer while she and Jim and Mother were staying there. Francis and I would sit on the deck with them, conversing while admiring the river before us. Various members of the family came and went, joining us on occasion for talk and meals.

Our nephew, John, would take us on the river by boat. Francis and I felt especially privileged when he brought us a few times to the historically interesting tributary of the Saint John River called the Nerepis River. That was an Indian name which meant, he pointed out – "near pass." After passing through its narrow entry, John slowed down the motor so we could slip into the river's quiet waters without disturbing canoeists or anglers, or the silence itself.

REUNIONS AND SHRINE SUNDAY

Francis and his siblings, with us their spouses, kept our family ties strong by scheduling a family reunion every summer. At first we spent a weekend together at a motel in Bangor, in mid-eastern Maine, since it was approximately halfway between our homes. But in more recent years, we chose for our meeting time and place, the weekend that

McGillicuddy family reunion.

includes the second Sunday of August, called Shrine Sunday in Canterbury, New Brunswick, Canada.

Once settled nearby in a hotel on Friday and Saturday nights, before and after dinner, we congregated in one of our rooms. Nieces and nephews crowded in too. Bringing in extra chairs if needed, we would sit on the edges of the beds, talking, sometimes in small groups, sometimes as one audience, listening to and relishing stories of the past. One of the gifts given me by my entry into the McGillicuddy family through marriage was its stories. In their recalling them, I again got to appreciate, even cherish, some of them. I would bring up some that others hadn't mentioned yet – like the way Francis' father had given his mother her engagement ring. Since he was in New Brunswick at the time, and she, in the United States, Francis' father Bill had carefully placed the ring in an envelope and put it in the post for delivery to Margaret.

The Irish wit of cousins.

On Saturday afternoons, Francis and siblings along with us in-laws, assembled in three or so cars and drove north to Johnville to visit cousins like Cecelia Boyd. After visiting the cemeteries with them in that town, we'd go to Cecelia and Arnold's home. Cecelia's brother Buddy and Francis enjoyed these refreshing stops as much as the rest of us.

For one or more of those Saturdays before Shrine Sunday, we visited the old homestead and recalled poignant stories of the family's move from the first to the second home of Francis' childhood. My eyes brim with tears even remembering one of them – how Francis' older brother, Lou, rode on a wagon driving two horses while Francis' father and brother Charles chased the cows to direct them on foot to the McGillicuddys' second home. The next day was Shrine Sunday, an annual event with a unique and long history.

Francis' great-grandfather Daniel McGillicuddy who had emigrated from Ireland had deeded to the Catholic Church in 1876, a corner of the family farm in Canterbury near Skiff Lake. In 1923, Father MacLaughlin, a name I heard Francis' older siblings mention many times, established it as a shrine to St. Francis of Assisi. Francis was born on that land in 1927, and given the name Francis Assisi Lawrence at his baptism in that little chapel.[2] Over the years, it became a historic Franciscan Shrine and a pilgrimage site that still draws hundreds of people on the second Sunday of August. Hence its name – Shrine Sunday. The McGillicuddy clan continues to come from near and far to participate in the activities. (Clan is an expression I often heard – "We're clannish," they'd say.) We bring our lawn chairs and set them up among the long wooden benches placed beforehand on the grassy incline. Seated there, we participate in a mass celebrated on a portable outdoor altar that is set next to the chapel itself at the bottom of the gentle slope.

As the time for mass approached, Francis would leave his picnic chair and walk to what resembles a wooden gazebo, called Pilgrim's Rest. He never explained why he did this, and I didn't ask, but I understood, and I always joined him. Sitting next to each other on one of the benches, Francis and I would participate in the Mass from there. The entry into the Shrine's chapel faced us.

Picnic lunch regularly followed and then two more religious activities – a ceremony of the blessing and anointing of holy oil, and the public recitation of the rosary in several languages besides English, for example – French, Maliseet, Spanish, Tagalog (Filipino), and Polish.

It was Francis who urged me to gather with this handful of people standing behind the altar praying the first part of the Hail Mary's over the loud speaker. I was actually waiting my turn to use one of the outdoor toilets when someone announced they would welcome other people, too, if they spoke in languages different from those named. "Why don't you go and offer to recite the Lord's Prayer in Aramaic?" he nudged. So I did that day and the next three Shrine Sundays of Francis' life, and ever since.

---

[2] Later in life Francis would joke: "I was named after saints, both deacons, who were never ordained to the priesthood." What's more, Francis so identified with his patron, St. Francis of Assisi after whom he was named, that in a love note he wrote to me in 1988, he signed it: "Francis Assisi."

CHAPTER FIVE
Sabbatical Doorways and My Convent Past

When practicality and interest sparked my idea of asking for a sabbatical, I was unaware it would open doors. But the time for it was ripe. English had been my major in college, and I was teaching principally composition at Thornton Academy. Yet, without formal training in Journalism, I was also teaching an elective course in it and given the job of advisor to the yearbook and school newspaper staffs. So I seized the sabbatical opportunity for the purpose of further training, having crafted my own plan and itinerary.

For the first six months of 1979, January to June, I would engage in two projects: spend over a week to observe and become an apprentice reporter at each of three Maine newspapers – two dailies, the *Biddeford-Saco Journal* and the *Portland Press Herald*; and the weekly statewide alternative newspaper, *Maine Times*. (Francis and I had marched with its founder, John Cole, during the Vietnam Moratorium demonstration ten years earlier.)

Then I would visit twelve prize-winning high school journalism departments. The Columbia Scholastic Press Association had provided me with a list of nine high school newspapers they considered unrivaled in the nation. Of these I visited four: two in Illinois, one in Iowa, and one in Long

Island, New York. From a second list of twenty-two high schools recognized on the *regional* level, I visited eight: six in Massachusetts and two in New Hampshire.

I had to pay my own travel expenses, but I was given full salary during that second school-year semester off. There were two stipulations: that I write a report about my investigations and experiences, and that I continue teaching at Thornton Academy for at least another two years.

The Association's *School Press Revue* published my final sabbatical report as a six-page feature article entitled "Other Staffs Down the Highway." The cover, a charming black and white drawing, depicts a woman's hand holding an encased electric typewriter, and next to her shins and low-heeled shoes – a suitcase emblazoned with logos of the schools I had visited.

VENTURED ALONE

After hands-on work at established newspapers, it was time to visit the high schools. I decided to begin in New England since I could drive to those locations by myself. For the schools at a distance which I would visit later, Francis eagerly agreed to share in my adventure.

The various newspaper advisors and staffs had been alerted about my role, dates of arrival, and length of stay. I got in our Volkswagen Bug and took off for Boston and environs, alone. But not without some trepidation. I had driven there by myself before in search of a job (when I thought it was over between Francis and me), eight years earlier. It had taken some courage, though I was unaware how much, then. But now that I knew what it was like driving on the helter-skelter streets of Boston, I was deliberately challenging myself.

My life until now had been very sheltered. After living for seventeen years in a small Maine town, and one year at a small college in New Hampshire, my next fifteen years were not only shielded, they were semi-cloistered. Admittedly, once out of the convent, the two years of living in an underground relationship had introduced me to a new independence. That self-reliance had matured me. But even under the loving eye of my husband, both when underground and then proudly public, I was still living in a kind of shy, if not protected, state. This sabbatical, on the other hand, had me take another step into broadening environments. That was the first, unexpected, "sabbatical doorway".

MY CONVENT PAST

The second was this. It was only when I had arrived in the Midwest that I realized the high schools I'd be visiting were located within manageable reach of every one of the convents where I had lived. Since these were not high schools I myself had selected, but rather, designated ones I should visit, I couldn't help but appreciate the serendipity of it. It was Providence! – not just for me, but (and this was the best part) – for Francis, too. He could now see for himself where I had been hidden away from him during those fifteen years.

We arrived in Chicago on a Friday to give us the leisure of a weekend exploring this "windy city" before my visiting the three high schools. Lyons Township High School was in La Grange, Illinois, outside of Chicago. But University High School was in the city itself. Francis and I walked along the Navy Pier, went up the Willis Tower, and took great interest in exploring the Art Institute. We were awed, standing dwarfed by Picasso's mural-sized painting *Guernica* and its sketches looming before and around us. The facsimile of *Guernica* that we bought and framed hangs on my living room wall.

It was while visiting West High School in Iowa City, Iowa, we got the idea: With a second free weekend ahead of us, why not drive to Festus, Missouri – to the Novitiate! Yes, we would. Twenty-five years earlier, I had spent two and a half years there, from July of 1954 to January of 1957, apprenticing to be a nun during six months as a postulant and two years as a novice. Francis and I rented a car and headed south, without even a toothbrush. Although the drive was six hours away, but thinking we'd just look around, we had not even telephoned ahead.

ON TO THE NOVITIATE

As we entered the long driveway on Glennon Heights Road that led to the long tall building ahead, I remembered walking here during morning meditation. The Ursuline nuns had given us some flexibility within the disciplined prayer life in which we were trained. We were allowed to walk outside if we wished, before chanting the psalms antiphonally in what we called The Divine Office (aka the Liturgy of the Hours) after which a priest would come to celebrate daily mass. As a parish priest, Francis had used a breviary to pray the Psalms privately instead of in community as we and Order priests and monks did. This visit occasioned our comparing experiences.

A sign I'd never seen before came into view: Ursuline Provincialate – House of Prayer, I read aloud. "So it's no longer a Novitiate!"

Francis drove along the curved end of the road and parked the car. Here was the Novitiate, now the Provincialate building, high on a bluff overlooking the Mississippi River. We looked down at the woods along the steep bank leading to the river. "We used to love walking down there," I told him. "Every week we'd pin up our long habits and veils behind us and go for a hike." Francis and I walked down a path a short ways and returned. "See those windows at the two ends of the building?" I pointed to the third floor. "On Saturday nights we were entertained seeing the river lighted up with pleasure boats that intermittently sounded their horns." In 1954 we had numbered as many as seventy-two novices and postulants, half of us in one of two dorms at each end. "I was in that north dorm," I said as we walked toward the front door and rang the bell.

I was prepared with a short introduction, having no idea who would answer the doorbell. But here before us stood a sister from my own band. That was one of the glories of the Ursulines. Theirs was an international Order. Being centralized under a Mother General in Rome, specifically because it was under the Vatican's control, had its drawbacks. But it also had its benefits; this Novitiate included young women from every corner of the United States. And here was one from Texas.

Sister Ursula McGann gave us a warm welcome and then led us to one of the parlors on the second floor so we could talk. By now, late afternoon, she insisted we stay for dinner and even overnight. (She offered us toothbrushes and toothpaste along with towels.) We did not refuse but followed her out of the parlor, past the rotunda and down the stairs to the refectory (known in other venues as the dining room).

The small group of nuns assembled there included members of the Provincialate and directors of this House of Prayer. Here, during meals, I told Francis, we took turns reading aloud to our fellow novices and postulants while they ate in silence. On Sundays and feast days, though, we talked at table; that was the monastic style. "During my seminary days, we did the same," Francis said.

OVERNIGHT

Sister Ursula brought us to the guest room for the night and invited me to show Francis around. "From a Novitiate for aspiring nuns to a Provincialate and a House of Prayer for the general public – you'll see," she told me, "many things have changed here in twenty-five years."

Francis was as pleased as I to take a little tour. We started with the piano room next to ours and a few parlors. Then we entered the library where Sister Dawn Mestier of New Orleans and Sister Donna Hyndman of Illinois and I had sat doing research on the Psalms in preparation for teaching our peers. Since we were more than thirty in our band, each of us would have had about ten novices in our classes. It made sense to have us start teaching even before finishing college studies, since the Ursulines are a teaching Order. Francis, an avid reader, lingered over the books.

Mother Leah Kearney came to mind. She was the nun who taught us scriptures. We loved this tall, brilliant woman who would almost blush with enthusiasm and good humor when talking about St. Paul and his Epistles. Francis mentioned his own pleasure studying scripture with an inspiring professor in the seminary. "We were both lucky, that way," he said, "to have had good teachers." Francis and I walked out of the library. "Let's go to the rotunda, now," I suggested, my voice rising. "It's there that we practiced for and put on plays."

As it opened before us, Francis swept his arm to indicate the marbled floors beneath our feet and the opening into the third floor above us. I told Francis that the Ursulines had a tradition of offering opportunities for drama not only for their high school students, but also for their young nuns. At every one of these three levels – high school, Novitiate, and Juniorate – I had participated in plays, four in French: *Le Papillion Bleu, Les Dames Aux Chapeaux Verts, The Martyrs of Valenciennes*, and Paul Claudel's, *L'Annonce Faite a Marie*. My favorite was Menotti's musical *Amahl and the Night Visitors* in which I was given the part of Melchior, one of the three kings en route to find the Christ child.

Once descended to the lower floor, because of changes in the building, I had to conjure up for Francis the scenes as I remembered them. The boiler room was at the North end of the building and next to it the laundry rooms and the sewing room where all of us got lessons in using a sewing machine. Francis commented as we walked into the next one that it looked like a comfortable room. I agreed, saying it's good that it was because we spent a lot of time here. I pointed out the wall onto which our individual cubicles were set, the other side of the room where large tables and reference books offered room for research and, on the Mississippi River, the eastern side of the building, where wooden chairs had remained in place. "Several of our classes were held here," I explained, "the points for meditation class and the Gregorian chanting practice, as well as our scripture classes."

As we walked along toward the southern end of the building, Francis peeked into what had been the trunk room. "Can you picture a room holding just that," I asked – "seventy-two trunks?" I went on: "Remember the trunk that sits in our cellar at home? It once sat in this room," I said. When we were transferred to a new convent, our nun's trunk would follow us to each one, holding all our material possessions.

Francis admitted it wasn't done quite that way among diocesan priests. They had more than one trunk to accompany them to new assignments. But in his own way, he added, he had experienced the advantage of simple living. For example, when he was moved to a new parish, he left books behind – though later, he acknowledged, he did miss some of them. In that Novitiate trunk room, we shared a sense of wonder at how our lives had changed.

When we reached the Refectory where we had had supper earlier, we walked up to the second floor to sit in the Chapel for a while. This was where we postulants had walked in procession, all of us dressed as brides before we were given the habit and white veil of the novice. My mother had come by plane alone to Missouri for this ceremony, bringing with her my white high school prom dress she had altered into a simple bridal gown.

The chapel was where I had been given the privilege of chanting the Martyrology in Latin in the middle of the aisle at Christmas time, a memory I had recalled only ten years earlier while struggling with my decision to leave the convent. Remembering how moved I had been chanting in like-fashion one of the prophet Jeremiah's haunting *Gregorian Chant Lamentations* on a Good Friday, I recognized and admitted to Francis: "This love of chant was one of the most enduring gifts given me during my years as a nun."

Francis and I walked back to our room in silence, I feeling thankful for the good in my past, but abounding in gratitude that I had left the convent and married him. And what about him? Holding me in his arms that night, I understood that his gratitude, for these same reasons, was no less deep than mine. Francis and I rose early the next morning, bade Sister Ursula goodbye, and walked toward the car for the long drive back to Iowa City.

EN ROUTE BACK

Along the way, Francis and I reflected together about our decisions to enter, for me, the religious life, and for him, the priesthood. The first hints of Francis' being attracted to the priesthood came, he said, with the death of a young priest in his early thirties who had impressed him with his vibrancy and sense of humor. He had felt profoundly moved at his funeral. "I was also drawn into the mystery and mysticism of the Latin Mass," he said, "but being in my late teens, I needed to get on with my life."

Two years later, Francis went on, he had read Thomas Merton's *Seven Storey Mountain* just after it was published. "That account of a bright, educated young man who entered the Trappist Monastery stirred my soul," he said. "This time, I really began to wonder if being a priest might not be my vocation." Francis reviewed for me the journey he had taken after consulting a priest. It was a nine-year educational journey: one year in preparatory school in Boston, two years at Holy Cross College, and six years at St. John's Seminary in Brighton, Massachusetts, after which he was ordained

Francis' ordination picture.

in Boston by Cardinal Cushing in 1958. "One week later, in the parish where I was graduated from high school," Francis said with some feeling, "I celebrated my first Solemn Mass."

We agreed our vocations had been real and our motivations genuine, but we also acknowledged they were mixed with other complex factors. In his case, though he had had a girlfriend he might have married, he could not see himself settling down to married life in a small town. My entry into religious life was also partly due to the example of another religious – my homeroom teacher Mother Lorraine Pomerleau, who had been a missionary in Cuba.

After musing further, as Francis drove along, I mentioned the boyfriends I had had in high school and the fact I had even been engaged to be married, "as a senior in high school, no less," I said. But what stood out, I confided to Francis, was my memory of how relieved I had felt, once arrived at the Novitiate . . . yes, *relieved* was the word – relieved to feel free of guilt.

We Catholic youth had heard talk (in those pre-Vatican days) about venial as opposed to mortal sins. The nuns would bring us to church every month (or was it every week?) to go to confession. I had had the impression that all sins of the flesh were mortal sins. I had never had sex, had never, that is, "gone all the way" before falling in love with Francis. But, as a teenager, I wondered – was "making out" a *mortal* sin? In the Novitiate, without boys around, there would be no more occasions for this concern.

Yes, my vocation had certainly been a genuine vocation. But the motivations that led me there were indeed, also mixed.

CONVENTS BACK EAST

Wantagh High School in Wantagh, Long Island, New York, was the next high school I visited, with Francis as my companion. It was natural to stop off at the College of New Rochelle before returning home, since it was literally en route. Again, I prized this opportunity to show Francis around the sites *here*. I had lived first, at the relatively small and packed Juniorate house off campus on Meadow Lane, and then, after graduation and the profession of final simple vows – on campus at "The Castle" itself where the teaching Ursulines lived. (I left the convent before going to Tertianship, the final, formal period of formation during which Ursulines took final *solemn* vows).

I showed Francis the courtyard where I used to do my daily half hour of spiritual reading and the dogwood tree where, on Easter Vigil nights when we had stood outside under the stars, I had felt deeply moved by one of the lines in the Exultet chant, in praise of Christ "the morning star that never sets".

The highlight of this visit, however, was my reunion with Sister Amadeus, my beloved superior for six years, and Sister Irene, my college English professor and friend. Three sisters from my band were also present: Sister Bernadette, Sister Jean Baptiste, Sister Stephanie, and Sister Kathleen. With this encounter, Francis felt the strongest pulse of my convent past.

I had already visited the high schools in the Boston area – Newton North and Newton South – but the last one I wanted to show Francis, the Ursuline Convent in Dedham, Massachusetts, was also conveniently along our route home. "I especially want you to see this convent," I told Francis, "because this is where I lived for six years before meeting you." I pointed, as we drove up to what had once been a mansion – "See that building up the hill there? That's it – the convent." Francis drove up the road and parked our car on the rounded driveway near the front door. He looked down at the long grassy area at the back of the school building below. "That was once a polo court," I said, indicating the expanse before us. "Quite beautiful, with the pond at the end of it," he remarked.

Turning to face the convent itself, I told Francis what he already knew, that it was not uncommon for religious communities to acquire homes of

the rich to house their members. Spacious buildings like this accommodated well a whole community of nuns. Entering the lovely wood paneled
chapel, Francis guessed right away it had once been a large library.

I then thanked the sister (one I didn't know) who had allowed us to look
around. As Francis and I walked out and onto the courtyard outside, I told
him I had fond memories of the spirited Ursuline who had been our superior
for too short a time – Mother St. Mark Sullivan. On the other hand, I confessed, the highlights of my six years in Dedham had been the five summers
I was away studying: for four of them – religious studies at Providence College; and for one eight-week summer – French at Assumption College, in
an intensive National Defense Education Act program to ameliorate the
French of Franco-Americans like me. Back in our car, having come full circle,
we got on the road again, quite happy to get back to our own home.

ONE LAST SABBATICAL DOOR

My sabbatical brought me through many doors – more than only high
school doors. In daring to set out on my own, driving around a bigger city,
I had learned how to fend for myself with more confidence, even alone,
and Francis and I had also walked through all the convent doors of my
past, together.

But there was a third door I only got to peek through at this time.
During my visit to Phillips Academy in Andover, Massachusetts, I stayed
at my cousin's, Pat Plante's, home. His wife, Linda, introduced me to her
friend, Sue Luby, who had recently opened her Sue Luby School of Hatha
Yoga. I went back later, and *that* decision would take both Francis and me
into a veritable new world.

CHAPTER SIX
Offspring

L ike a mother who names her children in the order of birth, even though I was an only child and childless, I found myself counting ours. They were: peacework, yoga, the Dances of Universal Peace, and permaculture.

PEACEWORKS

Francis was converted to working for peace after he agreed in 1966 to speak in court in support of two young men who could not in conscience participate in the Vietnam War. The conscientious objector status they obtained as a result, exempted them from going to that war. The attorney who represented those two Catholics, a member of the Society of Friends (a Quaker), was Cushman Anthony.

In the early eighties, during the so-called Second Cold War when the Nuclear War Scare became a full blown crisis, this same Cushman Anthony took it upon himself to give a talk on war tax resistance (WTR) at the Portland Public Library. Since it was he, in 1972, who had also invited me to join him on a televised panel discussing war and peace issues, just before

Francis and I were married, we were eager to attend.

CONVERSION OF TWO "QUATHOLICS"

Cushman's talk so moved us, we accepted his invitation soon after to join a gathering at the Friends Meeting House in Cambridge, Massachusetts. Its focus was on the Peace Tax Fund (PTF) bill, which, if passed, would allow the taxes of those conscientiously opposed to paying for war, to be redirected to nonmilitary, or peaceful purposes. Beginning with that meeting, we gradually became, in a sense, the "Quatholics," some of our friends jokingly called us – because we worked actively with Friends (Quakers) for eight years to pass the PTF bill.

In Francis' love note for our wedding anniversary that year, he wrote: "Elaine, my Beloved: Happy Anniversary! Here's a quote from Antoine de Saint-Exupery: "'Life has taught us that love does not consist in gazing at each other, but in looking outward together in the same direction.'"

Once Francis and I became members of the New England Committee for the Peace Tax Fund campaign, we drove to Cambridge six times a year to discuss the bill and strategies for its passage. When we heard it was the custom of this committee to spend one long weekend a year together at the Friends Meeting House in Falmouth, Massachusetts, we smiled at each other. That southernmost area of Massachusetts by the ocean was one by which we had driven en route to our first honeymoon near Provincetown.

Vacations like this, in the Friends' modest little summer house close to the dunes where we cooked our own meals and enjoyed long hikes, deepened our relationships. We became not just a committee working for a piece of legislation, but a group of friends. Two of our members, a couple from the area, were scientists. Rudy and Amelia Sheltima gave us a tour of their workplace – the Woods Hole Oceanographic Institution. We were privileged to learn firsthand through their stories something of their fascinating work. We heard some of those tales after supper sitting on the sofa and comfortable chairs in the small living room.

Francis and I worked closely with Quakers to the point of traveling to Washington, DC. There we came together with

Francis in Philadelphia.

longtime director of the Campaign, Marian Franz, along with a few directors of the Friends Committee on National Legislation and made contact with our Maine Senator George Mitchell to urge him to pass this conscientious objection bill for taxpayers. We also met with Friends at Bryn Mawr College in Philadelphia to celebrate the 50th Anniversary of Conscientious Objection.

Without question, the influence of our Quaker friends imprinted itself on us, especially Alan Eccleston's. Alan had made his own a particular quote of Quaker preacher John Woolman: "The process of ministry is like a man walking in a miry place, heavy with mist. He must take one step at a time to see where next to step." We did too, for Francis and I referred to it thereafter, at watershed moments in our own lives, beginning with that time when we decided to become conscientious war-tax resisters.

CONSCIENTIOUS WTR – NEW YORK PEACE RALLY

Our own Catholic Archbishop Raymond Hunthausen of Seattle also inspired us to act. Whereas he withheld half of his income tax to protest the stockpiling of nuclear weapons and the Trident missile program, Francis and I withheld, for three years – our portion of payment for nuclear weapons, $300, and for five years more – the "symbolic" amount of $25.

We were instructed at workshops and retreats by people experienced as war tax resisters how to calculate the correct figure. After simply subtracting the $300 amount from the taxes we owed, we wrote a note on our tax form, and attached a letter explaining why we were opposed, in conscience, to paying for war. Since, in the end, the Internal Revenue Service garnished Francis' wages, it might have seemed pointless, but what mattered was the public witness against the war.

One step Francis and I took was displaying our homemade sign, Mainers Against War Taxes, while walking in the streets of New York during the Peace Rally of 1982. We were two of the one million people participating in one of the largest political demonstration in American history demanding worldwide nuclear disarmament and an end to America's Cold War arms race with the Soviet Union. Even in our fatigue (we had tried to sleep overnight on the bus from Portland to New York), the atmosphere was electric. The march led to Central Park where we listened to, not only speeches, but Bruce Springsteen, Jackson Browne, Joan Baez,

and other musicians who had come to perform for us. Parenthetically, Francis and I vowed we would never travel that far overnight in a bus again without equipping ourselves with a least a pillow. He joked he now understood what Jesus meant when he said he had nowhere to lay his head.

The resulting publicity of our public witness – front page stories in the *Portland Press Herald* and the *Maine Times* – launched Francis and me into an eight-year period of both campaigning for pas-

Front page – Portland Press Herald.

sage of the Peace Tax Fund bill and answering invitations to give talks about the action we had taken. We gave seventeen presentations during that time (three of them during and after Protestant church services in Portland). Referring to the young conscientious objectors who had sought Francis' support, and who in doing so radicalized him, he told the people who came to hear us at one of those presentations: "My life could never be the same again. It was that young man's way of saying 'If you are trying to love your enemies, as Jesus taught, you do not prepare to kill.' *That's* what opened my eyes."

Francis explained that the military establishment brings legal pressure to bear solely on eighteen-year-old males. That specific population was the one put in jeopardy if they refused in conscience to register for the draft, he pointed out. "Elaine and I want to join them in civil disobedience in this way," he said, "by redirecting our taxes." We did exactly that by putting them in the "Maine War Tax Funds for Life" which we co-founded with another couple, Larry Dansinger and his wife, Karen Marys daughter. They are still active in creative new ways as well, promoting peace and justice. On tax day, those refused dollars placed there by us and by others were publicly donated on April 15. One year, the money was given to a shelter for battered women, and in another, for a children's playground in a low-income school in Portland.

Mainly for our own work as conscientious war tax objectors, in 1989, Francis and I were given by the Maine Peace Campaign, the Seeds of Peace Award. We hung in our home the framed quote of the award: "Liberation is an awakening of the consciousness, a change of mentality for ways of thinking so that the person no longer thinks what their present society wants him/her to think but rather learns to think and act for himself/herself in dialogue with others in order to create a new world in which it is easier to love." (Magaly Rodriguez O'Hearn)

CATHOLIC PEACEMAKERS

The peacemaking spirit alive among the Friends was just as passionate among people in our own Catholic tradition. Francis and I met Suzanne Belote and Brayton Shanley before they co-founded with Fr. Charles Emmanuel McCarthy in 1982 the Agape Community, a lay Catholic peace community which is still thriving. Their weekend retreats profoundly influenced us over the years, for Suzanne and Brayton do more than resist the violence of the status quo; their counter-cultural life-style (modeling nonviolence, simple, sustainable living, and service) creates the Beloved Community we need.

When a friend in Portland invited us to her home to hear Father Gower speak about forming a local chapter of Pax Christi (*Peace of Christ*), the international peace movement begun in France in 1945, Francis and I looked at each other with incredulity. "This has *got* to be the Father Gower whom Francis replaced when he was assigned to the Waterville parish where I met him!" I told our friend, adding that Father Jim was so well loved, the Armory had to be rented when it seemed the whole town of Waterville came out to honor him before he moved to another assignment. "You can imagine how I felt," Francis quipped, "trying to step into the shoes of this giant of a man."

All of us who gathered in our friend's living room that night, including the new people we met, agreed to form a local chapter of Pax Christi. That was in 1980, the year Father Jim began his two-year trek traveling with another priest, driving throughout the U.S. to found more local chapters.

Over the years, Francis and I worked with our new Pax Christi friends, Denny Dreher, Bill and Ursula Slavick, Sue and Bob Ewing, and Anne and Erik Johnson, among many others trying to live by Jesus' non-violence. For example, we persuaded our city council to pass the Freeze Campaign resolution and sent a tractor trailer full of supplies to the people of

Nicaragua during the Iran-Contra affair. But those were only early projects. In a period of more than thirty years, in collaboration with other friends out of town who formed Pax Christi/Maine, we organized annual retreats led by well-known peace advocates. In our present world rife with violence

Demonstrating against Iraq War.

and war, Pax Christi's work of peace and justice continues.

Francis participated in protests at a Maine shipyard – Bath Iron Works – along with other Pax Christi members for many years whenever warships were launch-ed. This was more his project than mine. He would hold up a sign: "Each cruiser = 840 Hiroshima-sized bombs." When the Berrigans began engaging in several Ploughshares Prince of Peace Actions in Bath, however, I joined Francis and Pax Christi in supporting them both in Bath and during their court trials in Portland.[3]

Always a good storyteller, Francis, when talk turned to peace issues, liked to tell the first of these two stories about the Bath Iron Works ship launchings. One particular one, he said, was etched in his memory. It was presided over by Cardinal Archbishop John O'Connor of New York, since the ship itself was named after a Jesuit priest chaplain. "The fact it was named after a priest," he'd comment with displeasure, "is one indication of the acceptance in Catholic culture of such massive armaments." A Catholic Maine artist, Ray Shadis, was so outraged by this naming of the warship, Francis related (and related well, since he had witnessed it) that he held a sign for the cardinal to see as he walked out into the streets at the end of

---

[3] The Christian, pacifist anti-nuclear Ploughshares Movement took its name from the passage in Isaiah 2:3 about "beating swords into ploughshares."

ceremony. It read: "Jesus would have puked!"

On another occasion at a Bath Iron protest, Francis said he never forgot standing near Philip Berrigan when federal marshalls took him into custody for a previous Plowshares action there. "Whenever I see a US flag displayed near the sanctuary in Catholic churches," Francis acknowledged, "I am reminded that the swastika was also displayed in German churches during Hitler's regime."

THE BERRIGANS' INFLUENCE

Francis and I certainly knew about the Berrigans. The *New Yorker* article about them he had shared with me in the teachers' lunchroom only days after we met had been one of our first ice breakers, though of course, there was never any *ice* to *break* between us. As Father Gower did, the Berrigans were entering our lives again, but now – with us as Mr. & Mrs. McGillicuddy.

We had read about them, then – how Philip and Daniel Berrigan, both priests, had burned draft files in Catonsville, Maryland, the previous May, 1968. Now in the eighties, we were beginning to be involved with them in specific ways, and not only with them, but also with Philip's wife, Elizabeth McAllister, a former nun who had married this once Josephite priest the year after Francis and I were married.

A weekend with Jesuit priest Daniel Berrigan came first. Our Pax Christi group chose him to lead our fourth retreat in 1983. Daniel's sister-in-law, Elizabeth, had recently gone to jail in New York state for a Ploughshares action, so Daniel's weekend had a special edge to it. After the retreat, I awakened that Monday morning at 4 A.M. to find myself in tears. Francis woke up too. "I've got to leave my job!" I said, suddenly knowing it was something I had to do. I didn't exactly know why, but the conviction was strong, that after thirteen years at Thornton Academy, it was time for me to give up academic teaching. I had done it for twenty three and a half years. Following a period of discussion and reflection with Francis, I told our principal that I would be leaving in June of 1984, at the end of the next school year.

Soon after, when Francis and I were feeling vulnerable about my quitting my job, we got a phone call from a company calling itself Security First. After telling the caller "No, thank you," we laughed aloud about the call. We were delighted the expression highlighted where our real security lay. Living on one salary was our choice.

Elaine, Dan Berrigan, and Francis.

UNCLEAR

My desire to teach yoga was stronger than ever by now, since after my year of sabbatical in 1979, I had returned monthly to Sue Luby's School of Hatha Yoga in Andover, Massachusetts for workshops by a yoga teacher from Cambridge, Carol Nelson, whom Sue featured at her school. But being still unclear about the direction toward which I might be called, I floundered.

I thought at first I was meant to work in a shelter for the homeless. A wealthy couple, Louise and Claude Montgomery, had recently decided to create such a shelter for the homeless in Portland. I spent over a year, along with Denny, helping Louise to set it up from scratch. We tore up old linoleum, painted walls, and did whatever was needed. Dorothy Day had also given a talk in our parish about her Catholic Worker Movement, right around that time, as if to give me a sign. But I was struggling, still unsure.

When Francis and I heard that Phillip Berrigan and his wife, Elizabeth, were giving a retreat at the Rowe Conference Center in Massachusetts, we thought such a retreat would give me direction, as Daniel's had done a few years earlier. Elizabeth had recently come out of jail for her Ploughshares action. Maybe I needed to be led this time by these other two extraordinarily committed Berrigans who shared our priest-nun background.

I returned from that retreat, however, needing to see a chiropractor. Dr. Sheila Littlefield, who soon became Francis' and my good friend, understood what was going on. I had been wondering if I myself were called to more direct action, the way the Berrigans were. I had heard them make the point that they were *not* "extraordinary," that they were "ordinary" people like us, like me. Of course that was true, but I took their comment seriously, as applying to me in particular. Without realizing it, I was putting pressure on myself. Dr. Sheila knew what I was thinking. "You're not cut out for going to jail," she said.

That comment of hers lifted the scales from my eyes. The deep knowing came. I realized I had been viewing yoga as a kind of inferior choice, in comparison with either direct action or working with the homeless to which others were called. I was not called to either of these things, except to help out and to support both, as we were doing. No. I was called, instead – to yoga.

I saw it now, and Francis could see it too. While I had been pursuing my yoga studies for seven years, he had been reading *Yoga Journal* and many books about yoga we had bought. Because of this yoga-study journey that I took before fully realizing why, and because Francis shared it with me as well, both of us understood in a more personal way now – that the ancient practice of yoga is a genuine way of peacemaking: It takes people out of their reactive ways of living which lead to conflict. Ahimsa (non-violence) is the first of the Yamas from the Yoga Sutras of Patanjali, known as the father of yoga. Nonviolence is at the root of Jesus' way and Gandhi's.

It's as if Francis and I vaguely sensed what Walter Wink wrote in his

2010 book *The Powers That Be* about what can happen to people in the peace movement: "Our very identities are often defined by our resistance to evil. The impatience of some activists with prayer, meditation, and inner healing may itself betray an inkling of what they might find if they looked within. For the struggle against evil can make us evil. . . . Prayer protects us against that contagion of evil." (p.126) For Francis and me, then, Yoga became Peacework's sister.

YOGA

It was Francis' remark originally, in 1978, the year *before* I met Sue Luby, that had set everything in motion: "You know what?" he had exclaimed, after having seen a yoga demonstration for low-income seniors at his workplace: "Yoga massages the internal organs." I was so intrigued by that concept, I bought a book – Richard Hittleman's *Yoga in 28 Days*. And within those twenty-eight days, I was won over. It had gotten me started taking two weekly classes from a local yoga teacher.

My education in yoga may have started from a book and those local classes, but the studies with Sue and Carol in Andover only whet my appetite for more concentrated training. Sue had told me that if anyone asked me what kind of yoga she taught, I should tell them it's "a preface to Iyengar Yoga."

YOGA IN SAN FRANCISCO

I had been an avid reader of *Yoga Journal* and a follower of Judith Lasater's regular column, "Asana" (Sanskrit for postures). She used the expression "Iyengar Yoga," so I got the idea of telephoning to inquire if this master teacher would give me private yoga classes during the weeklong spring break at Thornton Academy. I reasoned that, since I was starting yoga later in life (I was 46), I might as well study with someone of Judith

Lasater's caliber. Judith agreed, so Francis and I flew to San Francisco where he joined me for a few of my private yoga classes.

After one of them, Judith said, "You know, you two are very different." We joked that was one reason we complemented one another so well. Later, when we took the Myers Briggs Personality tests, we discovered we shared three of the four characteristics: Intuition, Feeling, and Judgment. So we were not that different, after all.

When I bade Judith goodbye, she urged me to return the following summer to take the six-week training program at what was then called The Institute for Yoga Teacher Education (and later – Iyengar Yoga Institute of San Francisco). Francis encouraged me. His mother would stay with him in our home, not for the usual two weeks that year, but for the whole of my time away. This was the training that gave me reason to think I was equipped to teach yoga before the breakthrough moment when I realized yoga itself was calling me.

There I was, in San Francisco then, for the summer of 1982, without Francis this time, enrolled in an intense program of yoga practice and study. By now I had done preliminary study of my own, printing the names of basic yoga poses along with their Sanskrit names on 3 x 5 cards, one card for each pose. My text book was B.K.S. Iyengar's classic, likely the most comprehensive book on hatha yoga – *Light on Yoga*.

In addition to classes in Asana, we had two classes of anatomy, one by Dr. Frank Wildman of the Feldenkrais Institute called Seeing and Understanding Bodies. In the other class, Marcia Stefanick, a professor of anatomy at Stanford University's School of Medicine (where she still teaches) and a yoga practitioner herself, gave us take-home tests every week. We had to describe what muscles were used going into and out of the basic postures taught. I loved all of it.

I was nevertheless homesick for Francis and for the sounds of crickets which seemed to be nonexistent in the Mission District where I had rented a room.

Only weeks before, I had participated with Francis in the 1982 New York Rally; it was the period of Reagan's "nuclear scare." I found myself having the wild fantasy, visualizing myself – if we got hit with a nuclear bomb – walking across the country to reach Francis and my mother. (My father had died three years earlier, in 1979).

When Francis met me at the airport after my six weeks away, we were unable to speak at first. We just held one another. I would have returned for this good yoga training all over again, but now I viewed homesickness with new understanding.

IYENGAR YOGA CONVENTION

When the North American Iyengar Yoga Convention of 1987 was announced, I knew I'd sign up, and Francis was up for doing the same. He had learned yoga from me, since my foray in teaching it began with him and my mother as my first students. We three had practiced hatha yoga together during our week of vacation in the summers. Tailored

Francis using chairs for yoga.

for each of them individually, I had created charts with stick-figure sketches of yoga poses – different postures for every day of the week. I had even made audiocassette tapes for Francis so he could follow my voiced directions while he practiced in the kitchen before going to work. In this sense, it was perfectly timed for us.

The convention was conveniently located, moreover, just a two-hour drive south to Cambridge at Harvard University. Hundreds came from all over the country, Canada, and abroad. This was a chance for Francis and me to meet and interact with one of the world's foremost hatha yoga gurus, B.K.S. Iyengar. He was called simply Mr. Iyengar at first, but also, later – Guruji. He was and still is, at 95 now, a genius at using yoga poses to "cure" physical problems.

Classes were taught in many different rooms on the Harvard campus by the most experienced Iyengar yoga teachers in the United States and Canada. Mr. Iyengar, with his mane of white hair, wearing the ankle-length white garb of Indian men, acted to some degree like the lion some called him. He would walk in and out the classes accompanied by four or five of the local advanced teachers who were familiar with the class locations.

The master could draw tears from the teacher that he would observe during his five or ten minute stop, if her or his teaching did not meet his high standards. This lion also had eagle eyes. But that was the point of the convention. He wanted the teachers who taught yoga according to his *Iyengar Way* (also the name of a book), to be totally alert to their students' conditions and needs. About him and the coming of his entourage, a participant used the expression which spread like a forest ablaze; "The Yoga Gestapo is coming." Francis loved that story.

DECISIONS

The convention made an impact on both Francis and me. In fact, it secured Francis' yoga conversion. "In the dog days of August," he would tell people, with amazement in his voice, "in August, usually the worst times, when allergies kick in – even then," he emphasized, "during that week, I felt *very* good!" The yoga regimen had been intense, too, so Francis took the lesson to heart: "The more hatha yoga I do," he concluded, "the better I feel."

Returning home from that convention with a wooden backbender kit ready to assemble in our car's trunk (intended especially for Francis), I was in the throes of my own conversion. I had to face it: I must go to India to study yoga with the Iyengars. Part of me fought against the idea, remembering how homesick I had felt during my six weeks in San Francisco away from Francis. But the feeling of being called to go was so solid, once I recognized it, it was irresistible. And, as if to validate the call's genuineness, the way ahead was fully opened. I was told when I signed up that I would be assigned to join a group of yoga teachers from New York, led by a master yoga teacher, the late Mary Dunn. They would be departing in late September of 1989, two years hence. I didn't mind waiting; it would give me time to deepen my practice, and the delay would give Francis and me time to find a place to open a yoga studio.

COMMITMENT WITH A PLACE

We looked around, then, for such a place. The moment we walked into the third floor room at 616 Congress Street, just one hundred yards from the Portland Museum of Art, we knew this was it. The veritable wall of windows on the right looked down onto Portland's main artery. The dramatic and beautiful Baxter Building housing the Portland Public Library from 1888 to 1978 stood almost directly in front of us across the street.

It was in that library, sixteen years earlier in 1971 that I had read the *New York Times'* news on the celibacy debate. And we could see to its left, the tall building where I had rented an apartment for less than a year, during our underground period. It seemed a good omen to have those buildings reminiscent of our past – where Francis had come to me incognito – facing the studio space we were considering.

We readily visualized how the two rooms could be used for weekend workshops by master yoga teachers from selected parts of the country. That very thing happened under both our directorship and that of subsequent new owners of the studio. In fact we joked that the teachers we brought in to teach those workshops were training our competition. One yoga student called our studio – "the citadel of yoga in Portland."

What is it that would cause us as a couple to found a yoga studio? The decision to have a baby is much more straightforward than what we went through. The idea of doing so in order to be generative, or, for a childless couple to leave a legacy, did not come all at once. In fact, the steps that led us there, like life, were circuitous and unsure.

The year we got the peace award, 1989, was the year we founded Portland Yoga Studio. We realized then it would be too complicated to continue the war tax redirection we had done for eight years. Or at least not in that way. Once the time would come, however, we would figure out another way to express our objection to war making, as owners of a yoga studio.

HIP STORY

When I was five-years old, a moving car came within inches of hitting me while I was crossing Main Street in Springvale, Maine. It left my right hip muscles in trauma. Though no obvious scars marred my body, those muscles went into a deep contraction that wouldn't let go. As a result it became, and remained, fibrous at the core. Chronically contracted, numbed tissue in a state of amnesia, creates pain. As an adult, its nagging was low grade, since it was largely dormant. No one could find anything wrong with it. It was something people had to live with, I was told.

But after ten years of yoga practice, begun at age forty-three, the postures began unearthing the pain. Unbelievably the hip was reaching for release after all those years. Mr. Iyengar had adjusted my hip in a posture during the convention, but when I went to his own yoga center in Pune, India, the following year, even he could not solve my problem. It would take me another ten years to understand what had happened. Although unable to cure me, body workers helped. What I assimilated from my anatomy teachers, and in particular from Tom Myers, was invaluable, even if it was my own body that guided me toward a satisfactory solution. It was not eagerness to perform advanced poses for their own sake that led me into a deep yoga practice, it was the relief the postures provided by eventually transforming tough fiber into flesh. (In the early stages, to describe the changes in how a specific muscle complex felt in that process which took years, I used the similes: a metal cable, a fiber rope, a rubber hose, and then, thera-band resistive tubing.)

I will never forget, nor cease to be grateful for, Francis' patience putting up with my talking about my hip, especially in the early years. I tried to hold back in his presence when talking with friends by saying, "Poor Francis, he hears about my hip all the time." He appreciated the fact that my experience helped me understand my students' physical problems. He saw for himself also how much it encouraged them to hear and see for themselves that it's possible to change chronically contracted muscles. ("Persistence pays off is my motto," I told them.) But Francis *had* to be charitable to hear me recount the latest development he had already heard about at home.

He told me at some mid-point in the process, "You'll always have this; it'll never end." No wonder it seemed unending – it took me thirteen years to reach and release the core of the contracture or "knot." I was as gratified as he when, in 2003, it reached that point. Now, although the muscle tissue repeatedly shrinks back into its old knotted state daily – a daily yoga practice just as dependably unbinds it. I count it a

Elaine in Eka Pada Raja
Kapotasana II.

115

blessing, too, that this regularity of practice keeps me fit.

It must be noted, too, that Francis was very proud of the good results my tenacity brought. Before other teachers joined me to teach classes at the studio, for our brochures, we used photos of me in some of the poses that had helped release my hip. He kept extra copies of them in his leather, male purse to hand out when someone inquired about yoga. The one he liked to show off was the photo of me in the One Foot King of the Pigeon Pose – Eka Pada Raja Kapotasana II, a backbend in which the practitioner's two hands bring one foot onto the head.

JOURNEY TO INDIA

I left for Pune on September 28, 1989. A week before, Francis wrote in his notebook, "I am not feeling any joy about your going to India. Mostly it's the reality of everyone getting sick while there." He told me when I returned that he had shed tears after dropping me off at the Mermaid Transportation van's office.

En route to the airport, I sat in the back seat. Since the five people seated ahead of me knew each other and were joking around, I was glad they were occupied among themselves. After Francis' and my sad separation, I wanted to do other things, like read the newspaper he had marked up for me. This was just another endearing habit of his. Francis had noted this passage – "There is probably no discovery on earth happier than the realization that you are in love with the person you happen to be married to."

I then wrote the first entry in my India journal. In 1989 there was no email to connect us. During the whole nine weeks, all that Francis and I had was a few expensive telephone calls cross-continent, and frequent letters. My entries, then, reads like an ongoing conversation with God.

Next to the date, I would write both the number of days I had been away, and those remaining before my return. For example: September 28

(1/63). For the third heading, I recorded from the parish missalette, what I called my "scripture mantra" for the day. On the day I left, I chose verse 15 from psalm 31: "My days are in Your hands, my God."

In Pune, I lived at a Christian ashram called Christa Prema Seva Ashram. Its sylvan setting had once included many types of trees which rare birds visited. Small rooms, a library, meeting room, kitchen, and open dining area on three sides looked onto a circular pond at the center. Pond lilies and a garden at the fourth side added beauty and a contemplative air to this monastic setting, which included a small chapel where daily mass was celebrated. We were told that when Gandhi visited the Ashram in 1933, he had stayed in the room I now shared with an Indian nun, room one. Our small cells and beds on opposite sides of the room were delineated by curtains. Mosquito nets enclosed our beds near cement walls whose windows were opened or shuttered.

To reach the Ramamani Iyengar Yoga Center, the handful of us who lived at the ashram instead of in a hotel, had a pleasant walk (free from the pollution of crowded streets) through the Agricultural College. To welcome us students who had come for the new term just begun, Mr. Iyengar, his daughter Geeta, and son Prashant held a reception.

I had come to India under the impression my fullest poten-

Elaine in India with B.K.S. Iyengar.

tial would be drawn from me by the fierce yoga master who asks for perfection. But my journal reveals an even deeper motivation which I discovered only gradually. Because I was tasting "the full brunt and bitterness of my separation from Francis," I came face to face with the reality of death. The trip to Pune from Mumbai in itself had done that. From within our bus, as it drove along the Deccan Plateau, we had seen an overturned car or two left in place down the mountainside.

Recalling a specific moment early in our marriage when I was lying in Francis' arms, "How safe I had felt there, with the fearful world shut out!" I mused. Realizing I was facing my fear of Francis' death, I wrote to advise myself, "I cannot put my trust in Francis' comforting arms alone. The source of my life must go deeper still. It must be founded on God's Love itself."

It was as if I was directly seeking ahead of time, strength to face it – Francis' death. I called it "the cross," and viewed my time in India as a purification that would prepare me for that, or for anything.

On November 1, about a month before I was due to return home, I wrote my scriptural mantra for that day in large print, personalizing it by paraphrasing this passage from Romans 8:15: "I have not received a spirit of slavery to fall back into fear, but I have received a spirit of adoption through which I cry 'Abba Father.'" My commentary verifies what this journey was all about: "this is the release for which I came to India – release from 'fear.' Now I know," I went on, "but I m not ready to return home; You are not finished with me yet. What remains now is for me to live this reality."

I credited the bhyjans in great part for this answer to my prayer. The fact that I found in these devotional chants "one of the deepest experiences for me here," seemed to authenticate what Carol, my seat mate on the plane had called me – "an ecstatic type of person." (I bought many cassette tapes of bhyjans to bring home with me.) I felt an affinity with Carol, a writer from New York City. She had been to Pune before and had told me that each person's experience is unique, but nevertheless "transformative." The insight about fear felt lofty enough as a "transformative experience." But the following incident proved, for all its down to earth practicality, to be no less supportive.

I journeyed to India very unsure of myself, in reality, lacking self-esteem.

The New York group with which I had come, returned to the US after four months, whereas I was staying for five more weeks, along with one other New Yorker with whom I'd be traveling back home. Since she and I were the only Americans among others from various parts of the world, we saw more of each other. A few weeks before our scheduled return, this no-non-sense person said to me, "Want to know what I've noticed about you? You ask everybody's opinions." I asked myself then, "What's wrong with that?" The encounter, nevertheless, shook me up. But through journaling I under-stood that this person had done me a favor, actually a big favor. Reminded by her unsolicited comment of my counselor's advice during the Clinical Pas-toral Education course I had taken the previous year with Dr. Alexander Cairns, I took it to heart anew – "Trust your own judgments."

FRANCIS' COURSE

Francis registered for a course which started just after I left for India. Focused on the history of the participants' experiences as members of groups, the course was called Personal Growth Group. His handwritten responses to the many questions given indicate he was doing, as I was doing on another continent, a lot of personal reflection.

Referring to me, Francis explained that his life was not normal in the sense that I, his "partner," was temporarily out of the country. Noting that "there are therefore few occasions for me to share on a deep level," he nev-ertheless expressed satisfaction toward the end of the course that his expe-rience of solitude had been positive.

The groups Francis chose to focus on were the priesthood in particu-lar, but also Pax Christi. About the first, he admitted he was still grieving to some extent the loss of the sense of awe he had experienced as a priest during mass. He missed "the mystery, a certain sense of the mystical."

Francis recognized, however: "There's a satisfaction now and even a joy that all of the above are still somehow part of who I am, but now in the place where freedom is experienced."

In discussing members' responsibilities in the groups they had joined, Francis brought up his "refusal" to take on a facilitator's role when we Pax Christi members were taking turns doing so at our meetings. "I see myself as shedding all clerical roles of leadership as I experienced them," he wrote, confessing, "I probably have some sorting out of those issues still to come."

On the question of personal handicaps, Francis indicated that his centered around being an introvert and "the consequent shyness and uncertainty about myself that follows from that." Speculating further about this shyness, he revealed that he felt "frustrated that sharing (himself) and speaking before others was a struggle." On the other hand, Francis sounded proud to report that he had made "efforts" and could see some "progress in explicitly recognizing occasions" when he could consciously speak first in a group, rather than last.

Francis' final jottings demonstrate the fruitfulness of his inner journey through this group course process: "An overall tranquility of spirit as a result of having descended into my past experiences, especially in the priesthood. A feeling of healing and then moving on."

I was returning home from India freed to some extent by having explored my own fears. For his part, in considering the question, My Fears and My Fetters, Francis concluded: "The only fear is the shared fear that all pilgrims experience – not knowing exactly where the path leads each day."

When I returned home to the Portland International Airport dressed in a Punjabi dress, Francis and I were again overcome with emotion. We just held one another until we were able to speak. I slept on him that whole night long. But the joy and peace we were experiencing, because of our inner work, had more depth about it than reunion alone.

FRANCIS – CO-DIRECTOR OF PORTLAND YOGA STUDIO

Our yoga studio was officially opened in the spring before I left for India. We had temporarily used the name Yoga Lifeline, but when I told Francis what name had come to me while in India, he preferred it. We announced in our Winter 1990 brochure, the definitive name for our yoga center was – Portland Yoga Studio.

Opening of Portland Yoga Studio.

It was only when Francis felt he had broken through what he called a "kicking and screaming early stage" of hatha yoga that he declared: "It's my pearl of great price now!" adding that he admired the students who immediately took to yoga. Not so for him. But once he had gone through that perseverance period, since it took away his back and neck pain and improved his breathing, he made the best advocate for yoga.

Francis not only participated in the classes I taught, he allowed me to use him to demonstrate some poses. After he died, a former student who had been in our class, Willa Wirth, referred to him as "the epitome of willingness." How could hesitant students, especially men who tended to be outnumbered in the classes, possibly resist trying poses if this 6'1" tall man,

Co-directors demonstrating poses.

who started yoga at fifty-two, was demonstrating them? One of our male students told us, "Francis is imitable!"

By the time other yoga teachers had increased our teaching staff, our student and photographer friend, Bill Gillis, took photos of the six of us and Francis at Fort Williams' Park in South Portland. He photographed us as individuals and in groups. We chanced climbing up and over the craggy rocks for photos atop the highest ones overlooking the Atlantic Ocean. Bill had us all chuckling when he referred to group shots as – "Francis with his harem".

I took pride telling a few stories about Francis, in talking with friends, for example, how he kicked up into his first handstand at age sixty-two. And how he handled the following situation which happened seven years before he retired from the Portland Housing Authority. Since Francis' office was a short distance from the studio, he would meet me there after work. I, in the meantime, would take the bus at the end of our street and meet him at the studio in town. Once, perhaps because of the snow, the bus was greatly delayed. By the time I got in town, it was past time to start the class. I knew Francis would at least have the door unlocked for our students, but I was unprepared for what I saw next.

When I opened the door to the inner, larger studio – there was Francis standing facing the class, and giving them verbal instructions, all the while doing the yoga pose with the students, as a trained yoga teacher might. I could hardly believe he had taken over like this, because, witty and intelligent as he was, Francis was, as mentioned, also

Francis with his "harem."

shy. Yet, he *had* had good teacher training simply from tagging along with me for ninety percent of the many workshops I continued to take, even after my yoga study in San Francisco and India.

After Francis' retirement from the housing authority, he liked to joke, "I'm working for Elaine now." He not only continued to take care of our yoga studio finances but worked with me as co-director for the remaining nine of the sixteen years that we owned it. That oft-repeated remark reminds me of another response Francis liked to use when people inquired if he also would become a lector at church: "No, I think it's better for the priest's wife to be up there on the pulpit."

Francis using the "pelvic swing."

YOGA TRAVEL STUDY

Once we opened the studio, we got a novel idea. In place of the symbolic war-tax resistance we had done in the past, we would do a kind of *legal* war-tax resistance. We did that by deliberately spending whatever profits came to us through our studio as a DBA (Doing Business As). At year's end, as a consequence, we would give each of the teachers a bigger than normal bonus, and we would participate in more yoga workshops and retreats than we might otherwise have done.

There *were* profits, but, as we saw it, those profits brought a three-fold benefit. They obviated payment of war taxes, Francis and I grew in knowledge of and experience in yoga, and the teachers were more than satisfied.

When the time came to sell the studio sixteen years later, though, the "books" didn't look very impressive. "Not a profitable business," we were told, but it was a small price to pay since we preferred a simple lifestyle anyway. Our luxury was to study with selected master yoga teachers in the United States and abroad.

In a cenotes - Yucatan Peninsula.

This decision, likewise, had far reaching consequences. Yoga would lead us to both the Dances of Universal Peace (DUP) and to permaculture, in that serendipitous way, once again, Providence guided, even dogged us.

For eight consecutive years, Francis and I participated in weeklong yoga intensives at Feathered Pipe Ranch in Montana. These were taught by Francis' and my principal teachers (and friends) whom we followed to sites abroad as well to their own yoga centers – Patricia Walden's in Cambridge, Massachusetts, and John Schumacher's in Bethesda, Maryland. In both places, we made new friends who also followed Patricia and John. Some of these friendships continue to this day.

For the week of yoga in Negril, Jamaica, my mother joined Francis and me, sleeping downstairs in our individual cabin near the ocean. For yoga on Isla Mujeres, in Mexico, our classes were held in a large open-air palapa. During that week, Francis and I also visited the cenotes (deep, natural pits, or sinkholes characteristic of the Yucatán Peninsula) and the Mayan ruins of Tulum.

Francis and I also participated in several annual five-day yoga workshops taught in Yellow Springs, Ohio, by Judith Lasater. Judith was the one who had invited me to return to San Francisco for the six weeks of yoga training. Her yoga workshops were focused on Anatomy, Kinesiology and

Asana, the title of her most recent book. Like the anatomy training I had received from Tom Myers by taking his 400-hour course in The Broadreach of Bodywork, the anatomy directly geared to yoga which I absorbed from Judith also helped me and my students with their physical problems. I took pleasure hearing Francis share with others some few key principles he picked up from Judith, for example: "The knee is the prisoner of the hip," meaning that some knee problems can come from tight hip muscles.

YOGA AS JAIL MINISTRY

Before Francis' retirement, I held (gratis) a weekly yoga class for two groups – Yoga for People with AIDS (for five years) and then Yoga for Seniors at the high-rise where my mother lived nearby. But once Francis had retired, we taught yoga weekly at the local Cumberland County Jail for eleven years.

It all started in 1996 when Philip Berrigan and four other Ploughshares members were incarcerated for yet another action at the Bath Iron Works shipyard. Francis visited Philip in the "men's pod" as it was called, and both of us visited Susan Crane, the only woman in that Ploughshares group. When we discovered that the women had fewer opportunities for activities in jail than the men, Francis and I decided to fill in that gap.

The jail personnel treated us like regular personnel. We left our drivers' licenses at the main desk before being allowed entrance beyond the first of several doors. Through the glass enclosed room where two jail personnel sat looking at monitors, they would see us coming from one section of the corridor, nod to us, and we'd hear a clang unlocking the next metal door ahead of us until we reached the women's pod where we had another button to press to get in.

To those who inquired why we did this, we would explain that both Francis and I had had happy childhoods. "It's something we need to do," we'd say. "We need to be educated about the realities from which we've been sheltered," adding that we received more from it than we gave.

In reality, and by way of example, Francis and I were touched by a lot of the people we met in jail. One inmate wrote us a thank you note after his release: "You both gave me the gift of providing a sense of safety to tap into my inner self in an otherwise unsafe environment. I looked forward to being with you every week because you reminded me what I gave up for drugs and more importantly that I could return to Self and Spirit."

One of the women with whom we made friends was an artist. She gave us a thank-you gift before she was transferred to the Windham Correction Center. It was a four-inch statue of St. Francis that she had made out of white bread. After squeezing it hard and letting it dry, she had used coffee grounds to dye it brown, the color of St. Francis' cowled habit. The statue depicts St. Francis feeding a bird in his hand. For the bird's food, bread-crumbs, she had used toothpaste. Francis and I were so struck by her gesture we alternated our visits – one week to the county jail, and the other to the correctional center, to teach her, and others, yoga. When she left prison, we invited her to our home and to join in our yoga classes. The strikingly beautiful painting she gave us called "Mother" hangs at the foot of my bed.

It wasn't unusual for us to meet some of these former yoga students on the street. Once, when I was called by a clerk at the Bureau of Motor Vehicles to come for my turn, I saw another woman called by another clerk, and I said, "I know you!" She then responded loud enough for all to hear: "Yes! At the Cumberland County Jail!"

YOGA LED TO DANCES OF UNIVERSAL PEACE

When turbulence rocked the aircraft we were on, en route to India in 1989, Chicago yoga teacher Gabriel Halpern and I briefly held hands in fear. He had joined this New York group as well. Nine months later at the

Iyengar Yoga Convention in San Diego, Francis walked into our hotel room and said: "I had the best yoga teacher yet!" (Gabriel was a master yoga teacher himself.) What a surprise to hear we had met the same person independently of each other, someone we both respected. I invited Gabriel to conduct a weekend yoga workshop in Maine, then, and the tradition holds – Gabriel in Maine.

I had never before heard about the Dances of Universal Peace. But at that first weekend workshop, Gabriel, who called himself "a Jewish hippie from Brooklyn" who learned the Dances from California Sufis, had a different kind of activity in mind for us. We had been doing yoga since Friday afternoon, but for Saturday night, he would lead us in those Dances. It was my first experience walking in a circle chanting "Allah, Allah, Allah, Erachman Erachim," that is, "the most merciful and compassionate" in Arabic. Although it made me feel uncomfortable – "It feels pagan," I first thought – the experience was unforgettable.

For several years I had been leading a "Yoga By the Sea" weekend retreat at Bayview Villa, a house of prayer in Saco. Wanting to do what Gabriel had done on the Saturday night, I did some research on the Dances of Universal Peace and purchased several cassette tapes to teach myself the movements and chant melodies. But I couldn't quite get from the instruction booklet, the movements for the Lord's Prayer in Aramaic. Hearing that the Aramaic scholar who had put Jesus' words to music, Dr. Neil-Douglas-Klotz, was giving a weeklong retreat in Illinois, at a Christian retreat center, I telephoned Gabriel. He encouraged me "Yes, come!" he said, "and stay overnight with me and my family." I did. The retreat, organized by a Dominican, Brother Joseph Kilikevice, was held in Plano, Illinois, outside Chicago where Gabriel lived.

The next morning I was sitting in my room in Plano. What was I doing here? I wondered. I knew no one. But, as was my custom, first thing in the morning, along with recording my dreams, I looked at the scripture reading for the day and did what I had done while in India: select a line that spoke to me, one that would give me guidance. That's why I called it my daily mantra. I saw that today's reading was the gospel about the rich young man. (Matthew 19:16ff) He had asked Jesus what actions bring eternal life. To Jesus' advice that he keep the commandments, he responded that he already did. Then he asked Jesus: "What more do I lack?"

When I read those words, I was stopped short. I didn't even bother to finish reading the parable because my heart was pounding. I put down my copy of the New Testament. It wasn't the parable that I focused on, but the words "What more do I lack?" I had my mantra for the day all right. In fact, I suddenly knew what I was still lacking in my life – the Dances of Universal Peace! It astonished me to discover in myself such a visceral response.

During the retreat, I found the Lord's Prayer and the Beatitudes chanted in Aramaic so compelling I didn't quite know what to do about it. In doing these dances, the lines of both the Lord's Prayer and the Beatitudes were repeated mantra-like over and over again. Saadi (Dr. Douglas-Klotz' Sufi name) said they are not really dances, but spiritual practices. Done in this way, it would take about an hour to pray the whole Lord's Prayer with simple movement and chant. (There are several YouTube videos online – under "Abwoon d'bashmaya" – of Dr. Neil Douglas-Klotz leading the Lord's Prayer in Aramaic.)

There were two couples there, both former nuns married to "inactive" priests." They had become certified as leaders of these spiritual practices. Obviously, I was feeling drawn to do the same, and their having my background made the idea attractive. "But I'm too old," I told myself, having turned sixty the previous year. My kind of internal push-pull went on all week.

As Saturday approached, when I asked a woman from Quebec with whom I felt an affinity, if she planned to go for certification as a leader of the Dances of Universal Peace, she answered, "No, I'm going to wait until I'm sixty for that." I couldn't believe it. What other sign did I need?!

FRANCIS AND THE DANCES OF UNIVERSAL PEACE

Flying back to Maine alone with the Aramaic Lord's Prayer and Beat-itude chant words and melodies filling my mind, I felt ecstatic. When I got home and sang them, Francis took to one of my favorites. In English it's "Blessed are the pure in heart for they shall see God." In the singing of it in Aramaic, Dr. Douglas-Klotz had added the word Allaha (the Aramaic word, similar to the Arabic, Allah) sung twenty times. To my further de-light, Francis immediately began singing it around the house. I didn't waste any time telephoning the person whose name was given me when I had asked who could teach me this prayer and these Beatitudes in Aramaic. It was Radha Tereska Buko who lives in Vermont.

After determining I was serious about this, but without having met me, Radha agreed to become my mentor. We talked on the phone for an hour every week for the next two years and met at retreats. Radha was my mentor for three years after which Brother Joseph Kilikevice became, and still is, my mentor. (Sufis themselves initiated giving Brother Joseph the Sufi name Shemduddin which I use.) Radha then suggested we meet at a convent for a weekend retreat in Ontario, Canada. It would be taught by the same Dr. Neil Douglas-Klotz whose Sufi name I now began to use – Saadi. I had just made a weeklong retreat with him, but now, in a few months, Francis was willing to go with me for that special weekend retreat with Saadi.

The site of the Loretto Convent, a five-story building, overlooked Ni-agara Falls. From the large room that accommodated close to one hundred of us from all over the East Coast and Canada and beyond, we could see the mist that looked like smoke rising from the falls. During break times Francis and I walked down the steep hill a few times to view the falls close up from the Canadian side. Earnestly hoping Francis would like the Dances, I would glance at him from time to time, since he was not always standing next to

Francis by Lawrence Brook.

me in the circle. During the "Kalama" dance when I looked at Francis' face, I saw his moist eyes. He told me that night in our private room upstairs that many of the Dances held for him some of the mysticism to which he was attracted, actually, mysticism that had drawn him into the priesthood.

From 1996 on, I participated in Saadi's five-day retreats, annually. For his later weekend retreats, Francis joined me – for example, in San Antonio, at the Rowe Conference center in Massachusetts, and many in Ohio sponsored by Munira Elizabeth Reed. Francis also came to Saadi's exceptional five-day retreat sponsored by our new Sufi friends, Halima and Abraham Sussman.

This retreat was held on a large tract of land in the woods which Halima and Abraham still own in Royalston, Massachusetts. Many retreatgoers camped out, but Francis and I slept, as some others did, too, in the main house. Three times a day, we gathered for the Dances in a large yurt. The yurt abutted a nature preserve. During break times in the afternoons, Francis and I and another couple, our friends Jane and Julien Olivier who share our background, would walk through the woods and down the steep hill to sit by Lawrence Brook.

Elaine by same.

It felt like a transformative week. The theme, focused on Saadi's *Genesis Meditations* (the title of one of his books), was especially relevant to our time. These creation dances, fifteen in all, were chanted in Hebrew.

At our New Year's Eve Dances.

Francis fully supported me when I myself led the Dances. "I lend my voice to hold up the men's voices," he told our friends. Once, while leading junior high school students in the Dances after mass at St. Bartholomew's Parish, we both secretly chuckled (we told each other later) to watch the faces of the boys as they joined in. How could they not? Here was tall Francis holding hands in a circle, going along with this! So they did, too. With young people like that, I selected livelier dances that naturally engaged them. I had spent a week in West Virginia one summer focused on leading the Dances for children.

This ministry grew, and although Francis didn't come every month where I led the Dances of Universal Peace at the studio, he participated at special times such as on New Year's Eve. He also cheerfully joined me every time I was called to lead the Dances elsewhere, as we were, by various denominations, namely Catholic, United Church of Christ, Unitarian Universalist, and Quaker. Even the Maine Jung Center

The Dances taken outdoors.

asked me to lead a Dances workshop alongside others offered at one of their annual members' nights. At a weekend conference on ecology in Belfast, Maine, I led the Dances out of doors.

YOGA LED TO PERMACULTURE

The road from yoga to permaculture led Francis and me, not just out of state, but out of the country. Francis and I flew first to Rochester, New York, for a weekend workshop with Francois Raoult, because we appreciated the way he taught Iyengar alignment, or *aplomb*, as this native Frenchman called it. When Francois offered a two-week yoga intensive in France, I wanted to go, being bi-lingual and of French descent myself, and I didn't have to importune Francis. We had visited the site of my Goulet ancestors in Le Perche region of France, a trip he had valued as much as I. This two-week yoga workshop took place at Fermes des Courmettes in Tourettes-sur-Loup. We were in the Maritime Alps. When taking hikes up the mountains above our high perch, we could see Cannes far below and mountain goats scampering in the woods around us.

We learned that the large building where we slept (without screens) had once been a farm, but then also a homeopathic hospital. (Many herbs grow in the mountains behind and above it.) The building was large enough to accommodate several retreat groups the size of ours. We saw that some of them were young musicians because they were practicing outside. A music school! we thought. Exploring the spacious grounds during free time, I found it curious that varieties of plants were intermixed in what looked like an untidy garden. I noticed, too, the use of mulch everywhere. It was a pleasant, relaxed garden all told, and best of all, we were serenaded day and night by bull frogs.

Before returning home, Francis and I discovered that this center, called by its website name, Permaculture Eden, is now one of Europe's most developed permaculture sites. It's there Francis and I got our first glimpse of permaculture. When fifteen years later, we participated in a daylong conference at the University of Maine in Orono, we were ready to act.

TWO YOGA CELEBRATIONS

Ten years after founding Portland Yoga Studio, in 1999, we called for a celebration. First came the free yoga classes we teachers taught in both the front and inner studios. To crown the evening, before refreshments, we had prepared a yoga dance similar in concept to the one I had created for my 50th birthday party at home (to the music of *Jesu Joy of Man's Desiring*). For this one, several of us moved through yoga postures in sync with the rhythm of Ravi Shankar's *Inside the Kremlin*.

Six years later, in January of 2005, after I took a five-month personal "sabbatical of discernment," Francis and I decided sixteen years had been long enough to co-direct the studio. A big transition like this called for another celebration. We called this one Passing the Torch.

I turned seventy that fall and Francis, seventy-eight. Yes, it was time. Let the younger teachers take over now the upbringing of this still young Portland Yoga Studio. It would undergo new, interesting stages of development which it was our joy then, and mine now, to witness.

PREGNANT ENCOUNTER

At this Passing of the Torch ceremony, during refreshments, Francis and I saw our good friend Lynn Kuzma walk into the studio. We were not surprised. An event like this was not something she would be missing. By now she had become a special person in our lives. A professor of political science at the time who later became one of the deans at USM, Lynn had joined our Wednesday morning yoga class. She was more than an excellent yoga student, she assisted us in a number of ways.

One of the most helpful where the studio was concerned, was Lynn's arranging a meeting with me and her roommate, Sharon Pieniak, a talented artist and web designer. With Mary Melilli and Bill Gillis' yoga photos in hand (the ones we had mailed out as the covers for seasonal brochures), Sharon used them to create an award-winning website. She positioned a different photo to head each of our website's sections. There was even a link on the original Portland Yoga Studio website for the Dances of Universal Peace.[4]

It was also Lynn, when my mother had died five years earlier, who had helped me clear her apartment and select which items to give away, which to use, and which to store in my old convent trunk in our cellar. Lynn's own grandmother had died within a week of my mother's death, so we wept together. Francis and I knew her even before she married Lee.

She arrived for this Passing the Torch event tonight, however, accompanied by her husband Lee, holding their nine-month-old daughter Rowan in his arms. Since Lynn and Lee's wedding had been scheduled during Francis' and my participation in an Irish folklore tour, we had missed it. This was then, our first opportunity to meet Lee, a handsome blond Englishman. Lynn, whom her family calls the pretty one, has dark, naturally curly hair. They make an attractive couple.

It's a nice beard.

I held out my arms to take blond baby Rowan from Lee and brought her to Francis. But his beard frightened

---

[4] Portland Yoga Studio's website has been changed under new ownership. Information about the Dances of Universal Peace, however, can be found here: http://www.dancesofuniversalpeacemaine.moonfruit.com

her, so I sat down, talking to her on my lap. Soon I rose with her still in my arms, came closer to Francis and pet his beard. He just smiled. "It's a nice beard," I told little Rowan, trying to demonstrate it was safe. Our friend Jan caught this scene with her camera. The look on Rowan's face is still uncertain.

Some months later I was forcibly struck when reading the questions at the end of a particular chapter in Meredith Jordan's book, *Embracing the Mystery*. The expression "your loved ones" was repeated in three of the five questions. "Who *are* my loved ones?" I asked myself. Of course, there was no question, Francis was preeminently my loved one. But, knowing that family members in the plural were being referred to here, live-in members of the family including young children – I suddenly felt bereft of such additional closer relationships.

Then, just as suddenly, I thought of Lynn, Lee, and Rowan. So I picked up the telephone and tearfully asked Lynn: "Could I be Rowan's godmother? Could you use a babysitter once a week?"

Lynn responded as eagerly as I. She explained the timing was perfect because after both being on sabbaticals since Rowan's birth, she and Lee (who is a professor at Rutgers' University in New Jersey) were now about to return to the classroom. Lee would be commuting there for weekday classes and she also would be returning to her classes at the University of Southern Maine (USM).

Weekly babysitting for Francis and me began that month – September, 2005. Rowan was seventeen-months old. I would pick her up at the Child Care Center nearby and drive her to our home. I noticed one day when walking into her classroom, that the photo of her with me and Francis (the beard- reassuring photo) had been posted on the wall by way of identifying me.

So now it was public. It felt and would become more official all the time. Francis and I gave Rowan two words by which to call us. Thereafter,

I was *memere* and Francis, *pepere*. We figured, since these were French words (even if they do mean "grandmother" and "grandfather") they would not encroach on Rowan's blood relationships with her maternal grandparents in Ohio, and her paternal grandparents in England.

PERMACULTURE OPEN HOUSES

The permaculture seed had been sown in France at Les Courmettes during Francis' and my yoga retreat in the 1990's. Then, at a July 2006 workshop on Permaculture by Australian born, Julia Yelton, it was germinated. (Permaculture originated in Australia, and Julia knew one of its founders, Bill Mollison.) Home from that Orono conference co-organized by Hugh Curran on "Ecology, Spirituality, and Peace," Francis and I discovered, via the Yeltons' website, that the Portland Maine Permaculture Meetup group was holding its monthly potluck the next night. We immediately cooked up a dish to share and joined this community focused on sustainable living. Its co-founders, Lisa Fernandes and her husband David Whitten, became our friends for life.

The awareness alone of challenges that children, including Rowan, will face because of global climate disruption, propelled us to act. Julia created the all-important permaculture design for our 8,000 sq. ft. lot. It was something I learned how to do after spending a total of three weeks taking the basic, and then the following year, the advanced,

Sheet-mulching the garden.

permaculture design courses. When Charles, her husband, told us it could take from three up to fifteen years to implement the design, we decided, because of our ages, it seemed wise for Francis and me to go the three-year route.

We then hired two neighborhood "tweens." They helped us sheet mulch the front and side lawns with newspaper and straw in preparation for an orchard. Once eight fruit trees, blueberry bushes, and grapevines were planted that fall, the per-maculture way of life took root in our soil. We also hired a neighbor to dig down at least three feet to create a pond in our backyard. It was three-feet deep, fifteen-feet long, and nine-feet wide, kidney shaped. Its solar-powered waterfall is enchanting. This same neighbor also welded pieces of rebar to form a stunning

After 2007 permaculture work party.

grape trellis. It was modeled after organic gardening expert Eliot Cole-man's.

Many permaculture work parties followed. It was amazing how much work could get done in three hours followed by a potluck – and what fun in community! While some built the cold frame and hoop house, others posi-tioned a liner in the pond and filled it. We used, not only city water, but also buckets of water harvested from the seven rain barrels we had erected under downspouts, one of which fed into the pond.

The first frog found the pond by itself six days later. Since there was talk of frogs being endangered, Francis and I were pleased. The pond became our magnet all summer, and by hibernation time, we counted nine frogs and one bullfrog.

Between 2007 and 2009, Francis and I held at least six open houses called Introduction to Creating an Edible Suburban Ecosystem. But the loveliest of all was the first of four, in the summer of 2008 when the eighty-six perennials, plus 103 daffodil bulbs planted the previous fall were in bloom.[5] When

Francis eating strawberries.

Matthew Ryle, who lived at the end of Avalon Road, offered to help me with this planting, Francis and I made a fast friend. (Matt then became our yoga student. We thought it made for a very fair trade.)

Viewed as a generative enterprise, the permaculture ecosystem Francis and I put in place is perhaps one of our most enduring legacies. Installed not only close to home, it created an eden *around* our home. The semi-dwarf fruit trees demonstrate one can have an orchard on one's front lawn (and have less lawn to mow as well!). The strawberry patches and grape vines should continue to yield fruit along with the blueberry bushes, kiwi, and two paw paw trees. The J-shaped chicken run also invites the keeping of backyard hens for the sake of their tasty eggs, their manure (composted), and the entertainment they provide when they dust bathe in the sand. The solar hot-air panels will also continue to provide virtually free heat.

---

[5] The 2008 open house was filmed and made into a five-minute video by Eben Metivier, a student at USM's Muskie School of Public Service and a member of the Bioneers, a community of social and scientific innovators from all disciplines working to advance solutions for a more just and sustainable world. Eben posted it on YouTube under the title "Permaculture at the McGilicuddys" (but one must type our last name with only one "l" in order to get to it).

PERMACULTURE FOR
ROWAN AND FAMILY

"All this," I told myself and Francis as we worked, "is for Rowan." It was for her sake we got our first chicks in the summer of 2009, in time for her fifth birthday. Rowan suggested names for them, and with Abi-

Rowan pointing out frogs for *Pepere*.

gail, her playmate from across the street, they learned how to pick them up properly with their hands over the wings, to pet them. One day when Francis was sitting on a lawn chair watching them, Rowan quietly sat herself on his lap. I reached my camera in time to catch the moment.

Visiting the chickens was the first thing Rowan wanted to do when she arrived, or else she would run to the pond to see the frogs. Often I would tell people, "Rowan's going to inherit this house, you know," proudly announcing the fact Francis and I now had an heir. We even went to an attorney to make it legal.

Since Rowan loves pancakes, to this day they're preordained for supper. As a very young child, unable to handle well a jug of maple syrup, for each pancake, Rowan would come to Francis seated on a kitchen stool, eating his own, and ask him: "*Pepere*, could I please have some maple syrup?"

Francis with Lynn, Lee, and Rowan.

139

When Lynn arrived to pick up Rowan, she would occasionally take supper with us, and during summer vacations when Lee was free from commuting, so would he. Sometimes the two of them would arrive with a take-out meal for us to share as a picnic. Sitting there on the deck, we could see and hear the waterfall, notice how the vegetables had grown, and hear the chickens clucking. Sometimes we would reach overhead to pluck grapes for dessert. Before they left for home, we gathered vegetables and whatever ripe berries and fruits were ready for Lynn, Lee, and Rowan to take.

Little did we know when we set the timer to ring in three years that Francis' energy would gradually begin waning after two, and quite obviously, after two and a half years. We had trusted we'd both see Rowan growing up beyond the five years which Francis, in the end, was limited to spend in her presence.

During the 2009 summer Open House, Francis had to sit when people stood, or lean on a sturdy stick, when we walked around to the orchard. Before the last piece was added to our realized permaculture design, namely, installation of solar hot water, we wondered if he would get to experience it. It had to wait until the spring after Francis' death on January 3, 2010. I would oversee that project alone.

These, then, were our "offspring" – Peacework, Yoga, the Dances of Universal Peace and Permaculture – the four areas of work in which Francis and I engaged. These communities, our "offspring," became our "family."

CHAPTER SEVEN
Elders Up For Anything

He was only retiring from a job in 1995 when Francis left Portland Housing Authority, not retiring from life. With fifteen more years ahead of him, he was still "up" for more adventures. More than that, Francis was still in his stride at sixty-eight, when he started "working for me." Taking care of finances at Portland Yoga, driving me to the studio, participating in, and even demonstrating selected poses during the classes I taught, didn't take up all his time. So Francis shaped a schedule for himself that suited his tastes.

FRANCIS' LIFESTYLE

He'd retire for the night and rise in the morning earlier than I. While en route to and from the bathroom to get back to bed, I would see Francis sitting in his rocking chair in the kitchen. For breakfast he would have drawn toward him our small custom-made table that slips over the rocking chair's armrests. Reading the newspaper there after breakfast, he'd half listen to public radio, but we'd smile at each other as I walked by. I knew Francis liked to have his own quiet morning space. I had learned early on not to interrupt it. We had the whole day to talk, and we did that with the ease of an intimate married couple.

About Francis' prayer habits, he wrote five years after we were married: "After you leave for work, I often turn off the stereo and enjoy the morning silence for reflection." For the last four years of Francis' life, after we took experiential classes on meditation taught by Dana Sawyer, I would see him, for the first activity of his day, sitting in silence on the futon. If I was turning over in bed, in the next room within view, I would prop myself on one elbow and gaze at him briefly before settling back down to sleep.

Jogging was on his schedule in the mornings. Our home is close to a small Jewish cemetery. Francis tried out this one at first, but settled instead on the larger Evergreen Cemetery about a mile from our home. There, he'd run for up to an hour down to and back from the cemetery pond. After that, he would drive to Starbucks and read the *Boston Globe* over coffee. After Lynn saw him there, on occasion she'd buy him coupons for Starbucks. Later in the day, Francis often told me about his conversations with our friend, Michael Brennan (now Portland's first elected mayor). They didn't just smile as they passed each other while jogging at Evergreen, they'd talk religion and politics since Mike was State Senator at the time, as well as a member of Portland Pax Christi.

IN OUR EVERY DAY

Both before and after quitting our respective jobs and then moving on to new things, Francis' and my lifestyle fell into place naturally. We readily agreed on a division of labor. I planned the meals, but Francis cooked many of them, in fact, at the beginning of our marriage, during the short period when he was between jobs – *all* of them. When it was time to replenish our freezer with more homemade spaghetti sauce, we would pull out a restaurant-sized container in which to make it, using the authentic recipe my parents had gotten from an Italian woman. It was Francis who cut up fifteen onions while I opened the cans of tomatoes to which he would add a long list of the called-for spices. He had his specialty, too. Whenever we ate Italian White Clam Sauce, Francis took over completely. Lee said that that dish never tasted as good as when Francis put it together.

I washed the dishes, but Francis put them away. He put the clothes in the washing machine and hung them out to dry, but I was the one who put them in the closet and kept them in order. He did a lot. Each spring, Francis would paint the wooden clapboards on one side of our bungalow. He was always helpful, for example, he would drive my mother to Dr. Kevin Zorsky's office out of town and back.

Paying the bills, getting the groceries, going on errands, in addition to going to the bank and credit union, and to Hamilton's Garage for car maintenance and to Fogg's for a touch-up paint job after removing rust on the car – he did all that. Francis cultivated good relationships with the people who served our needs. I remembered his references to Chris at Hamilton's garage, Martha at the bank, and Theresa at the credit union. Especially after Francis died, seeking out those people by name when I took over these jobs, gave me a sense of comforting support.

READING AND FRIENDS

For Francis, reading was a passion. In the afternoons he often retreated into the living room to read again, in addition to reading in the evenings, when we were not out for an evening at symphony, or Portland Stage Company, or even watching a film at home. Francis would also note for me articles in newspapers which he knew I'd appreciate. He did the same when it came to everything else he read – the *New Yorker,* the *Atlantic, NCR,* and a stack of other periodicals.

Francis, then, was better informed than I. In the mid-seventies, while feminism was spreading around the country, I was just getting adjusted to, and absorbed with, married life. So I had not kept up. I tried to catch up later, however, in a small way. Riane Eisler's *The Chalice and the Blade*, for example, opened my eyes to the place of women in history. I was passionate in exploring and reading one book after another by progressive theologians, but such subjects are more conducive to a discussion group. On the other hand, with the trove of information that Francis had from his wider reading, he had more to share than I in more informal contexts.

I held my own in conversations all right, but Francis' greater ease engaging in the kind of small talk in which Irish wit shines, also made up for my lacunae. Part of that gap, I'd tell our friends, if I was ignorant of a past cultural event alluded to, came from my having been in the convent at the time. "Oh, that's why I don't know!" I'd say. Priests, on the other hand, and especially diocesan priests like Francis, were closer to the secular world than I had been in a semi-cloistered Order. That distance from the world had augmented my tendency, growing up in a small town, too (if it's fair to blame the small town), to be innocent, sometimes even gullible.

Francis' friendship with Bob Mottau and Gus deBaggis went back to seminary days where they were classmates. During their priesthood years, they had visited together places like Pemaquid Point, Maine.

Bob had even spent summers at Camp Pesquasawasis when he was not on assignment in a parish, but teaching . That friendship, renewed after a long hiatus during which Bob and Gus left the clerical priesthood, now included me. Gus and Bob visited us a few times, and we, them. After Gus' death, I joined Francis on a bus trip to Boston, every now and then, to spend the day with Bob. Once I spent an overnight with Francis in Bob's apartment. But after that visit, I didn't return when Francis stayed overnight, because of Tweetie, Bob's parrot. We deduced Tweetie didn't like women.

Francis had a handful of close friends. One of them was, of course, Joe Brannigan, my longtime friend as well, along with Claire. When Joe ran for and won seats as a democrat in the Maine Legislature (for six years as a Representative, and for six more as State Senator), we supported him by leaving fliers at people's doors in Joe's district. Francis regularly had breakfast with Jerry Banner, another longtime friend we had both met as charter members of Lifeline's physical fitness program at the university. Jerry was a librarian. Even after retirement from the housing authority, Francis also continued going out for lunch with a small group of men friends who still worked there.

He was an active member in the Voice of the Faithful organization which supports survivors of clergy sexual abuse, priests of integrity, and structural change within the Catholic Church. Michael Sweatt, whom we met through this organization, became another good friend with whom Francis had lunch. (Michael later gave the eulogy at Francis' funeral.) We also went to a unique retreat about simple living organized by our friends, Georgia Kosciusko and the late Jim Harney, an indefatigable peace activist and photo-journalist.

After that weekend, Jim stopped by for a few overnights en route to or from his home in mid-Maine, for another reason besides friendship: Jim found well-being in practicing the yoga postures he learned from us, even after his cancer diagnosis. It was his pleasure and mine to have Francis also teaching him.

Some of Francis' longtime friends like Barbara DeCoste became my friend, too, but we were introduced to several new ones through our work and activities. Annual and periodic workshops for yoga and the Dances of Universal Peace, both closer to home and out of state, enabled us to cultivate our relationships with friends who shared these interests, for example Elizabeth Agnew of Indiana. We counted among them Celeste Roberge, a well- known Maine sculptor, Susan and Joe Christian, and Jean Henry, an

With Elizabeth at Deering Oaks Park.

art historian who is also a gifted photographer, as is Jan Born who took many photos of Francis and me over the years. Our permaculture friends live locally. Progressive Catholic communities also willingly commanded our allegiance, that is, Call to Action/USA and *CORPUS*.

CORPUS

Francis and I were invited to a house meeting in Portland in 1990, which turned out to be of consequence to us. Bill Manseau, a priest of the Diocese of Boston who had married a former nun, Mary Doherty, would be coming to talk about an organization called *CORPUS*. (It had been founded in 1974, two years after Francis and I were married.) We had

Jean's photo after serving us dinner.

heard about it before, but, mistakenly thinking without investigation that their only goal was the reinstatement of married priests in the church, we hadn't taken the initiative to give it a deeper look. Bill's coming was an opportunity we would not pass up now, however, especially since he was coming from Massachusetts to Portland to meet with us.

We learned that its acronym stands for Corps of Reserve Priests United for Service. Francis and I were very pleased to discover that *CORPUS* was a pro-active kind of community. Its goals, for example, had evolved (nudged by their own wives), to include not only more active participation by women, but support of women priests. It is currently characterized as "a faith community affirming an inclusive priesthood rooted in a reformed and renewed Church." It is, moreover, one of the oldest reform groups in the Catholic Church.

Francis and I not only joined, we went to their next annual national *CORPUS* meeting held at the World Trade Center in New York City. I say "we," but in actuality it was Francis who participated in that whole weekend. Since I was occupied taking my Iyengar yoga certification examinations in the city that very weekend, after my own sessions were concluded, I joined him at the conference.

Further, close to every year from then on, Francis and I participated in their annual national meetings. We found the speakers inspiring and the gatherings a singular opportunity to make friends with remarkable and gifted people. We deepened those friendships over the years. Its members were people with our own background. It didn't matter at all that some of the married priests' wives had not been nuns, though it seemed to us that most of them had. Annual *CORPUS* conferences took us to different states including Ohio (at Kent State), Minnesota, Rhode Island, and Texas.

What especially delighted Francis and me was reconnecting with Dr. Anthony T. Padovano, the priest and seminary professor who had supported us during our underground period. We knew, incidentally, that he also had left the clerical priesthood and married a former nun. In fact, we had even met him when he came to Maine shortly after we were married, to speak at a Confraternity of Christian Doctrine conference.

As regular conference participants, we caught up with some of Anthony's initiatives: He had been part of a dialogue with a number of priests in the Chicago area which lead to the creation of *CORPUS* in the first place. What is more, he had served ten years as its first president, and then became – and still is – its ambassador, speaking at national and international meetings. But now we were able to meet his wife, Theresa, a former member of the Sisters of Charity of Leavenworth, Kansas.

Two of our annual conferences had a different feel about them. One, held in Atlanta, Georgia, was joined with that of the International Federation of Married Catholic Priests. Francis and I enjoyed interacting with Europeans who shared our backgound.

The other conference was the national 2008 Joint Conference held in Boston for the following communities besides *CORPUS*: Women's Ordination Conference, Federation of Christian Ministries, and Roman Catholic Women Priests. *CORPUS'* own married priest, David Gawlik, publisher and photographer, posted multiple photos of this conference on www.corpus.smugmug.com, as he did for many other conferences. After this one, Francis and I drove with a few friends to the Church of the Advent to witness the ordination of yet another Roman Catholic woman priest and deacon.

PETER'S TELLTALE PHRASE

Francis and I bought Peter Manseau's book *VOWS: The Story of a Priest, a Nun, and Their Son* from the Harvard Book Store. While in Cambridge for a yoga workshop in 2005, we were staying for the weekend, not in a hotel but, according to our longtime custom, in the guest room at the Friends' Meeting at Cambridge. That night, Francis stayed up late, unable to put down Peter's book. This was rare for him, regular as he was in his sleeping habits. He discovered we were mentioned in the epilogue.

Francis and I had met Peter the previous year. We had given a daylong Aramaic Lord's Prayer retreat for the assembled *CORPUS* members of New England. It was Peter's father, Bill, who had invited us to come give the retreat, the same Bill who had traveled to Portland to tell us about *CORPUS*.

Peter had come to observe his parents at this retreat, looking for material for his *VOWS* book. Referring to me in the epilogue as "a former nun turned yoga teacher," and to Francis as "her married-priest husband," Peter described Francis as "a good sport, slender and tall, up for anything. He was in quite good shape for a man near seventy, still wearing a crisp little beard like the beatnik priest he once had been."

Francis especially liked the "up for anything" part. "His comment about me," he said, "is more far-reaching than Peter can know." Francis was thinking of his parents, how from his birth in 1927, they seemed to have tried every new idea doctors could come up with to control his childhood asthma.

It was *them* he credited for this central characteristic in his personality – his openness.

During the rest of the weekend, Francis got other insights into how his parents' approach had influenced him. It came down to this: Now he had the instinct for and had developed the attitude of examining and testing rather than prematurely rejecting new ideas or practices. He would take the time to discern whether or not they were meant for him.

Peter's comment felt like a gift. In revealing this much about Francis, it gave us besides, a light by which to interpret and appreciate what we had lived through in our past thirty-three years together.

HIS OWN PERSON

Granted, I had initiated key projects in our life, but what good would that have been without Francis' support? For this major "new thing," yoga, which in turn connected us to both the Dances of Universal Peace and permaculture, it was he, Francis, who had introduced me to the very idea of yoga. He brought it up, and I ran with it. But he made yoga his own. For the other two as well, he tested, found them to his liking, and then entered

Twin photos of Francis and Elaine . . .

in, but always on his own terms – when it came to his participation.

Francis did what he wanted. It always seemed reasonable to me. But more than that: He was the wise one in our family of two. I consulted him. For everything. It was our way to talk things over. From the beginning, having

agreed not to let the sun set on misunderstandings between us, discontent had nowhere to sprout. Francis did not need to appear like the dominant male in our relationship. On the contrary, he was proud of my leadership. Though he was naturally kind, perhaps one reason he did not need to appear strong is that he

three years before Francis died.

was, in fact, already the guiding light in our life as a couple.

Together with all this, Francis was his own person, going on some weekend retreats without me – one on Centering Prayer and several with the late Michael Dwinell, a well-known Episcopal priest and counselor for both laity and clergy.

Because of his sensitivity, Francis had a lot of anima, and he didn't fear allowing it naturally to show. For example, he didn't mind holding my purse in public when I was doing something. Many men took our yoga classes, but they were usually outnumbered by the women, and sometimes

150

there were only a few, or no men, in class. This occasioned my joking with our students that Francis' ease gave a sign he was secure in his masculinity.

It was no wonder then that our students laughed aloud after class over one person's comment referring to Francis. I had asked her privately if the blind date which she had recently had, had gone well. She answered loud enough for others to hear: "No, I'm afraid not. The kind of man I would want would be one like Francis."

INITIATIVES AS ELDERS: YARMOUTH YOGA STUDIO

Never did Francis and I expect we would be founding a second yoga studio. On the contrary, in grief after my mother's death, I wanted us to let go ownership of Portland Yoga Studio altogether. But I bowed to the wisdom that it's not a good idea to make major decisions after a loved one's death. Instead, Francis and I hired a part-time administrator of the studio, Patricia Sperber, to ease the work load. Shortly after we made her job full-time and were feeling a little nervous about that decision, she shocked us with her suggestion that we open a new studio in Yarmouth, north of Portland. Showing us the ad announcing the space's availability, she marshaled the arguments: the location was good, the rent reasonable, and there was parking, to boot. The clincher was this: because we had a large database, the organizational structure was already in place.

Like those times in life when jaw-dropping changes arise from outside ourselves, Francis and I recognized we were called to take this unlooked-for path. The small, lovely Yarmouth Yoga Studio we opened in 2003 was dedicated to my parents because the modest legacy, recently bequeathed to me by my mother, was used to finance it. In addition to *how* it happened, what especially surprised us, was the energy with which I took on the task of actually becoming its "general contractor" – overseeing such things as selecting the floating hardwood flooring, and directing the carpenters by specifying what we needed, for example, in yoga prop cabinets. Francis, my sidekick consultant, cheered me on.

ANTI-TORTURE VIGIL

By now I had begun to retrench my yoga-teaching schedule. In contrast to the many workshops I had offered at Portland Yoga Studio over the years, such as on backbends, forward bends, yoga for shoulders, knees, and to prevent back pain, I would now offer only occasional workshops. From teaching four yoga classes a week, I now taught two, one of them on Wednesday mornings. With President Bush and Vice-President Cheney in power the following year, I felt called to demonstrate against the torture in which our government was engaged. Francis immediately agreed.[6]

We started an Anti-Torture vigil then, at Monument Square in Portland, every Wednesday after our yoga class. In doing so, we acted quickly, without consulting even our Pax Christi friends, but to their credit, they soon joined in along with many others, including members of Amnesty International and American Civil Liberties Union, and Quaker Friends like Cushman Anthony, our friend since Anti-Vietnam War days.

After two years, we merged our vigil with another peace vigil recently started and held by Protestant ministers dressed, there at the Square, in their clerical robes. One of these was Bill Gregory, a retired United Church of Christ pastor, a contributor to our local paper's weekly "Reflections" column, and a person Francis and I had long admired for his creative good works in the community. He stood with us next to his wife, Nancy, at Monument Square. Bill was to figure prominently in Francis' and my life in ensuing years.

---

[6] At that time, only progressives were saying what now in 2013, as I write this, official reports point to: "Indisputable evidence" that torture was used by our government.

ACTIVITIES AS ELDERS – COURSES

Francis and I had time now to take advantage of Senior College. At this Osher Life Learning Institute (OLLI), we took courses, he, for example, on Irish theater after which we both enjoyed a play put on by AIRE – the American Irish Repertory Ensemble. I took a class in Spanish and another on the Psalms, taught by Rabbi Sky who had founded Senior College. The Poetry of Soul course, however, is one we took together. It turned out not only an especially enriching course, it brought us even closer to its teacher, Bill – Bill of the peace vigil.

A year after Bill's course, he asked Francis and me if we would be willing to be interviewed on Portland Community Television for a program about what active elders are doing in their later years. He had helped produce "The Second Act." We agreed, because having let go directorship of Portland Yoga Studio by then, we had been pondering that very thing – what we were about to do and become, now, in our senior years.

TRAVELS TOGETHER

Tom Fox, publisher and editor of *NCR* was keynote speaker at our June 2005 *CORPUS* Conference. After his talk, Tom invited those assembled to tour Vietnam with him and his Vietnamese wife, Hoa, the next spring. We could not say no.

In anticipation of this trip, Francis and I reminisced. Our trips overseas had been interesting and worthwhile. To be together while taking in the ways of other cultures and new terrains, like the canals of Venice, and gardens on the terraced hills of Italy, gave our experiences significance. I took pleasure in Italian on my lips, letting the words I could pronounce fairly well, roll over my tongue. When Francis laughed about the name of a building in Rome, Banco Spiritu Sancto, I took a photo of that bank. We enjoyed saying words in Italian like those, or like the word *ristorante*, by "landing" with a heavy accent on a particular syllable, typical of that melodic language.

Sites where excavations revealed something about the past held import for us. For example, in Rome we saw the ruins of the ancient city in the Old Forum, the catacombs of St. Callixtus, and the church of San Clemente. Our guide took us through the past on three levels of this structure. Francis and I walked from the present upper 11th century basilica down to the middle 4th century basilica and descended further to view the ruins of a 1st century Mithraic shrine at its base where we heard a rivulet still flowing.

In Israel, too, there were ruins to see, such as Megiddo overlooking the Jezreel Valley. Having read James Michener's novel *The Source* before Francis and I left for that journey, I was fascinated learning there were twenty different layers there containing the remains of about thirty different cities. We saw ruins on the other side of the surprisingly small Sea of Galilee, too, in the town of Capharnaum, after viewing the stone house of Simon Peter, the apostle. It was there where Jesus had cured Peter's mother-in-law. "Aha! Francis joked to fellow travelers when we saw that house – "the first pope had a wife!" I added: "Did you know that thirty-nine popes were married?"

A priest had guided that tour of Israel during which we retraced Jesus' steps. In Jerusalem we walked the narrow streets of the Way of the Cross to the Praetorium where Jesus was kept before his crucifixion. Standing there in this authentic site where he had stood before Pilate, deeply moved Francis and me. I was so stirred by it, that when Henry Gosselin asked me to write an article about it for *Church World*, I did.

An incident happened one afternoon, one we would always relate in telling friends about our tour of Israel/Palestine. Our Israeli guide took us inside a military bunker. From within this cave, we heard what sounded like a distant cannon. "It's from the Golan Heights," he told us. Then he led us to the hill where it was said Jesus gave his Sermon on the Mount and the Beatitudes.

The town where Francis of Assisi was born naturally drew Francis and me. Feeling a personal connection with this saint, we walked the winding cobbled streets and sat quietly in the lower church. It was the earliest one built in this Basilica of San Francesco. We looked on the original frescoes before they were shattered by the earthquake of 1997. Francis and I came home with small icons of St. Francis to give to his mother and to Aunt Irene after hanging a few on our own walls.

FAMILY RELATED TRAVEL – IRELAND

Interesting as these were, the travels that created longer lasting impressions on Francis and me were those that connected us with our ancestry. During Mick Moloney's Irish Folklore Tours, we saw McGillicuddy's Reeks and went to Donegal, where Francis' mother's forebears came from. It was in this region we saw a gigantic outdoor cauldron in which food was cooked for the poor during the potato blight. Viewing at the *Irish Famine Museum* at Strokestown Park photos of the Irish being evacuated from their homes was hard to take. But seeing close-up John Behan's "coffin ship" was even more unforgettable. Sitting outdoors, his bronze sculpture is the largest in Ireland.

Francis at a peat bog, Ireland.

Enchanted by an earlier visit to Tory Island, Francis and I were grateful that our last of four tours took us there for a second time. This sparsely populated island lies nine miles off the northwest coast of County Donegal. By now we had made friends with a few other couples who, like us, participated in more than a few of Mick Moloney's tours. The Dumans and we kept up the relationship. Les and Elsie visited us in Portland, and Francis and I

Francis doing yoga on slate bench.

flew to Philadelphia in 2003 to join them for their Seder.

Tory Island was a site we four appreciated. The Island is small, only three-miles long, and yet, according to long-standing tradition, they have a king. Every night we had Irish music in the hall, the only hall in the only hotel on the Island. And the king was there! His daughter, he told us, was currently a college student in the United States. Francis and I sat on the benches at the perimeter of the hall, and occasionally joined in the dancing. Once in our room, he told me the old timers among the locals were just like those he knew growing up in Canterbury, New Brunswick.

The Connemara Mountains so affected me, I awoke in our Clifden hotel in the middle of the night in tears. Achill Island conjured up a similar kind of mystery, as did The Burren with its Neolythic Poulnabrone Dolmen (portal tomb) located near where, before he died a few years later, the Irish poet, John O'Donohue was living. During

Francis at Yeats' grave – County Sligo.

156

the Celtic Spirituality tour, we visited Brigid's Well, named after a goddess in Celtic mythology. Once home, Francis and I hung on our walls a few depictions of the Irish coast, one in needlepoint.

FRANCE

The International Celtic Festival coincided with one of our Irish Folklore tours. For this one, we spent most of our time in Brittany, France, also a Celtic region. I was delighted for the opportunity to speak French which my parents had assured I spoke even before I spoke English. Francis was as pleased as I discovering we would be participating in the annual Breton dancing festivity known as Fest-Noz (night party), a tradition since the middle ages, recognized by UNESCO as a "cultural heritage."

"Bully pulpit" in Brittany.

Hearing from our guides that our bus would be returning to the hotel much later than usual, Francis and I lounged on the grass for a while in the late afternoon. While large tables for our communal meal were being set up, we watched a pig being roasted over a fire. The centering nature of the circle dances in which we participated late into that night mesmerized us.

On another trip to France by ourselves, from information Aunt Aldea had given me, Francis and I had found the small town, Normandel, near Mortagne, in the Perche region where my Goulet ancestors had lived. This area, we heard, hosts the world's international black pudding championship. Having grown up eating crispy, dry *boudin noir* (blood sausage), I ordered some in a small restaurant and was surprised to find myself feeling emotional – "just eating *boudin*," I told Francis, smiling through my tears. It had suddenly struck me: This food tradition my parents had kept up, and their parents' parents, on through the years, had originated, not just in Quebec, Canada, but it had come from France!

The following spring, after further research and inquiries, Francis and I located the Goulet farm on L'Ile d'Orleans in the St. Lawrence River, east of Quebec City. The Goulets had emigrated there from France. We met their descendants, the Goulets who lived toward the center of the oval-shaped island, not at its river's edge where the original thatched roof house still stood. So Francis and I drove down the dirt road toward the water to see the house. We met the architect who had bought the original 300-year-old home. He told us that although birds had begun to take over, he was able to restore it and keep it intact, in its original style.

Once back on the mainland in Quebec, Francis and I found and bought in a bookstore, a book commemorating the 300th anniversary of the founding of Quebec City. The pullout-map in it indicates the strip of land owned by my Goulet ancestors who had emigrated from Le Perche in the 17th century.

Heartened by these memorable trips, Francis and I now looked forward to touring Vietnam.

VIETNAM

I had lived for nine weeks without Francis in India. But now we would spend three weeks together in another Southeast Asian country, Vietnam. It would prove to be for both of us as exotic as India had been for me fourteen years earlier.

Like Hoa, his wife, Tom also spoke Vietnamese. He had met To Kim Hoa while working as a reporter for the *New York Times* during the Vietnam War. First Francis and I flew to San Francisco where we met our group and Tom and Hoa, our guides. Our plane was headed for a stop in Taipei en route to Hanoi. In addition to Tom and Hoa, we had two Vietnamese guides, one for the whole three weeks, and one for each of the three regions we visited.

With a new digital camera in hand, I took close to 1,000 photos. From these, on our return, I culled the hundred best ones and gave a slide presentation to the Audubon Society's Travel Club. For that event, Francis and I wore clothing custom-made for us in Vietnam. The buttons on Francis' blue heavy silk jacket, like those on my maroon silk top, were cloth covered.

HANOI AND NORTH VIETNAM

The first photo I showed that night depicted people on bicycles waiting to cross an intersection; their lines were wide and deep. Francis and I especially loved the picturesque Old Quarter in that city. We saw someone on a bicycle transporting a dead pig in a basket; a woman carrying at two ends of a pole objects heavier than she; a girl shucking snails with a pick; and on and on – plus scenes that showed the communal nature of this society we admired, for example, families eating dinner and doing dishes on the sidewalks near the booths where they sold their wares. We saw teeming life, close-up. During our own first restaurant dinner, musicians played traditional Vietnamese instruments. To our delight, Vietnamese music accompanied many of our meals.

HA LONG BAY

Tom, Hoa, and guides had arranged for us to go by boat to Cat Ba Island in Ha Long Bay, also a UNESCO World Heritage Centre which features limestone karsts. Never having seen anything like this, we were bewitched. En route to Cat Ba Island, we had stopped at one of the limestone karsts and descended into its caverns and grottos of stalagmites and stalactites. Upon exiting it, I took a photo of a breathtaking scene below me. A semicircle of boats attached to a wharf on the left curved around towering karsts. Five other karsts of different sizes receded into the distant center background leaving "paths" of bay water around and between them. A range of more tall karsts rose on the right. Single boats on the water, a few of them with colorful reddish orange sails, added another romantic touch to an already rare scene. Francis bought me some pearls during our stay on Cat Ba Island.

A photo I took of Francis standing by the sail on the deck of our boat shows him in a thoughtful mood. A photographer friend who created a slide show of Francis' life for his wake used this photo which hints at a mysterious adventure.

CENTRAL VIETNAM

In Hue, the ancient capital of Vietnam, home to royal tombs, we visited the citadel there which encloses the Forbidden Purple City, modeled after the Chinese Forbidden City. Two married priests among us, Tom and Sam, had come here when in the military after the TET Offensive. It was an emo-

Francis on deck. – Ha Long Bay.

tional trip for them. For us who had demonstrated against what the Vietnamese call the American War, we too were disturbed when we saw victims of Agent Orange.

Tom and Hoa had also arranged for us to visit, in Hue, the Office of

Genetic Counseling for Disabled Children. Agent Orange disabilities had skyrocketed after the Vietnam War. When we met with the doctor who oversaw the work of the hospital, he explained they arrange surgeries for brain tumors, heart operations, eye problems, and other conditions.

Francis and I found Hoi An, with its historic graceful architecture, one of the most colorful places along the coast. We walked the cobbled streets, past eighteenth-century houses, pagodas, and assembly halls in pristine condition.

The Vietnamese people offered a variety of personal services. Two such services provided us fascinated Francis and me. We and our tour group were on a small open boat heading to an island. While Francis sat at the outer edge of the boat, I was seated on one of the several benches in the middle, with one bent knee lifted, and that foot propped on another bench as a Vietnamese woman performed a service I had never witnessed before. Not having particularly hairy legs, I didn't regularly shave them. But out of curiosity as well as to support her, I paid her a fee to remove hair from my legs by using a thread.

The other service that both Francis and I took advantage of as well, was offered in our hotel in Nha Trang: ear wax removal. I had had more difficulty hearing in my left ear for a few years. But after one skilled practitioner removed a small lump of hard brown wax, my hearing noticeably improved.

The Cham Museum in Danang held great interest for me because I had spent time in India and had also read a few books about a goddess tradition. Francis and I learned that the Cham people, originating from Java and southern India, had a unique history. In the feminine-looking Shiva statue, for example, we saw remnants of the Cham people's matriarchal society.

From a special shop, Francis and I watched every step that had created the large silk wall-hanging we bought, framed, and hung on our dining room wall. We saw silkworms eating mulberry leaves, and artists, each in turn, harvesting their cocoons, spinning the silk, dyeing it, and weaving the threads. Against a black background, the wall-hanging depicts two Vietnamese women dressed in white *ao dais* and conical hats, walking over a bamboo bridge.

SOUTH VIETNAM AND THE MEKONG DELTA

Once settled in our hotel in Ho Chih Minh City (Saigon), our tour group was given a talk on the history of Saigon. "Did any good come from the Vietnam War?" Sam, one of our veteran travelers asked the professor. "No" came the quick answer. With anguish in Sam's voice, he repeated – "Nothing?" The professor repeated in turn, "No." But then he paused, smiled, and added, "Yes – the marriage of Hoa and Tom!"

At The War Remnants Museum we saw a sculpture of a woman bearing a deformed child. The Children's Art celebrating peace brought Francis and me close to tears. I apologized on behalf of our country a few times in talking with a Vietnamese. But the people of Vietnam hold no rancor toward us Americans, only kindness. Our Mekong guide responded: "That's a sad story, but it's past now." A middle-aged man without hands told us – "You come back next year." Francis and I felt overwhelmed by the graciousness of the Vietnamese people.

We were charmed by our long boat ride on the Mekong River Delta. One fascinating sight after another interested us, like house boats on which clothes were hung to dry, or passing boats with painted eyes intended to be, we learned, a kind of scarecrow for crocodiles. We stopped often to tour small enterprising cottage industries, like the making of pottery.

We were en route to the rustic hotel that would house us for a few nights. Our bamboo huts had thatched roofs secured with polished bamboo saplings. Their foundation was also made of bamboo – sturdy stilts plunged firmly in what looked like a small tidal flat over which the adjoining rooms stood.

That water reflected the trees. "What a way to awaken," Francis said, "looking up at this cathedral bamboo ceiling!"

Flower pots were hung from trees along the river. In fact, flowers were everywhere in Vietnam, at entrances, within the buildings. And in public bathrooms – orchids.

PREPARING TO LEAVE

Returned to our hotel in Ho Chih Minh City, I went shopping for a shawl one afternoon to replace the one I had inadvertently left behind at the Taipei airport. As I walked along to the next shop, two children approached, inviting me to buy the cards they held up, handmade by their mothers. I was grateful to do so, since the cards were lovely, and the children, sweet. They spoke impeccable English. I asked their names. "Hung" and "Lang," they told me. I learned that Hung was eleven-years old.

Then Hung begged me to go with them to a store on the other side of our hotel to buy something their families needed. Agreeing, I walked along with them, each small hand in mine on either side of me, trusting they'd know better than I when to cross the street. We had learned earlier that traffic-light observance was minimal in Vietnam, since residents, it was obvious, knew when (when a large enough group had formed) and how to charge out into the street to get to the other side. The cars dutifully stopped for the children and me. The store was a mall, and (I couldn't have imagined it) what they picked out – was powered milk.

Walking back toward where we had met, I stopped at the en-

Hung, Lang, and Elaine.

trance of our hotel and asked them to wait a few moments while I went up upstairs. Francis willingly left what he was doing, charmed to meet my two young friends he was pleased to photograph. It depicts the three of us standing before the entrance of the Continental Hotel where Graham Greene stayed while writing part of his novel, *The Quiet American*. I muse, in looking at that photo: Hung and Lang must be close to twenty-one years old by now.

Our last dinner in Vietnam a day or so later, coincided with a participant's sixtieth birthday. The already celebratory air of our departure night included, then, a birthday cake for all the guests on the roof of the Rex Hotel. Lighted lamps shone above, illuminating tall bushes around us. We were dressed for the festivity; I wore a two-piece sleeveless purple silk dress, and Francis, the grey silk shirt and black trousers, also made in Vietnam which I had bought for him on the streets that day. There was nothing shoddy about the quality of clothing made in Vietnam.

During our meal, a roving singer serenaded us. After dessert and clearing away of the dishes, Tom gave a little talk. Then roses were distributed to each of us with the invitation to exchange the rose with another person's. Someone took a photo of Francis' and my exchange, before he gave me a kiss. It holds a prominent place in my home: Francis' hands are holding mine. Each of our roses is held in that clasp while we look into each others' eyes.

Francis and Elaine exchanging a rose.

It was fitting this was Francis' and my last trip together, though of course we didn't know that then. We had agreed years before to visit foreign countries first, and then, we thought, we'd explore our own. Although that was not to be, we had at least made it to the East together.

THIS THOU PERCEIVEST . . .

Spending three weeks in Vietnam had signaled the slower, more contemplative pace of life that gratified Francis and me in recent months, even if I continued preparing handout fliers for the weekly anti-torture vigil. Perhaps now we would resume annual treks to Tanglewood as we had done during pre-yoga years, or participate in more Audubon programs, like a wildflower walk, or a tidal-pool exploration.

As septuagenarians, Francis and I, in entering the diminishment of elderhood now, were aware of it. Aunt Irene and Aunt Aldea had died, so monthly visits with them slipped into the past along with their deaths and the deaths of one relative and friend after another. On Sundays, we had taken my mother and her Polish friend, Irene, to lunch, or on an outing. When my mother's last sibling died, who still lived near Springvale, we had fewer occasions to visit my hometown. Through the years, and especially after my mother's death, our schedule was changed.

Our last Poetry of Soul class was held at Bill and Nancy's home. Francis and I drove to Yarmouth and crossed the causeway to Cousin's Island where they live. Sitting on couches and chairs in their living room, we took turns reciting a poem of our choice. Bill had alerted us ahead of time to select one.

The poem I had chosen was Shakespeare's "Sonnet LXXIII": "That time of year thou mayest in me behold . . ." The three quatrains depict, each in turn, images of endings – autumn, at summer's end; sunset, at day's end; and a dying fire. The final couplet is the most poignant: "This thou perceivest, which makes thy love more strong, / To love that well which thou must leave ere long."

My selecting it did not come about as a mere response to an assignment. This was a sonnet I had held dear since introducing it to my senior English students at Thornton Academy. I had lived with it, too, for the past four years, ever since Francis' seventy-fifth birthday party in 2002. At that celebration, I had recited a different Shakespeare sonnet – CXVI in the presence of our guests: "Let me not to the marriage of true minds / Admit impediments. Love is not love / Which alters when it alteration finds . . ." The pleasure of that experience, even just the process of memorizing and reciting it from memory was so strong, I decided to memorize others.

On the last night closing a weeklong yoga intensive at Feathered Pipe Ranch, as my contribution to the program that summer following Francis' birthday, I recited yet another Shakespeare sonnet – XXIX: "When in disgrace with fortune and men's eyes . . ." It stirred one of our close friends from Kentucky, Judi Rice. "We saw it was clearly for Francis," she told me, quoting a few of the lines: "Haply I think on thee, and then my state, / Like to the lark at break of day arising / From sullen earth, sings hymns at heaven's gate, / For thy sweet love remember'd such wealth brings / That then I scorn to change my state with kings."

Of these three, for that last Poetry of Soul class, it was "Sonnet LXXIII": "That time of year . . . ," I recited. It had struck such a chord in me, resonating in my soul, it even recited *itself* in my mind. I was speaking it aloud in the car en route to appointments, and when no one was around, during my daily walks to the Jewish cemetery nearby.

Logs crackling in the fireplace as Bill and we classmates sat in a circle, created a haunting atmosphere for me that night. Francis was sitting quietly listening as I recited the sonnet. I knew to whom the *that* in its culminating couplet referred: "This thou perceivest, which makes thy love more strong, / To love that well which thou must leave ere long."

A STARTLING QUESTION

While working in the garden one summer morning after our Passing of the Torch ceremony in 2005, a thought, given rise by nothing in particular, occurred to me: "What if Francis dies before I die? What would I do, then?" The question had so much energy, it gripped me. "Would I reenter the convent?" I pondered the question for a while, yet I knew my answer in a relatively short time. In fact, in a *very* short time. Because the question rekindled reflections I had had while sitting in my Augusta apartment after leaving the convent, the feelings I had experienced then, returned. With no uncertainty, I knew: No, I would *not* reenter the convent, not one organized as they were during pre-Vatican days. The freedom of a secular life suited me more than what I myself had experienced as limiting and confining about the convent then.

During subsequent days, this question led to musing about my life with Francis. Perhaps the constraints I had felt in the convent explained why I had wanted (and Francis had agreed) for us to be connected to a variety of non-live-in communities – like those promoting peace, yoga, the Dances of Universal Peace, and permaculture. I seemed to fear being hemmed in, by a self-enclosed society, a subculture.

Then a related question arose: "But would I remarry, if Francis died first?" I thought, if remarriage was meant to be, for me, that is to say, if it were to happen *naturally*, well, why not? I have always depended on what I call Providence – what organically evolves, what I have not devised for myself. At several important junctures in my life, I have experienced certain unexpected developments as a kind of visitation from God.

Aware, however, that the basic elements of monasticism were already at the core of my life with Francis, even if placed in a position different from this order – prayer, study, work, and recreation – (which characterizes *formal* monasticism), I thought I'd probably be content living a kind of largely monastic life at home. I shared all these thoughts with Francis.

SENSE OF MORTALITY

"This thou perceiveth, which makes thy love more strong, / To love that well which thou must leave ere long." I did perceive this in a piercing kind of way. It was keen for Francis, too. It came into play when we caught sight of each other through the glass door as he returned from around the corner of the garden shed, or when, in warm weather, I would give him a haircut outdoors. When it came to trimming Francis' beard, we would sit on the deck steps, I, one or two steps higher than he. That way, with his head resting on the barbershop cape on my lap, knees apart to support him on each side, I could reach to shave the edges of his beard under his chin.

Corners seemed to come into play for some of these moments. Seeing Francis' car rounding the corner of our Avalon Road, or when we looked at each other through the kitchen window as I approached the corner side door to take one of the grocery bags from him – I was aware of *this*, then, too.

Becoming an elder had created in Francis and me a sharp sense of mortality. But it was intensified by our having married later in life. We discussed this and decided that we would not let a day go by without lying in one another's arms, even if briefly, at times. And even if I was fully dressed because still working, and he in his pajamas, since he retired to bed earlier than I. We would relax together for a while talking about the day at every day's end. This was our way of assuring we made time for each other, while we still had each other "here."

As early as on our thirteenth wedding anniversary, close to my 50th birthday, twenty-four years before we discovered he had cancer, I had written in my notebook for Francis:

"Someday – whoever predeceases whom, we will have to face bodily separation. I know that that reality alone, even though it will have to be gone through, lived through only once, will give me to drink all of the dregs of Jesus' cup. . . . I thank God for the intimacy He gives us – for His uniting us so deeply and fully as soul mates as well as man and wife. I'm referring to a kind of spirituality *à deux* that we've experienced. But the deeper our love is, my beloved – the more we will suffer at our time of physical separation. Yet the depth of our love will also reach down beyond the grave into the heart of the Lord 'whose imperishable spirit is in all.' And we will find one another there." (Wisdom 11:26)

On Francis' part, he wrote me on Christmas day in 2007, two years before his own Passover period: "Listening to the poignant Christmas music, I deeply appreciate the gift of being alive in this mysterious, beautiful world. Yet at this stage of my life, I am more and more conscious of the fragility and preciousness of each of our moments, hours, and days together."

Francis' and my life together was a very active one. We had co-founded and directed Portland Yoga Studio for sixteen years and Yarmouth Yoga Studio for two years. After we let go these responsibilities, we relished the more contemplative pace of life that was now ours, aware all along that our hold on them was utterly fragile. I am grateful we were given five more of those leisurely years, together.

CHAPTER EIGHT
Crossroad

I felt sure Francis would live a very long life – even into his hundreds, because of his Aunt Irene's example. She died two months short of 105. I thought he had had in him that McGillicuddy gene of longevity.

He had, after all, overcome asthma which had dogged him since childhood, in the sense that he no longer used medication on a regular basis – and only rarely, an inhalant. That freedom was quite an accomplishment for someone who, in the days before he practiced yoga, was on a regimen of prednisone. Even his pulmonary doctor, less than a year before Francis died, was impressed that Francis was off regular use of medication. That doctor's remark created a story he loved to tell. "'Well, take this inhalant,' my doc told me, 'At least, it'll make *me* feel better,'" Francis related. He nonethelesss topped using the inhalant altogether, except for occasional cold-air-induced asthma.

For that victory over asthma, we credited yoga in general and his use of the backbender in our home. We had bought it at the 1987 North American Yoga Convention at Harvard, the convention that had made Francis a yoga practitioner thereafter. By reclining supine over this whale-shaped prop, with his feet pressing against the footwell, Francis' chest could arch over its upper part, while his arms reached overhead and back down toward the floor. In keeping his rib cage muscles more pliable, the back bender improved his breathing.

ANOTHER HEALTH CHALLENGE

After asthma, Francis had a more serious challenge to encounter. My memory is indelible of the pain on his face when the news that he had adult onset diabetes hit him, and, loving him – me. That diagnosis came in 1993 when we returned home from a week of yoga at Feathered Pipe Ranch, located in the northern Rocky Mountains of Montana. We were blaming the high altitude for his excessive thirst and increased urination. Once home, we learned in his doctor's office, since his blood sugar was 700 (a normal reading would fall between 60 and 120): he could have died.

Both of us valued holistic ways to maintain good health, but "Now I'll have to depend on mainstream, Western medicine," Francis lamented. "I'll be tied to it!" The news he had diabetes depressed both of us, at first. But participating in the education sessions that were offered gave us tools to cope with it.

At Francis' follow-up doctor's visit with Dr. Louis Bove, now retired, we must have looked alarmed at his high blood-sugar reading because Dr. Bove felt the need to reassure us, "Don't worry," he said, "you'll get used to this after a while." That calmed us, and especially hearing what he said next, "You know, one of the best ways to live a long life is to get a serious disease like diabetes and to take really good care of oneself." Francis had already learned from dealing with asthma his need to avoid getting overextended, or overtired, so hearing that, our spirits were lifted.

Eventually, even without perfect results (since Francis did have some low blood-sugar readings, though many fewer highs), he acquired a management of diabetes that was recognized by members of the Diabetes Center as close to stellar. At times he seemed to pride himself on his skill in balancing its tripod – meals, exercise, and insulin – as if it were a game.

Francis' own endocrinologist and diabetic specialist, Dr. John T. Devlin, was so impressed that Francis didn't suffer from some typical musculoskeletal disorders resulting from diabetes, such as neuropathy and frozen shoulders, he made us a novel proposition. Recognizing that Francis' being spared was likely due to his practice of yoga, he invited me to teach a course called Yoga for Frozen Shoulders in Diabetes. The good results demonstrated from this series of classes were published as a scientific study in an article written by Dr. Devlin and Dr. Donald Endrizzi for *Practical Diabetology*.

Demonstrating poses for participants and also assisting me during those therapeutic yoga classes, Francis became a model whom others who had diabetes wanted to imitate. Earlier, after his diagnosis, a friend had been eager to tell us that his uncle had lived with this disease until age ninety-five. At the time of the study in 2005, Francis was only seventy-eight years old.

Because of Francis' good control of asthma and diabetes, we had no idea something yet more serious would appear. It looked as if he had a recipe for longevity.

NEW ADVERSARY

As part of his yoga practice, Francis had taken pleasure daily reclining on the backbender. In the late autumn of 2008, and even more so by the following spring, it became increasingly uncomfortable for him. Noticing that Francis was avoiding the backbender, and ignorant of what was going on in his spine, I tried to clear up for him with selected yoga poses he was eager to try, whatever might have caused his new discomfort. The postures all gave him temporary relief, but nothing worked to remove the obstacle that refused to allow his spine to arch as it had in the past. So he gave up trying.

On babysitting Mondays, I would read stories to Rowan. When I saw her sitting on Francis' lap on the futon a few times, I was very pleased that he also was reading to her. As introverts, in the beginning, they had both approached each other shyly. I could see they enjoyed each other because the following week, I saw Rowan sitting straddled on Francis' shoulders.

With her legs firmly in place there, she had swung her upper body down and around to look at his face, her blond hair hanging like strands of gold. After Lynn and Lee had gone home, Francis told me he would have liked to continue reading stories to Rowan, but he couldn't. Doing so aggravated his back pain. But there were other ways they could interact. They rolled pennies together.

Rowan hanging out with Francis.

Although not at all a complainer, Francis began referring to his painful sacroiliac joint. He made appointments to clear up the problem with health professionals who served us, and who had become our friends – Dr. Sheila Littlefield, our chiropractor; Ron Lemire, a massage therapist; and even a rolfer for deep-tissue massage, Christina McChristian.

So pained to see Francis in pain, having to lie for relief on a blanket on our yoga studio floor, even before it was time for our closing relaxation pose, I readily took his complaint to heart. I wasn't just spurred into action as before, now I was *driven* to do all I could to get to the bottom of this. First came research on the sacroiliac joint, and yoga postures to assist maintaining skeletal and muscular balance for a pain-free lower back. My students benefitted, and those poses did seem to help him.

Francis also began using a tool that I suggested, a MA roller. Made of solid rock maple, this wooden cylinder with two knobs that fit snugly on either side of the spine, is designed for gently stretching the paraspinal muscles, like very deep-tissue work. Lying supine over it was so helpful, Francis thought we had found the effective remedy. In fact, it was so efficacious that when he was planning an overnight visit with Bob Mottau in Boston, I ordered him a MA Roller Mini, convenient for travel.

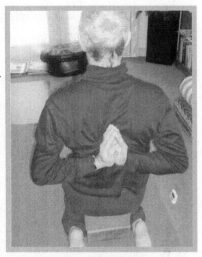

Francis – Virasana and Namaskarasana.

Overall, however, though alternative approaches did help, the relief they gave Francis was increasingly short-lived. Our multiple attempts to find the root of what we thought was a musculoskeletal problem were seesaw experiences. Discovering something that worked elated us; realizing it had ceased to work deflated us.

Annually, Francis took pride in going to Holy Cross College reunions. By now, since he and his classmates had already celebrated their 50th anniversary, it was in part a free weekend away for us. But in June of this year, 2009, he had to sit during the gospel reading.

It was the same for our own Sunday church liturgies. Unable to stand for long, Francis would sit on the worn wooden bench next to me while I stood for that reading. Then, for our weekly peace vigils, unable to stand for long, for the pain, Francis would excuse himself from staying in line the whole time. His back was bothering him, he said. He would go to the library instead, or buy vegetables at the Farmer's Market across the street, and then meet me at the end of the vigil. We would then stop for lunch at the little Chinese restaurant we liked, before returning home. The three-legged canvas folding chair I had bought for him never got used at the vigil. We found another (ironic) use for it later. I used it in the hospital when visitors occupied the other chairs.

It was Francis who started using the expression – "my condition." Giving it that name seemed to imply that the mystery was solved. Now, remembering the weeks he suffered increasingly nagging pain, just thinking of those words, "my condition" – makes my heart ache.

I half blamed, even upbraided, myself later for having tried first, all possible natural approaches instead of suggesting we see Francis' own doctor

sooner. But when we did, Dr. James Katz, Francis' primary care internist told us it had made sense to rule out musculoskeletal problems first. Moreover, later when I repeated my regret to Francis' compassionate oncologist, Dr. Roger Inhorn, he assured us it would not have made a difference.

Francis at dinner with our "family."

Once we knew the truth, however, we concluded it was better we were left in the dark about the real cause of Francis' pain. As it turned out, during the last year of his life, he was living as normally as he could. Had we found out sooner, we might have spent a year making the rounds, getting tests of all kinds for him,

Telling Lynn a joke.

and all to no avail. For this kind of cancer which his doctors considered rare – chemotherapy was not recommended. There was virtually nothing medically they could do to cure him of the cancer he had, mysterious until the end.

Sr. Irene – before Francis' diagnosis.

For the last weekend in June, Francis and I flew to Fort Worth, Texas, to participate in one of our favorite annual weekends, a *CORPUS* conference. The fact that Patricia Fresen was one of our keynote speakers caused some excitement; this Dominican nun had been ordained a Roman Catholic woman priest in 2003 by one of the two male bishops who had ordained seven women the year before. These had called themselves the "Danube Seven" because their ordination was held where no bishop had jurisdiction – on the Danube River between Germany and Austria. Then in 2005, persuaded by one of the male bishops who wanted to ordain Fresen a *bishop*, she became Bishop Patricia Fresen. The story of her initial reluctance was related in an *NCR* article, "Reluctant bishop ordained for North America." In that article Patricia characterized that ordaining bishop as one who was driven by a sense of justice, [one] who feels women have been excluded from the priesthood far too long."

In her address, Patricia spoke of the Lord's Prayer in Aramaic which she had learned from Dr. Neil Douglas-Klotz. I told her I also had studied with Saadi, this Aramaic scholar, yearly since 1996. Moreover Francis and I had chanted and presented it during the liturgies for four previous *CORPUS* conferences. For one of those, it was the Beatitudes in Aramaic.

The conference organizers, therefore, asked Francis and me if we could bring The Aramaic Lord's Prayer to life again during this year's closing Sunday liturgy. We assured them we could. All we needed was a brief practice. But when the time came on Sunday, Francis had to sit down. He continued to chant it with me while facing the assembly as I was doing, standing next to the altar. But I was going through the movements alone.

TAKING ACTION

Unquestionably, something serious was going on. When we got home, we called Dr. Katz. He prescribed pain medications and sent Francis to a specialist, Dr. Mats Agren. After ordering an X-ray of his spine, this orthopedic surgeon stood over Francis lying on the examination table while he palpated it, all the while engaging us in friendly conversation. As Francis slipped on his turtle neck, we looked at each other, reassured. Then Dr. Agren returned with the X-ray. He pointed to a spot between the first and second lumbar vertebrae that looked, he said, like a very old injury. "You must have had a fracture many years ago," he said, concluding – "but it doesn't have to hurt." Now *that* was an encouraging comment, so we left less worried.

But the hope was short lived. What was Francis to do *now* with this stubborn pain? It had become intolerable. We returned to Dr. Katz, then, who tried a different, even more powerful pain killer, since the previous one proved ineffective. By now, however, Francis was suffering nausea from the medicine itself, something that increasingly disconcerted us in weeks to come. As with alternative therapies we had tried for him, so with medications: they raised, only to dash, our hopes for Francis' relief from lower back pain.

In between trips to the hospital, we returned home on two separate days that week to receive guests for dinner. The first was John Wirtz, a friend stricken by the recent loss of his wife, Mimi, whom we also grieved. Obviously, Francis didn't want us to cancel that visit, nor the second one with Gloria Hutchinson, a close friend for more than ten years; her overnight stay had been prearranged. The latest pain medication seemed to be working. But again, Francis was forced to leave the table before the end of both meals. Such was his impossible pain.

Returning to importune Dr. Katz to do something, we were encouraged when he ordered an MRI, administered at Mercy Hospital's new campus. This would surely reveal the root of the problem, we thought, but I felt anxiety about what we would learn. The new building features a wall of windows overlooking the Fore River. In this light, with the sun streaming in, the expansive view might calm patients. I, along with a few others, who were likely also awaiting their loved ones, needed calming as well.

The air of urgency with which Francis was told to return to Dr. Agren's office as soon as the results of the MRI were available, and the manner in which we were ushered into his office without taking our turn in the waiting room, seemed to signify not just concern about the acuteness of Francis' pain, but the emergency of his condition. Yes, it was his "condition" – but a much more serious one than we could imagine.

TWO SCENES

Two scenes on that dark day, the eve of my 74th birthday, stand bleak, frozen in my mind: Francis is sitting in Dr. Agren's office with me at his side. Dr. Agren walks into the room with news about the MRI. "It's a cancer we don't know about," he says, wincing. "I want you admitted to the hospital immediately."

In the second scene (I don't even remember driving him to the hospital) – I walk into the double room, past the curtain to the other side of Francis' bed near the window. I sit close to him on his bed.

We simultaneously reach for each others' hands. His eyes seek mine as quickly as mine seek his, as if to arrive at assurance that all will be well. We hold hands and look into one another's eyes as in deep pools. Yes, all *will* be well, and we will return to our home, his spine healed, and our fears resolved.

But we have never before encountered a moment like this. That look between us reveals our mutual, stark awareness that a junction might be lying in wait for us at the end of this road. We might possibly be approaching the final, dreaded crossroad where we must physically part. That look between us, manifesting our mutual acceptance of this fate, holds, too, all our mutual knowing and loving regard of forty-one years.

FIRST HOSPITALIZATION

I went home in a daze, alone. Tonight I would sleep in our bed, also alone. But I had to notify Francis' family and our friends. He and I . . . we were also in need of prayer. I sat at the computer, then created group lists to include the names of our families and our friends, entitled the Subject line: "Please Pray for Francis," and wrote: "Dr. Agren told us it's a cancer we don't know about." [7]

I couldn't sleep that night. Francis had cancer! What would happen now? Would he become one among many who had survived cancer? Or would he die? If he did – what would happen to me? Would I remarry? If I did, I would have a second husband. The thought sounded so strange, I felt a little guilty thinking it. It came as a flash, and I dropped it in a flash. I remembered my long ruminations in the garden, generated as if out of thin air, four years earlier. I had thoroughly examined possible answers to those questions then. They satisfied me now, and that was a good thing, because Francis and I were now set in motion on a new path. To where would it lead?

The next day, when I visited Francis in the hospital, he said, smiling: "I'm not having dire thoughts, you know. I'm having a good time. I just stay in the present moment." I relaxed, relieved. In using that expression,

---

[7] A web search using our names – "elaineandfrancis" – will lead to the blogspot which Susannah Sanfilippo created for Francis and me. All the letters I wrote about our journey, and now mine, are posted there.

Francis was revealing a way of living influenced by Eastern thought which he had internalized from twenty-two years of practicing yoga. This was typical of him. Along with Francis' lifelong following of Jesus, this too, had guided him in daily life, as it was doing today, the first of his last one hundred days physically among us.

Even if he needed frequent naps, Francis continued to enjoy the *New Yorker* and the *Boston Globe* and looked forward to the *New York Times*, which Lynn and Lee brought him. He also engaged those around him, even teasing the student nurses.

Francis' sense of humor helped him in other ways, too, namely, with his roommate's loud snoring. When awakened by it at night, he told us he felt as if he were out at sea whale watching. Lynn and Lee came up with a solution: Lynn uploaded many of Francis' favorite musical selections on an iPod she gave him. Francis enjoyed the music and used it, too, when he was trapped again at "sea" with the "whales."

Observing how depleted Francis felt going from one test to another, he had the presence of mind to admit he did not want many visitors. In my next letter, I turned to family and friends: "The enormity of what is happening to us is sinking in for me," I wrote, "in spite of fervent hope that the tissue is benign."

I was Francis' advocate discussing the options with his doctors and communicating this information over the phone to one or more of three good friends in the medical profession. My telephone consultations with them gave me much needed support and reassured both of us that we were making informed decisions.

Francis' first biopsy report brought in a non-diagnostic result. There was speculation, for a variety of reasons, it might be small-cell cancer. But Dr. Agren, and Francis' oncologist, Dr. Inhorn, were puzzled. Dr. Inhorn would be telephoning me in the morning.

After they left his room, Francis' spirit, nevertheless, seemed trusting, even sweet. Because sitting up straight in bed caused him pain, even with the intravenous (IV) medications, he had to keep the upper part of his hospital bed down in a horizontal position. Since it was hard to eat that way, I fed him and flossed his teeth before returning home. This ritual, from then on until Francis died, was a tender exchange that never became a mere habit for us. Far from taking it for granted, I savored those moments, hoping he might all the more savor his food. And from then on, each easy, or demanding, act of assistance I gave him, comforted me.

What a blessing friends are! Following Francis' progress through my frequent letters, they rallied to help us. Examples multiplied of their loving concern: a casserole left in our refrigerator; my cousin George Remy's offering to bring and return our car to the garage; a neighbor's going on errands for us; the new owner of Portland Yoga Studio, Stephanie Abram's helping me sort out bills and write checks to pay them, neglected in recent weeks. During Francis' hospitalization at home, many friends like Denny Dreher and Grace Braley came to help. Michael Katz, for example, did some of our grocery shopping for us. The gestures of generosity and love surrounding Francis and me were very big to us. None of them was small.

I wrote in a September 28 letter – "I realized forcibly today we're not alone on this journey. All of us are caught up together in the big events of life's flow. Your love has drawn you into our piece of it."

THE DIVERSION OF CHICKENS

The chicks Francis and I had gotten for Rowan five months earlier were now pullets. When one of them laid her first egg, five days after Francis' hospitalization, it was not just a cause célèbre. Because this event coincided with our unease that Francis' puzzling case required a second biopsy, it gave all of us who love him respite from our distress.

The first egg was double yoked, so I fried it and brought it to Francis in the hospital. "That's the tastiest egg I've ever eaten," he said.

When our friend John Wirtz read about the first egg event, he wrote this note which delighted Francis and all of us accompanying him:

> *Dear Francis: From latest reports, chickens (or, if you want to be technical, eggs, double-yolk ones) have come to roost at your room at Mercy Hospital. In common with your made-in-heaven partnership with Elaine, I never once felt hen-pecked in all the years with my dear Mimi. True, once in a while, I might chicken out and let her have her way. To the point: I understood Elaine to say no visiting for now. Yet her last e-mail suggests otherwise. I'm not one to brood over such things, to suggest fowl play, or to say a plot was being hatched. Still, it sounds like you had a flock of visitors. And, if egged-on, Elaine should know I have a long memory. And, when you next see her, tell her that I don't consider this a yolk.*

SERIOUS MATTERS

When Francis and I learned that all patients are put by default into category "full code," meaning, for example, if the patient's heart stopped, staff members would rush in and get it started again – Francis chose DNR, "Do not resuscitate." It marked the direction he, and I supporting him, took. Dr. Inhorn agreed, putting it this way, "We would let nature take its course." At Francis' age, with this much unmanageable pain, even with medications, the prognosis was not good.

In the past, Francis had liked to repeat a friend's story. Tony Montenaro had asked his oncologist, "Can you cure me, doc?" His doctor's reply, "No, but I can treat you," elicited a quick response from our friend, Tony

– "Then, no thank you."

At a time like this, Tony's story, vivid in Francis' mind, bolstered his own thinking. As a hospital chaplain he had witnessed how taking extraordinary means to prolong life at any cost often only prolongs suffering.

HOME FROM THE HOSPITAL

A few days later, Francis was discharged from Mercy Hospital. In addition to oral medications for him, we received instructions in how to use another powerful drug to anesthetize his pain. Stronger than morphine, fentanhyl is administered through adhesive patches for absorption into the bloodstream. Every three days, a new patch had to be placed onto a different part of Francis' body.

To make room for the hospital bed's arrival, Paul Ridlon and Will Huntington, our neighbors on a nearby street, came right over and transferred the futon into the living room. This would now be Francis' room. Then they helped the delivery man maneuver the bed through the glass door.

Though we call it the yoga living room, Francis had also called it our cave since we spent a lot of time here, not just because of the TV, but for yoga practice, and I, for reading. Over the years, Francis had developed the habit of using three different chairs for his reading. He read the morning paper sitting on the kitchen's rocking chair, and, in the afternoons, to take advantage of the northern light, he chose to read in the living room. The maroon, stuffed swivel rocker in that room was hard to resist. But in the evenings, he would join me in this choice yoga living room, our favorite.

For a sickbed, none could be more comfortable and cheery than this southeastern corner room with one of the two glass doors opening out onto a deck overlooking the garden and chicken coop; and, on its southwestern side, a four-paneled bow window overlooking Canadian hemlocks. From his bed, Francis would be able to see, not just the chickens, but the sun streaming into our room at its rising, and circling around the room during the day, descending as it set in the west.

The next day, when I arrived with Francis in the car, Paul and Will met us to help him up the short flight of stairs. In gratitude for their help, I gave them two eggs lain that day. Pamela Ryan, a friend and yoga colleague teaching at Portland Yoga Studio, greeted Francis at the door. She had vacuumed the rug, cooked us a meal, and put together for Francis' room, a bouquet of garden flowers. She got the third egg.

SETTING THINGS UP

I soon learned it takes effort to navigate the medical system, and patience with delays, but we managed. The Visiting Nurses' Association (VNA) for which Francis' and my niece, Jane McGillicuddy, worked as director of Human Resources, were an indispensable help. When the physical therapist whom they sent arrived for his first visit, he transferred an antique chair with arm rests from the living room to Francis' room. That one was placed not far from his bed. With its back close to the glass door, the sun would warm his own back. Francis' favorite swivel stuffed chair was also brought in and positioned on the other side of his bed, requiring him to walk farther to get to it. "When you feel free enough from pain," his physical therapist told him, "go ahead and sit in the chairs, for five, ten, or even fifteen minutes a day." The suggestion was not lost on Francis. He tried out both of them on that first day, but only for a few minutes. All was now in place for Francis' hospital care at home.

I had massaged Francis' lower back before we knew he had cancer, because it relieved his pain. But now, since he had been virtually bedridden for almost three weeks, learning the importance of preventing embolisms, blood clots, and skin breakdown, I eagerly undertook giving Francis a daily massage with soothing massage oil.

To help me care for Francis, I organized, through my letters to local friends, what I dubbed The Favors Brigade. One of them who came to do garden and chicken-coop chores, did so shortly after the annual Pax Christi Maine weekend retreat we had missed. So our friend was able to report on how lovingly those present at the retreat had spoken about Francis. After she left, he told me, "I just had a black humor thought: People would die to hear such tender sentiments expressed about themselves!" Not to be outdone by distance, our dear friends in *CORPUS*, Allen and Sylvia Moore from Arizona, emailed to tell us they'd be in what they coined as the Prayer Brigade.

RADIATION TO THE RESCUE

Francis' pain, in the meantime, in spite of his strong medications, was increasing. Learning that bone cancer is "radiation sensitive," we hoped this therapy would alleviate more, if not all of his pain.

The night before his first radiation appointment, Francis wanted me to give him a bath. I had done it not long before in preparation for his appointment with Dr. Agren that had led to his immediate hospitalization. Although it was more difficult to get to the bathroom and back this time, Francis was determined. Leaning on my arm as we walked toward it, about twenty yards away – he made it. With the tub's support bar and me on the other side, Francis eased himself into the filled tub. Resting his head on its rear incline, he visibly relaxed in the water's warmth and began humming his pleasure in this relief from pain. I hummed in joyful unison.

It was comforting, for the early radiation appointments, to have our new friend Kathy Tosney's roomy car to taxi us to the center. Especially since, after having to find the correct hospital parking lot, returning to a different office to fetch a parking card, and then locating the office proper of Francis' Radiation Oncologist, Dr. Phillip J. Villiotte – I felt my face suddenly heat up. Looking into the bathroom mirror, I discovered why; it was flushed red. My reaction might have come as well from the fact that although the receptionist requested that Francis sit in the waiting room, with Francis' pain so insupportable, I had intervened to ask for a gurney. In a full horizontal position, he had relief. Whenever we arrived after that, the staff accepted his need for a gurney.

Seeing how painful it was for Francis to be transported by car to the radiation center, I did my best to make him comfortable. I would draw down the back of the passenger car seat and prop pillows around his waist and hips to cushion him from the car's jostling. But even with pillows, small bumps in the road caused him to wince. All I could do was cringe. And he would be getting a total of twenty-three treatments! When we came home from those appointments, moreover, all Francis could do was sleep for two to three hours. I learned from his nurse that radiation also causes fatigue. I began to understand. Although radiation can "come to the rescue," the patient must be rescued in turn from its side effects.

Our friends' gestures of generosity and love literally kept us going. One of them, for example, had stacked in our refrigerator several containers of fruit, and marked each one: "Breakfast to Go." How did she know I might have left the house without breakfast because of the work it took to prepare Francis to leave for the radiation center? Now I brought those containers with me when I needed to finish my breakfast there.

ALTERNATIVE THERAPIES

From the beginning, we took advantage of alternative therapies. When two friends volunteered to give Francis special treatments, he agreed. Dorothy Woods Smith was not only a teaching nurse professor who headed the Southern Maine University's College of Nursing and Health Professions, she had also studied in New York with Dr. Dolores Krieger, founder of Therapeutic Touch (TT). Dottie came regularly, to give Francis treatments of TT which she practiced. One day, sitting in the stuffed swivel chair as I watched her give Francis a treatment, Dottie offered to give me one as well. As she swept her hands in midair over me, I felt a wave of warm "healing energy," as she calls it, that I had never known before. That experience made me an instant believer.

Dr. James Melloh, whom we came to call just "Jim," also came to help Francis. Jim, a geriatric rehabilitation and hospice physician, had spent five extra years studying a one thousand-year-old tradition from Aztec medicine. He called it "gentle hands-on 'energy work'." He would light a candle, and with his hands placed on Francis' body, for example, on his head, chest, hands and feet, each in turn, he would chant. The chant was so soothing that I made it a practice, during this already silent time, to lie on Francis' and my own bed close by, listening. Mesmerized by my own fatigue and the healing chant, I often dozed off. I'd awaken from this restful respite and watch Jim's face deep in concentration. Before leaving after that first treatment, Jim generously offered, "Call me any time with questions, or even, if you otherwise need me," he added, "in the middle of the night."

Then there was acupuncture. I drove Francis to Yarmouth once a week, a thirty-minute drive north, for treatments with Dr. Fern Tsao, a Chinese doctor. A few times we piggy-backed a second appointment, just a bit further north to Freeport for a cranial osteopathy treatment with Francis' regular osteopathic physician, Dr. Kevin Zorsky.

ENCOURAGING DEVELOPMENTS

After Francis' first acupuncture appointment, he told me, once back in his room, that he had found it comforting. For the rest of the day, seated in his chair in the sun, he expressed astonishment to be feeling better than he had in weeks – and even in months. "In fact," he said, "I don't want to move, so I can savor being pain free!"

The next morning when my alarm rang, he called out to me on our bed nearby, "There's nothing like a natural sleep – eight hours with no sleeping pill! I turned a corner! The radiation two days ago helped (it had been his fifth), but it needed a boost. The acupuncture treatment gave it that boost. And boom! The acupuncture treatment said to the cancer: 'Get out of there!' WOW! This corner was extraordinary! There'll be more bumps on the way still to go, but a big obstacle was overcome here!"

Two days later, I was also able to report that, although Francis had lost a lot of weight, he had begun getting out of bed on his own and was walking around the house. A few hours later, after I parked the car at the radiation center, instead of using a wheelchair to go from parking lot to the building, and although he did have to bend his head a few times to control dizziness, he walked to the office holding my arm. Those two sallies, however, did wipe him out for the rest of the day. But, when the VNA nurse took his vitals later in the afternoon, she noted they had all improved. "All because of the walking," she said. So we were encouraged.

Although the previous day had been desperately challenging, it was obvious now that Francis felt a new kind of ease in walking. Before I knew it, instead of waiting for me at the foot of the side-entrance stairs, he walked ahead without me and down the incline to the car – with his arms out like an airplane.

In the letter giving family and friends an account of this joyous development, I concluded: "I want him to fly!"

The Cooking for Cancer Prevention class I went to one night did a good job of introducing me to the macrobiotic cooking I had only glimpsed before. David Handwerker, who regularly joins our monthly Dances of Universal Peace circle at the yoga studio, stayed with Francis while I attended that class. I was hoping a macrobiotic diet could save Francis' life. Hearing some extraordinary success stories even for people who already had cancer, only encouraged me. How pleased I was to see that Francis was open to trying it.

189

Friends like Katherine Morgan, already on the macrobiotic path, brought us their versions of macrobiotic mushroom barley soup. We both got to love it. Another friend (whom we met through permaculture), Tree Tenney, brought us medicinal mushrooms which she had gathered for us from her farm property. Our former yoga student and good friend, Sally Waite, even spent a whole afternoon showing me how to cook the macrobiotic way. When she came to say goodbye to Francis, he laughed and said: "I heard you two cackling in the kitchen."

We would soon meet also someone who taught classes in macrobiotic cooking. Meanwhile, with radiation treatments in process, when a friend used the expression that "macrobiotics can flush out the debris of destroyed cancer cells" – that idea also bolstered our hope. But then, discouraging *new* developments arose – nausea, inability to eat, weight loss, constipation, and low sodium. So Francis was readmitted to the hospital.

THE SECOND HOSPITALIZATION

For the first nine of Francis' radiation appointments, he had had to endure the insult of painful transport from home and back, by car. But, for the remaining twelve, he was grateful to be carried to the radiation center each day by a kinder method – the hospital ambulance. For this reason alone, Francis was relieved to be readmitted. He actually hoped he would be discharged from the hospital only after the last radiation appointment. And he was.

Francis was pleased by the treats I brought to supplement the hospital's institutional meals. We were used to eating popcorn on a regular basis. Besides, it provided good fiber to keep "things" running smoothly. I also deliberately made too much in order to share it with the nurses, both in Francis' room, and if there was some left – with the nurses at the main desk. One of them said I should market it. Seasoned with dill as well as with nutritional yeast, it's very tasty. Francis also liked the fresh greens and the pecan bread

Dr. Tsao had recommended. And of course he still relished the pullets' fresh eggs I fried for him, just before leaving the house for the hospital.

THE DEBATE

As the time approached for Francis' last radiation appointment, a quasi debate started: Should he be sent to a rehab center? Or return home?

By now, because Francis' intestines were already irritated by radiation – oral medications would not do. At home, he would have to use, instead, a pain pump called a PCA (a patient controlled analgesic) which would be connected to him under the skin. We both had to be prepared in how to use the PCA to better manage his pain. The little machine would be delivering him a continuous, small amount of dilaudid, a derivative of morphine. But Francis would also be able to get more if he needed it, by pressing a button. A lockout mechanism enforcing a ten-minute wait after each new press of the button would prevent him from getting too much of this powerful drug.

The debate went on for several days. It was both worrying and wearing. Francis looked at me one day and said, "We don't know what will happen." I sat close to him on his bed, and looked into his eyes. His words hung in the air. I knew he was right. But I tried to encourage him, "Remember when my mother was also debilitated like this after a stay in the hospital?" I asked, reminding him that even in her 80's, after that long stay, my mother had been able to regain her strength.

If Francis were to come home instead of go to a rehabilitation facility, he would have to regain some of the strength he had lost by being in bed. "We've got to rehab him," Jim told me in Francis' presence.

PHYSICAL THERAPY

For the next three days, I virtually lived in the hospital. Doing physical therapy with Francis was our priority. I wrote out a plan for him including simple things he could do while sitting, standing, and even reclining. I also trimmed his beard and nails, and gave him foot and leg massages. Since Portland Yoga Studio was only an eight-minute walk from the hospital, I would go there for a nap or two during the day. Sometimes I napped in our car.

Francis was as determined as I to build up his overall strength. That was evident in his reaction to what Dr. Jim recommended he try. As soon as Jim gave the following directions for this particular exercise, I knew Francis would respond. "While placing your hands or elbows onto some stable structure," Jim told him, "keep one foot firmly planted on the floor. Then bend forward at the hip so that the torso is parallel to the floor and," he concluded – "keeping the other leg straight, lift it up toward the ceiling, with the heel leading."

This was, in essence, a yoga pose we knew as Warrior III. It's not at all an easy pose, even if done with the arms supported rather than in midair. But Francis beamed, because, he not only knew about this pose, he had practiced it many times. Hence, he proceeded to do his best, demonstrating it for Jim. It reassured me. But more – seeing Francis' eagerness to get strong, my eyes blurred with tears in my pride that the memory of past yoga practice was still in his body. Yes, it was still in him to do it.

Yet one afternoon, after hardly touching his lunch because of nausea, Francis was eager to get a nap. Before going to the car for a nap myself, I sat on the large stuffed chair near the foot of his bed to watch him for a while. He looked so pale and thin as he slept, while walking out to the parking lot, planning to return in about an hour or so, I thought he would surely need to go for rehab after all. And this in spite of my earlier assurance.

But when I returned and saw him smiling, wide awake and refreshed, I was inspirited. He had good color now, and even, unbelievably, a very good appetite! To top it off, after his evening snack of popcorn, I learned from the nurse that his blood pressure had been much better that day, almost normal. My husband took me on roller-coaster rides, little and big ones, during his long last ordeal.

It was Francis' own active cooperation in doing physical therapy that created the progress which further encouraged him. Two days before his discharge from the hospital, he stayed up all day. After dozing periodically in the lounge chair, he read the *Boston Globe*. Because it was Lynn's birthday on this day, instead of eating my own lunch with Francis, I went out with Lynn, Lee, and Rowan to celebrate it. When I returned, the first thing . . . yes, Francis was itching to tell me – with the help of his walker and free from his PCA pain pump, he had walked on his own, the whole length of the hall, past the doors that lead into the doctors' office area, and back! And now, he wanted to do it again, with me walking beside him this time.

COMING TO A DECISION

In the end, the opinion of a doctor with more authority even than Francis' primary-care doctor tipped the scales. Even before he arrived, we were given the impression it was he, *the* person with whom we should consult for advice of the type Francis needed now. Dr. Blaizer's job was to figure out the dosage of pain medication Francis needed for his PCA. But he brought us more than technical information.

He walked into Francis' room with a pleasant energetic air. With only one look at Francis, he said, "I didn't expect you to look this good," admitting, "I thought you'd be slugging along." We smiled, gratified Francis' diligent work doing physical therapy had brought him this accolade. He obviously shared our sentiments in saying, "I'm pleased how well you look."

Dr. Blaizer also introduced us to a third method to reduce Francis' pain – the transcutaneous electrical nerve stimulation, or as it's known by its acronym – the TENS unit. This one, we were pleased to learn, was drug-free. He explained how and why it worked. When Francis wasn't sleeping

I would velcro around his waist a very wide waist band which was attached to a device through which we could set the strength of the electric current. We were told it would distract Francis' brain from the pain.

Dr. Blaizer's best line came just as he was leaving. When I told him some people thought Francis should go to a rehab facility, he immediately shot back – "Going home *is* rehab!" It was electrifying for us to hear this. "Yes," he added, "go home and do some things!"

Although he tried to hide it, I had noticed that Francis had felt somewhat uneasy about burdening me if he returned home. But now, hearing from Dr. Blaizer that going home *is* rehab, he repeated his words aloud: "Yes, let's go home and do some things!" I was ready also. Having caught up with my lost sleep in the past twelve days, I was ready for the next round.

TO BE PRACTICAL

I knew enough by now to ask myself, nonetheless: "How will I handle all these minutiae?" We needed a setup more efficient than even our revised homemade Favors' Brigade. Susannah, who had created the elaineandfrancis blogspot with Stephanie's help, found and set up for us an organizing tool that would improve on it: lotsahelpinghands.com. By including a calendar for all our helper-friends to check online, it met our practical needs.

In addition to this, Stephanie formatted in Excel, a Daily Care Log idea I had dreamed up during my first experience of being Francis' "home nurse." A checklist like this made it easier to remember Francis' scheduled needs, for example, keeping on schedule with changing the fentany patches.

In allowing us to detect patterns, the Daily Care Log also provided information that had several practical applications, for example, in keeping track of fluids to prevent Francis' sodium from plummeting while yet getting enough fluid to prevent constipation. What complexities the side effects of medications caused!

HOME!

I was euphoric bringing Francis home. Parking the car by the side door, we saw Susannah and Nicki Piaget waiting, ready to help. While Nicki started preparing supper, Susannah transferred from the living room the new egg crate mattress which Anne and Erik had brought for his hospital bed. Francis, however, took lunch, not in bed, but sitting on his comfortable chair with the sun at his back.

Meanwhile, sitting before our wide computer desk abutting his bed and close to his chair in what was a cheery nook, because of the sun and view – I read Francis emails from friends giving him a virtual welcome home.

For example, this one from Barbara DeCoste: "You both have worked with the many miracles medicine has to offer and now you can come home to deep healing which love and beauty provide." I responded full of hope: "I firmly believe that the love, prayers, and healing energy we are both receiving will melt whatever is left of Francis' cancer which the radiation oncologist admitted "radiation cannot completely get."

There it was – the caveat I quoted but did not consciously take in (what "radiation cannot completely *get*") because I so trusted, or convinced myself, that this love and beauty and prayers and the macrobiotic meals I would now prepare for Francis, and the several other alternative therapies waiting in the wings – they would, all, together, save his life.

The next morning after Francis' return from the hospital, his energy was so strong he sat in the kitchen for breakfast. It felt unreal. He was sitting up in the kitchen without pain. This was the first time since we knew cancer had struck his spine, that he was able to eat in the kitchen, to sit as he normally did, as he used to do – with his rocking chair pulled up to his small custom-made table for one. The contrast was so startling, it felt as if the last two months had been a dream. We were savoring these moments of normality. But then, after three good meals, perhaps because Francis behaved in too normal a manner by forgetting he needed to eat smaller amounts with lots of pauses between bites, we got caught off guard. He lost his supper.

Now we needed to turn to macrobiotic eating in a serious way. Francis was up for it, viewing it as I did, an adventure. In many ways, I reminded him, it wasn't completely different from the way we already ate. We had already enjoyed, years ago, our eating experiences at Masao's macrobiotic restaurant in Cambridge. So I asked Stephanie to post a message through lotsahelpinghands.com entitled: "Helping Elaine cook macrobiotic meals at home for Francis." We had no idea that a perfect stranger would be answering this email, one with more to offer than we could imagine.

UPSWINGS

Francis himself had expected more bumps or downswings along the way, and the nausea was a major one. But since his coming home, the upswings outdid the downswings. Five days after his return, he reveled in going out for acupuncture. Dr. Tsao said his color was better and his pulse was good. Thin or not, wearing his Greek hat and London fog raincoat, with his PCA in a case slung over his shoulder, Francis looked like a movie star. I could understand why he exclaimed, "It's good to do normal things."

Going for a ten-minute walk on the dead-end street near our home, and very briefly visiting the chicken coop, was another feat, even if Francis did need to sleep two and a half hours afterwards. Going to my cousins' home for Thanksgiving dinner was an even bigger *fait accompli*.

Unbelievably, even though Francis had been unable to keep his supper for two consecutive evenings, he surprised me while en route home from an acupuncture appointment by requesting we stop at our favorite Thai Restaurant near our home: he craved fresh spring rolls. So we did. Francis ate two pieces of spring roll and some of the dinner I ordered, his usual favorite – ginger tofu with vegetables and brown rice. Although he ate slowly, Francis didn't wait overlong between bites. And yet, this was a supper he did not lose.

OUR SUFI FRIENDS

In recent years our Sufi friends Halima and Abraham Sussman had come to lead us in an annual day of retreat using the Dances of Universal Peace. When Francis was hospitalized, instead of our cancelling the retreat, they proposed turning it into something different, quite unique, actually, which they called Community & Healing: A Benefit for Francis and Elaine McGillicuddy. The flyer read: "Join us for an afternoon of renewal, generosity, and healing."

Halima and Abraham also insisted on giving us all the proceeds. "It'll help defray your co-pays for Francis' expensive medications," they explained. "But what about your having had to drive from Cambridge, Massachusetts?" I pressed. "Wouldn't you at least take gas money?" We were awed they declined, and yet not completely surprised, for we had encountered our friends' generous spirit before.

Especially since the retreat was billed as a benefit for us, it didn't matter to Francis that he had been struggling for days with a myriad of complications. He wanted to go anyway, if he possibly could. So he calculated that with Joe's help he would be able to climb the three flights of stairs to the studio. One of us could gently support him from behind his back. Furthermore, Francis thought he could use the tripod fold-up canvas chair to help him sit for a short rest at each of the two stair landings. But, he had sensibly added, "All this depends on how I feel on Saturday." On Saturday, he was not up to it.

I went to the gathering, though even for me, since I was the sleep-deprived caregiver, spending about an hour with these forty dear people was challenging enough. I was uplifted by our community's support, nonetheless, and grateful to share the joy of it later with Francis.

Halima and Abraham and two other Sufis from Cambridge came to visit us, not only before, but after the day's retreat. They brought us the artwork which the participants had created for us. Some of the unique hand-printed designs are glued, collage-like on a poster. Others are attached to a long piece of yarn which I've hung vertically along one side of the living room door leading to our bedroom. The artwork includes messages like these: "We are with you along your journey"; "Francis, you are my co-pilot"; "Each day we rejoice in knowing you." And even – "Hen power." That outpouring of love blessed us then and continues to bless me now. When it was time for Abraham and Halima to leave, we were all in tears, aware it could be, and was, Francis' final reunion with them.

PIVOTAL DEVELOPMENT – MEG WOLFF'S GENEROSITY

"What a gift – Meg Wolff's appearance in our lives," I wrote to family and friends. "The queen herself of macrobiotic cooking has come to us!" Her website to this day is bustling with activity. Meg's teaching about the healing nature of macrobiotics is grounded in dramatic healings and recoveries of her own. Most startling is the cover of her book. It depicts her with her left leg amputated, replaced by a shoe and a metal rod (not yet wearing a more life-like prosthesis). Her arms are uplifted, and this beautiful woman is smiling. The title of Meg Wolff's book is *Becoming Whole – The Story of my Complete Recovery from Breast Cancer.*

Meg explained over the phone that because she was now recuperating from her third surgery, it would help *her*, to help us. I paused to take that in. She also invited us to her home. A few days later, Francis and I drove to Cape Elizabeth, the home of Tom and Meg Wolff.

While Francis lay on the couch facing the windows overlooking the ocean, Cuddly, their white poodle, snuggled in the crook of his arm. I sat in the kitchen with Meg where she discussed what she had in mind. All the while, she was preparing a dish with some locally grown navy beans for us to bring home. I was getting an education in the concrete – explanations along with pleasing aromas which in the eating proved Meg was concocting something tasty and good for us.

Some people had warned me that the macrobiotic diet can be rigid. When Dr. Inhorn had heard of our plans, he emphasized that Francis ought to be able to enjoy his food. But we wouldn't have this problem with Meg. She knew well how to follow the macrobiotic diet in its strict, healing version. But Meg's own approach to macrobiotic cooking, I was happy to learn, is just as she characterized it – wide. So wide, we would soon discover – it's gourmet.

Meg offered to hold a cooking class in her home to teach volunteers how to make one macrobiotic lunch, once a week (or more if they wished) to assist me in cooking for Francis. It was a plan she saw worked for one of her friends.

Not only that, Meg promised for the whole month of December to bring us dinner every day! Her plan was, at an appointed time, to leave the tray on the path to our door, but near the road. This project, she said, would begin immediately. I made a point of noting the car's arrival so I could meet her there outside daily, but because this wasn't always possible, the plan worked well to leave our dinner briefly on the ground. A few times I saw through the window, just before I made it to the porch, that Meg was not wearing her prosthesis. Yet she managed somehow to place the large, antique, wood tray wrapped in plastic, on the snowy ground. Often I met her in person to take it from her. Sometimes her nephew brought the tray, and several times, her husband Tom.

From then until Francis died a month later, we were regaled with Meg Wolff's meals. Even though at first Francis occasionally lost a meal, this happened much less frequently with food like this.

Meg's generosity was a matter of great consequence in our lives: Because of the appeal, variety, and taste of her multiple-course meals, with appetizer, soup, main course, after-dinner salad, and dessert, and even if Francis ate small amounts, they added up to more than he might have otherwise eaten. As a result, because of Meg Wolff, I am convinced that Francis' life was not only prolonged – his last days with me took on an unexpected character. They became our last suppers, with all of the implications of that pregnant expression.

FRANCIS' LONGSUFFERING

For now, as I told family and friends, though his steps are short, his posture bowed a bit, and his loss of weight visible, Francis had more energy since eating Meg's meals. He himself drew my attention, after an acupuncture appointment, to how much energy he had. "Look at how long I was able to go without needing a nap!" he tried to console me. When I told Francis how heartening it was to see him smile again, especially after what had looked like an unsolvable problem, he said with a humility I found disarming, "It was just a down spirit in keeping with what was going on."

"Incredible!" I thought, "after that seemingly intractable problem with his intestines." But he added, simply, "I'm glad I'm negotiating all the curves and doing a little reading in the meantime."

Yes, Francis was smiling again, even though he had to put up with several vehicles of pain control on his body. Besides the fentanyl patches, stuck in various rotating places on his body, he was attached to the PCA. And then there was the TENS Unit, whose sticky electrodes adhered to either side of his lower spine. The tubing for the PCA and the wires for the TENS Unit easily got entangled, or pulled out by the device for the TENS Unit which was hooked in front. So I devised a belt to prevent this snarl. All in all, it was no small thing for Francis to maneuver daily living, and then, what's more, to be patient about it.

That's why I said my longsuffering spouse had the patience of a saint. That's why I was surprised at what happened next.

UNPRECEDENTED CHIDING

As I've said, sometimes I can get too meticulous for my own good. One day, in addition to mounting fatigue from lack of regular sleep, there were extra snafus to deal with, like Francis' pain pump ringing a loud alarm every two minutes. While he was pressing the stop button each time it clamored, I was calling for a VNA nurse to come to our home. The message flashing on the screen read: High Pressure. It was easy to see why – there was blood in the tubing.

The whole episode took over two hours to clear up because the nurse got lost en route. Once arrived and unable to handle this complication, she had to telephone another nurse to come help her insert new tubing before she changed the needle. Apparently the nurse who had changed the needle earlier in the day had hit a small vein or capillary – it was all very tiring.

In any case, later on, as I lay on our own bed, with Francis in his hospital bed nearby, I was talking nonstop (he told me later). I was sharing ideas I had gleaned how to help him. That's when I heard him say two words which I had never heard Francis use with me in all our years together: "Shut up! Give us both a break!"

Of course, I was surprised, *very* surprised, even stunned. But I knew immediately there was no anger in Francis' admonition. And he was right. So I did shut up and even began to appreciate that this was exactly what I needed to hear: I did need to stop ruminating aloud and just relax.

Without another word, then, I let go gratefully, and it did me much good. I remembered my mantra and I remembered to practice Savasana, the yoga corpse pose which by definition is the practice of letting go. This beneficial little wake-up "slap" was a reminder I knew I wouldn't forget. We laughed about it later. And I told him, "Sweetheart, you're *good* for me!"

This incident, however (of two nurses' difficulties handling complications with Francis' pain pump tubing and needles), marked only the beginning of a kind of breakdown in Francis' body. The next day, after Francis' nurse, Tim Boothby, struggled once again trying to replace the needle of Francis' pump, he said in frustration, "His upper left leg simply can't support any more needles!"

A TURN IN THE ROAD – FIRST MEETING

Francis' deteriorating physical condition was inevitable. It occasioned Dorothy Smith's inquiring of Francis how he was doing. When he weakly answered "fair," she offered to bring in her friend and colleague, Dr. Ken Hamilton, founder of H.O.P.E. Inc.

When Ken arrived, he and Dottie sat facing Francis and me, with the glass door at our backs. It was an ordinary question Dr. Hamilton asked, but his manner immediately drew out Francis. "How are you doing today?" I wasn't surprised by Francis' answer because by now he had what his doctor called pronounced dependent edema. He told Ken he was finding himself writing his obituary.

Francis went on to explain that earlier he had had short-term goals he could meet. But now, he couldn't meet them. I knew what he meant since I also feared Francis was losing ground. I had had a sinking feeling of my own in the last week observing his desperate need, in rushing back from the bathroom, to recline as quickly as possible, whenever he had to stand. By now, even walking had become difficult again.

Francis replied that he felt discouraged, as if he were standing before a brick wall. When Ken repeated his word, "discouraged," pointing out that its root word "*courage*" had to do with the heart, "cor," Ken asked Francis, "If there were a song in that heart, what would it be? What would you sing?"

Francis' face softened. He looked at me wide-eyed. We both knew what that song was in his heart: his favorite Beatitude that he and I had chanted at national *CORPUS* conferences.

It was the Beatitude Francis had made his own, on the spot in 1996, when hearing me sing it upon my return from that life-changing weeklong retreat. With his good ear for music and his resonant voice, he had quickly learned it. So we sang it together for Ken and Dottie, in Aramaic: Tub-wayhun layleyn . . .

It's the beatitude we all know as "Blessed are the pure in heart for they shall see God." But one reading of the transliteration that I had pieced together from Dr. Neil Douglas-Klotz' textual notes, in his most popular book, *Prayers of the Cosmos*, is this: "Blessed are those whose heart has a deep sense of passionate purpose and the audacity to feel abundant inside. They shall see God, in a flash of insight – everywhere."

As Francis' rich voice joined mine, it was hard for mine not to break, because his face came to life with a look I will never forget.

That half-hour visit with Ken and Dottie turned everything around, not the cancer, of course, which was attacking him now without mercy. But now also, it was Francis' spirit which turned around in rediscovering within himself a wellspring in the words of Jesus. Twelve years before, singing around the house the beatitude's refrain, "Allaha" repeated twenty times, gave him a taste of joy that buoyed him from then on. We had been sidetracked because of Francis' hospitalizations, and so had not been singing as much. But recovered now, that Beatitude chant brought Francis an energy that in ensuing days some friends and I found astonishing.

A TURN IN THE ROAD – SECOND MEETING

This second turn in the road was our exchange with Tim Boothby, one of Francis' VNA nurses who was consulting closely with Dr. Inhorn. When Tim arrived, only hours after Ken Hamilton left, we told him what Dr. Inhorn had told us – he had no other great ideas for Francis. "*That* was Dr. Inhorn's way of telling you something," he said. "It's because they like you, that the nurses and staff at his office couldn't bring themselves to tell you that Francis already qualifies for home hospice care."

I was genuinely surprised. Living close to Francis as I was, it's as if I hadn't seen, or maybe couldn't realize, the implications of his body's regressive condition. Even as I witnessed it. People around us saw it, they saw the inevitable, weeks before we did. Interestingly, the truth gave Francis and me a sense of relief.

We had come to see that the radiation gamble had not worked in Francis' case. From the beginning, we all knew he had not wanted, at eighty-two, to take extraordinary means to prolong his life. The only reason he had accepted radiation was that it promised pain relief. Whereas once he could not sit in a chair without pain, now he could, so some good had come of it. It had also given us more time together. But now, it was time for hospice.

Tim explained that home hospice care is a superior program. It would offer more services than VNA could, and even more help for both Francis and me. He emphasized what their website explains: "Hospice affirms life and does not hasten or postpone death." After Tim left, Francis and I had a long talk with Lynn. She confirmed the same, by supporting us once again with helpful research. Having never walked the hospice path before, we needed this education. In response to my reporting this news, Anne Underwood emailed: "Everything happens as you are ready for it." When I read this to Francis, he shot back: "I'm ready!"

With hospice in place, the focus now would be wholly on Francis' comfort and the quality of his life. Accordingly, we hired Maria Willis, our neighbor up the street, to come during the busiest time – from 8:30 to 10:30 A.M. Maria not only assisted me so I could wait on Francis, this former emergency medical technician and secretary was funny, efficient, and smart, always insisting that I myself not overlook my own breakfast. Maria took care of the chickens, did the dishes and laundry – everything to free me for Francis.

Francis now stopped reading the newspaper, ate very little, and slept a lot. And saddest of all, his pain when standing was so insupportable, he spent all day in bed. When he *had* to stand, Francis' other alternative was to take four extra doses of dilaudid from his pump before getting up. And that took forty minutes.

One afternoon, I was sitting at the computer desk next to Francis' bed, typing his instructions for the financial tasks he used to do. Often stopping to talk, I would love him with my eyes, and he me with his. Suddenly, it startled me to notice he looked so well! For the moment, it was as if he weren't sick. It made me heartsick to realize he was. Hence there were these flips of the heart in which the reality of our situation shifted into a sense of unreality. Yet, heartbreaking as it was, we were at peace with what was happening.

Francis turned to me with a new seriousness. "You've heard me tell you, haven't you, Dear, what I learned as a hospital chaplain about the dying process?" I nodded, and he reminded me about evidence demonstrating that the last sense to go when a person is dying is the sense of hearing. "So, even though I might seem beyond your reach," he said, "sing to me, and I will hear you." My eyes welled up as I promised him I would. I knew which song to sing, not just the Beatitude chant, but especially, "Set me as a seal upon your heart . . . for love is strong as death." (Song of Songs 8:6)

Reality hit hard, too, when Pam Shay, Francis' new, head hospice nurse unpacked medications that were delivered to our door. She explained the use of each one. The package was called the Urgent Symptoms Hospice ComfortPak. Although it was reassuring to know we had on hand what was needed . . . and needed for what! – No wonder I felt numbed then by an equally strong sense of unreality since even as I write this, the rest of that sentence hangs in the air . . . but of course I listened to Pam with great alertness – how to use one or the other medication, if or when certain symptoms appeared. The medications in this ComfortPak would be utilized, I was told, under the guidance of a nurse through a phone call or visit, day or night. Some part of me operated on automatic to take in, and later, to follow all these steps. They are steps I don't want to write about, even now.

One of the most helpful things I learned at this crucial time came from our good friend, Dr. Ann Lemire. "The most common reason end-of-life patients go to Hospice House, or to the hospital, when the end comes," she told us, "is that caregivers can no longer manage at home. It's usually not lack of skill," Ann explained, "but lack of stamina or exhaustion." When Ann concluded with this: "Taking care of yourself is taking care of Francis," I took a new course of action. To accompany this information which I shared with family and friends in an email, I asked Susannah or Stephanie to post a new request on the lotsahelpinghands website: "Needed – a person to come to Elaine and Francis' home every afternoon so Elaine can take a nap." Yes, I was doubly determined to get the rest I needed, in order to accompany Francis, at home, to the very threshold of his completion, his fulfillment – his arrival.

DEEP TIME MESSAGES

When I told family and friends, "It could happen sooner or later, no one knows when," I didn't know then it would happen ten days later. Sitting at the computer typing, I was within arm's reach of Francis lying on his bed. Whenever he was awake and aware of what I was doing, I counted that a bonus.

Even though Francis was eating again, and "with some gusto!" he said, we were told to get ready for anything. I congratulated him for eating, praising Meg's meals for giving him the incentive. Hearing this, Pam said to me, for Francis to hear, "By the way, it's not just a macrobiotic diet and daily massages that have enhanced, or even prolonged Francis' life, it's you, ministering to him." Francis smiled and said, "Yes, that's my experience."

Pam told us something else I communicated to all, namely, that because people nearing death need time to do deeply personal work, visiting can be very tiring for them. Though they can rally for visitors, and even look good, they're exhausted afterwards. I could vouch for that, having seen it firsthand. After a visit with Father Mike McGarrigle, a close friend for fifty years, Francis had slept for the rest of the day. "Here's a way around this," she offered, describing an idea she had seen work well. To give friends an avenue to Francis without draining him, those who wanted to could send me an email with the subject line Message for Francis. I would then read him their messages when he was awake and rested. In response, many people wrote to Francis. Their messages were touching and he greatly appreciated them.

"WONDERFUL MOMENTS"

"Can you imagine," I wrote to friends and family, with incredulity, "what Francis said to me in his state of complete dependence?" Francis had been bed-bound for three days. Since standing or sitting in a chair were insupportable by now, he was forced once again, but permanently now, to lie fully reclined as he had had to do, repeatedly, in the previous *three* months. His spinal cancer pain had chained him to his bed. I had flossed his teeth, I had helped him pee.

And then he said: "This is another wonderful moment, going through with you the little chores of getting me ready for bed. My beloved is here with me. She is preparing me. You look good, you feel good, and you are so good to me."

How could I not love a man like this! I had met him in 1968, meaning I had been in love with Francis, now eighty-two, for half his life. And this was not the *only* wonderful moment. There would be many more extraordinary "ordinary" moments from then on until Francis died.

A special moment, indeed, happened when Lynn and Lee came for their next weekly visit. Visits with them not only did not tire Francis, they never failed to energize him. "Because with family, one can be even more relaxed," I suggested.

Lynn and Lee had brought us for lunch our favorite hot-and-sour soup from the Stir Crazy restaurant we had frequented. We had gone there as recently as earlier that year. After gathering around Francis' bed, enjoying the soup together, Rowan climbed onto it, and he showed her how to use the lever to raise and lower his hospital bed. Francis even encouraged her, showing her how to do it gently. That was a "Rowan-*Pepere*" moment to remember.

I told Lynn and Lee about Ken Hamilton's visit which had inspired Francis to reclaim and sing again the two chants we loved, not only his favorite Beatitude, but Saadi's other chant from Song of Songs – "Set me as a seal upon your heart, for love is strong as death." This book of the Bible is also known as *Song of Solomon*, or *Canticle of Canticles*. Francis and I had not only sung this chant at the bedside of a friend in a Hospice House, but I had led it as a chant-dance of universal peace at the yoga studio the day after my mother's funeral, and in the *Hebrew* version that time – "Shime-ny . . ."

I also related to them a suggestion our good friend Nicki had made the day before. During our telephone conversation, I had sung one of the chants for her. That's when Nicki got the idea we should record Francis and me singing them. I had thought of inquiring through lotsahelpinghands if anyone had the skills to do that for us. But when Lee and Lynn heard about this, and correctly sensing we might not want to wait, Lee offered to do the recording himself. He went right out to buy a microphone and promptly returned to set it up through the computer.

Then and there, Lee recorded Francis and me singing the entire Lord's Prayer in Aramaic. To see the earnest, proud look on Francis' face, to hear his voice increasing in strength and articulation as we went along – and then to see Lee and Lynn's expressions of pleasure in response to the beautiful Middle Eastern melodies, our joy overflowed. As our last note echoed in the room, we spontaneously cheered. The recording caught Lynn and Lee's ebullient "Yeah!"

Those mystical moments didn't get lost on Francis. When I greeted him the next morning, he was so happy, I picked up a pen to catch every word he said: "This is the deluxe way of getting up! Everything is falling into place! There are lots of wonderful moments, wonderful, wonderful moments now." Oh my God, I thought – what a gift to hear him talk like this. "They just keep coming!" he said, amazed at how much energy he had had the previous day. "It was unlike any other day," he emphasized. "After two hours I usually cop out. But I was *with* it all day. I couldn't believe what was going on, and on, into the evening. "What's more," Francis said, "I then had a good night's rest."

I knew the other cause of Francis' renewed energy besides the chanting because I shared in it: the bonds of our relationship with Lynn, Lee, and Rowan were sealed.

TALK ABOUT DEATH

Christmas was approaching, but the hospice team, nonetheless, directed us to begin making plans for what would come after Francis' death. We called Lynn and Lee to come for that discussion. Rowan was engrossed reading books in her library corner in our own adjoining bedroom. Within view and earshot of her, we were making preliminary plans for Francis' funeral, in his presence. Alternately and simultaneously we were weeping and nervously laughing.

Francis smiled at some of the details – for instance, our plan to set up audiovisuals for his wake and funeral reception. Once a month, in the early twenty-first century, CBS, Channel 13 television, had created a three-minute noon program during which I would teach one yoga pose, on live television. Francis was my model yoga student for that program. We did this for three years. I had joked it was this public exposure that had made us seem less "radical." Our reputation as conscientious war tax objectors, we thought, was now balanced in our fellow parishioners' eyes. We were seen now perhaps, as people who might be able to help them with a sore shoulder or a bad back.

HE ASTOUNDED US

We were entering into the anteroom now at the other side of which stood death's door – Francis' threshold into another life. I was anguished to see his gaunt and colorless face with that cancer look.

While learning from the nurses how to roll Francis from one side of the bed to the other in order to change his sheets, I viewed up close Francis' thin arms and skeletal frame. I saw firsthand the ravages of cancer impairing his body – and again, when Meg Nobel, our nurse friend arrived with her husband, Mike.

This teacher of hospice nurses with whom I had consulted over the phone, showed me other ways of working with a patient confined to his bed. She saw Francis' weight loss for herself, then, but when she witnessed how he still had the upper body strength to lift himself a bit when trying to assist us, she expressed pleasure about that.

Meg and Mike had come to our wedding. What a heartrending scene – this last coming together with a dying friend. Observing Francis was tired after that work, we walked quietly out to the kitchen.

As they were leaving, I told them about Lee's recording on Sunday, but that Francis and I needed to re-record two short chants which had turned out partly truncated. But, I added, saying the obvious – "Francis has no energy to sing now." Since Mike is a singer-song writer, I wanted him and Meg, however, to at least to hear the Aramaic Beatitude, the one I hoped, I said, we'd be able to re-record the next day. So I started to sing.

When I started intoning Francis' well-loved Beatitude for us three to hear in the kitchen, we were startled to hear a voice singing along in the other room. *Francis'* voice! So we hurried back to his bedside, dumfounded that he was ready to sing again. Mike, knowing how to do this kind of thing, went to the computer to finish the unfinished recording job. He even recorded two takes of our singing "our" Beatitude, as well as one take of the second short chant from Song of Songs.

As on Sunday when Lynn, Lee, and I were left open-mouthed by Francis' unexpected burst of energy, which moreover lasted the daylong, we this day, Mike, Margaret and I, were flabbergasted and thrilled to hear the strength of Francis' handsome voice.

SET ME AS A SEAL UPON YOUR HEART – FULL CIRCLE

The whole while Francis and I were singing "Set me as a seal . . ." we were looking into each other's eyes, letting our full voices express our love that *is* "as strong as death, its jealousy as unyielding as the grave." (8:6) This passage was among those I had copied for him as my Christmas card when I was still a nun. I had told him then, that they had originally expressed my relationship with God, but that – now, in love with him – I was applying them to him.

This Song of Song 8:6 verse was the chant, as Francis' body was wasting away, he had asked me to sing for him while he would pass. I would sing it for him about ten days later, several times, when he was in the process of dying. Two witnesses would tell me they saw Francis then, mouthing the words as I was singing them. But at *this* moment of its being recorded a second time, when he was fully alert – *that* was when it became (I realize it now) – our love-vow chant.

These love words, as a pledge when Francis and I entered into one another's lives in 1969 – and then again as he was beginning to make his transition from this life into another in 2009 – came full circle for us, forty years to the month, perhaps even to the day, on the edge of a new year.

CHAPTER NINE
Last Suppers

I t was a Christmas Eve like no other, but it was friends' gifts which provided the Christmas atmosphere that uplifted Francis and me. Francesco Sanfilippo and his wife Susannah, as well as Susan Christian, had brought Francis homemade ginger cookies. On behalf of the macrobiotic-meal cooking crew, Winnie Shivelhood-Kartez delivered a big wicker basket full of macrobiotic staples. (Besides Winnie, Jan Born, and Woodsie Enwistle, others helped out as well.)

Francis' room was made magical also by our neighbors' gift, an 8" glass square lamp into which Laurie and Ken Birmingham had placed Christmas lights. It stood on top of the wide bookcase which fit just below the bow window's four panes.

With the descent of darkness through those windows, Francis and I saw the magic extended outdoors because of the generosity of Shawn Clark of Clark Tree Co. As an expression of his friendship, Shawn, our arborist and new friend, wanted to brighten our Christmas. "I'd like to string up Christmas lights for you in the Canadian hemlocks," he offered. We had agreed, not realizing we'd be given a little show as well.

Shawn had arrived with his own equipment to get the job done. We had watched him in the first act – standing in the cherry picker lifted higher than our house by its fully extended boom, while he strung a festoon of lights. In the next scene, we saw Shawn, bent forward at the hips hanging over the vehicle, draping the rest of the lights over the branches. He had maneuvered all this without assistance, using remote control. "What a unique, thoughtful Christmas gift!" Francis said, warmly thanking Shawn. Those loops of white Christmas lights illuminating the Canadian hemlocks directly across from Francis' bed gave us comfort during the whole Christmas season.

These were all wonderful gifts. But the greatest gift was the exchange between Francis and me that night. He had slept all day on December 24, except to surface briefly for breakfast and lunch. At suppertime, I thought he looked weaker, observing the effort it took him, even with my help, to sit up. Once he was settled, leaning back against the raised part of his bed, I placed on his chest a small, white cotton tablecloth I had bought in India, and laid the festive tray Meg had brought, on his lap.

I sensed it was a special, unusual moment because of the way Francis looked at me. He seemed physically fragile, and also, somehow, more spiritualized, even while being very present with me. He appeared in a kind of altered state.

Francis paused before our meal and then started to sing on his own – "Havlan lachma . . . "the line in the Aramaic Lord's Prayer, "Give us this day our daily bread," often used as a grace before meals during Aramaic prayer retreats. We had used it in our own home on special occasions. I immediately joined in, so pleased he had initiated this meal-prayer chant.

Then I was caught off guard: Why was Francis starting to sing again? In a split second, I caught it: it was the "Allaha" refrain from "our" Beatitude. I took part in this, too, until all twenty of the "Allahas" were sung after which Francis and I began singing the Beatitude proper – Tubwayun layleyn . . . we sang. I was aglow with joy to see and hear him delight in the living love for God in his heart. "Allaha" gave him the words and the melody to express it in song.

Francis then told me he had had a dream, and that in his dream, he had awakened in the morning to see his obituary in the paper. "And I was glad!" he said, with feeling.

"Why glad?" I asked.

"Glad it was over," he said. I felt his sense of relief.

"Are you afraid?" I asked.

"At times," he answered softly.

"What comes up?" I probed.

"I'm not sure," he said.

"The unknown?" I pressed.

"Oh, yeah," Francis answered without hesitation. He then recalled for me what I had related to him the day before – Jim Lovejoy's telling us he had just put up in his office a poster which read: "Let go, let God." Francis looked at me intently. "*That* is the task," he said. "That quote helps me. I had never reflected on it seriously before. Everything is involved in that." He paused, needing as I did, to reflect on this.

"So the dialogue we're having right now is helpful," he said. "It's helpful to me because the two of us know I'm in that process. Other people don't necessarily know. But you know, and by dialoguing with me, you're helping me to bring it forth."

In the slow, contemplative pace of our conversation, I had time to savor his saying: "The two of us know I'm in that process." How that moved me, making me feel I was, on earth, the person closest to him.

I volunteered, then: "You can let go anytime, you know. Are you wanting to hang on?"

"I suppose, yes, in a way. I'm wanting to hang on, wondering what's going to happen to you with finances."

"Do you realistically think I'm at risk?" I asked.

With tears in his eyes, he said "Yes and no. It's there. But it's good to talk about it."

His concern, I then told him, reminded me of my mother's asking before she died: "Who's going to take care of you when I'm gone?" I compared her worry, motivated by her unconditional love for me, to his: "What's at issue here is your love for me, and your instinct to protect me," I reasoned, "more than a justified fear."

Francis went on speaking about the value of our dialogue by expressing the same idea in seemingly every possible way he could. His words are so dear to me, I want to include them all in this love story, in spite of their repetition (or maybe because of them), for the reader, too:

"This is a very valuable dinner conversation we're having," Francis said with obvious relief after my response calling his worry unjustified. "Most people don't have this. A lot of people . . . when they're dying – they don't have this." I knew from his having been a hospital chaplain, he was speaking from experience.

"It's very helpful to me. It all came from your asking me about my fears," he added. "Being with you like this, I can express that fear. It helps me to let go a little bit."

Obviously projecting the possible time of his death, Francis said: "I'm not thinking in terms of anything immediate, tonight or tomorrow. I'm just expressing an example of that whole process of letting go. Talking totally honestly is very helpful to me."

Seeing how my questions drew him out more, I asked, "How helpful?"

"It's just the fact we're having this dialogue," he said. "It's a step in my effort to let go, my effort to be free . . . just one step in letting go."

He looked thoughtful. "Sure, there'll be other steps. But it's very wonderful. You take what's given to you. You take the insights, the little gifts along the way."

Francis continued, "'Let go, let God' sounds like a cliché. I had never thought about it before. But – huh!" He made a face connoting something difficult. "Those things surface," he said.

"When do they surface?" I asked.

"During the night, sometime today." He had, I thought, slept all day. "Gradually they surface and make themselves known," he was saying. "It's just a matter of their bubbling up. It would be strange if that didn't happen."

After quoting Ken's comment about writing one's obituary and then getting on with life, Francis said with satisfaction, "We've been very open about this whole situation we're in. Now let's get on with our lives." With a "Yeah! Okay!" he asked. "What's the meal?"

I put a red cloth napkin under his chin. We both served ourselves, and then as we ate (he, slowly and in small amounts) Francis remembered there was more he wanted to tell me about his dream. "In my dream, dying was painless," he said, his countenance brightening. "I just slipped away in my sleep, and then I said to myself 'Oh! That was nothing!'" Hearing this, and especially seeing the confidence it gave him, my spirit lightened.

At this point I offered Francis one of Francesco's soft ginger cookies. "Oh, wow! I just got the smell of them! Mmm," he said smiling. "Tell Francesco that I swooned with delight. So, Francesco gets top billing tonight!"

With his eyes closed, Francis seemed to be sucking on the cookie. I was watching him, noticing his jaws chewing. As he was tasting it, I was cherishing every moment being in his presence. Since Francis had slept most of the day, I had been partially deprived of this. My whole attention was held by him; I was watching him, aware of this silence, deep in our time together that night.

Francis opened his eyes and looked at me with a warm, direct smile.

"I wonder about the consistency of these cookies," he commented. "Which do I prefer? Francesco's soft one? Or Susan's crisp one? For immediate sensation, it's the softer one. But for longer term, Susan's ginger

217

cookie hangs more in your mouth, though the flavor of each isn't a great deal different." I smiled, too.

Concluding his meal, "I've been very well served," Francis said. "It's very enjoyable. We've had a very satisfying repast. Your presence was deeply drawn into my soul, and so I am very happy."

I was almost startled by Francis' words, but he was going on: "Those things come like a gift. The whole thing just pulled together. It made for the nourishment of my whole being. It came to us from God."

I could hardly take it in, but he kept on speaking: "It was so important for me, for that single step I needed to take: 'Let go, let God.' There'll be many steps, but I took a step in that direction now. I need to feel that very strongly – that feeling of letting go. I'm glad I've taken a step in that direction."

"Does it take away your fear?" I asked.

"It's a beginning," he said.

"It's a process, isn't it?" I said, using his expression.

"Yes. But I do understand your gratitude for my sharing it with you."

Then Francis lay back to rest before starting our bedtime ritual later, when I would brush and floss his teeth, check his blood sugar, and massage his feet and shins with oil, since they were so dry from the medications.

We had had many loving exchanges during our forty years of marriage. But never one as poignant as this one. Francis' words "Your presence was deeply drawn into my soul, and so I am very happy" came as an outright, unexpected, pure gift. It marked for me, beyond anything I could have hoped for – the deepest fulfillment of our marriage.

Our extraordinary dialogue drew me so deeply within, I wanted nothing but to sit with it, so I did. Even the sound of revelers on the street couldn't disturb the room's rich silence as I sat, just watching him sleep. He had slept all day, aside from this meal after which he was now sleeping again before needing, probably in another hour, his personal night ablutions. I would be here for him wholeheartedly.

I was grateful I had intuited, at the start of this first holiday dinner, that something unusual was going on, and so I had instinctively reached for a pen and clipboard. Now, at the end of this wondrous conversation, I was relieved to have in hand, these written notes. Francis' words were now preserved. I cherished them already. Reflecting on the intimacy of our dialogue, I thought it better, in this instance, however, to discuss with Francis first, whether or not it was a good idea to share it with our family and friends. Should we bring them this close into our lives? Was it instead too precious or intimate a conversation to broadcast? Before writing my next email, I would wait. For such a thing as this, I wanted Francis' viewpoint. Later, Francis readily agreed it was a good idea.

When Dr. Devlin read my letter indicating I had taken down our conversation by hand, he brought us his small recorder to use. "What a thoughtful gesture!" I told him. Francis was very impressed that this allopathic doctor we highly respected, even loved, had noticed such a detail. And how generous of him to have taken the initiative to assist us in this way. Along with Francis' setup for future meals, I placed Dr. Devlin's small recorder on his tray. It would preserve our conversations, all unforgettable, during the next four evening dinners.

A PASTOR FOR THE "TRANSITION"

There was no festive dinner together Christmas night itself. Francis was in pain until he was catheterized. That morning, feeling as he put it "torn between

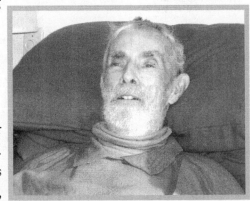

Francis during recording.

219

one reality and another," he was on the verge of tears, admitting, "I thought – Oh, this is dreadful! It's hard to take." Then, when he told me with a new earnestness I hadn't heard before that he needed someone to help him for the transition, I instantly called the hospice office to see if Jennifer, the VNA Chaplain was available.

Hearing she was not, I remembered how moved Francis was in thanking Bill Gregory for his Message to Francis. Bill was the retired United Church of Christ minister whose Poetry of Soul course we had taken the previous year. So when I asked, "What about Bill?" Francis immediately said "Yes!"

Just as readily, Bill called within the hour after receiving my email message. And shortly after that, he arrived at our doorstep. For Francis' first visit with Bill, I stepped into the kitchen to leave them alone. After Bill left, Francis told me, his eyes moist," He's the right person!" adding, "He held my hand, and I told him my story."

That night, after checking Francis' blood sugar before going to bed, knowing even when he looked asleep that he often responded to whispered questions, I asked: "Would you like some of that tasty organic yogurt?" I was pleased he did. While he was eating, I massaged his feet. The skin on his feet, ankles, and shins was the most dry.

Francis liked the scent as well as the sensation of the rich Badger Massage and Body Oil Lynn had bought us for this. I had seen by his expression how relieving it was for Francis when I gently scratched loose the dead skin from his ankles. Applying this pungent oil, piquant in that it had a cayenne extract in it, elasticized the new skin underneath and filled the room with a pleasing aroma. Its half-filled bottle sitting on my bathroom counter still, reminds me of those moments. We had just a handful of precious days left.

When we said goodnight, Francis thanked me for having awakened him. He said the yogurt had made him feel stronger. "Yes," he repeated, he was glad I had awakened him – "because it's not time yet." When I questioned his meaning, Francis told me – although in the morning he had felt torn between one reality and another, he just *knew* – "It's not time yet."

ANGELS AT OUR SECOND CHRISTMAS DINNER

When Bob telephoned him from Boston the next day to say goodbye, Francis told him about Bill and quoted him: "Call me every day as you'd like. I'm here for you." To Susan who came on the following day to say goodbye, Francis also told her that just Bill's presence had done him some good.

That Sunday night, Francis was ready for another gourmet macrobiotic Christmas dinner. When I brought in and opened a bottle of wine, his eyes lighted up. "I'm so glad to see you pouring yourself a glass!" he said. I was touched by his delight in my joy. Francis took a sip, but because of the opiates, he didn't take more. But neither did he express regret that he couldn't partake. Instead, he was happy to see me relaxing with him.

Meg's dinner was not off limits for him, however. The tray with Christmas tree napkins her husband Tom had delivered earlier included a hand-printed menu for this feast: "Cranberry braised tempeh; oven-roasted vegetables; wild rice with pecans; pasta with tofu and steamed broccoli seasoned with drops of rice vinegar; and for dessert – apple/blueberry crisp made with rice syrup. The cornbread was made with blue corn flour."

Inspiring Christmas carols from King's College, Cambridge, England, resounded in Francis' room as we ate. Christmas lights draped over Canadian hemlocks glowed within view of Francis, who was sitting up in the hospital bed which he would no longer leave after that morning's catheterization. It was of no consequence that our Christmas dinner was two days late.

During the meal, Francis was eager to tell me about unexpected memories which had arisen for him that morning because of two earlier visits with priest friends – Father Mike, still in the clerical priesthood, and John Munroe, a married priest.

Father Mike had told Francis a story he in turn related to me. It had to do with Father Richard Rohr's experience. "During Richard's visit with his dying mother," Francis recounted, "she had said to her son, 'You're not alone, Richard, I'm not leaving you alone. There's someone here with us.' Richard had said, 'Mother, I'm by myself. There's nobody else here.' 'But,' his mother said, 'Richard your guardian angel is right there beside you. You don't realize it, but he's there now.'" Francis repeated, "He's beside you now."

The sun was streaming into the room during Francis' meeting with John. Before leaving, John stood over his bed and gave him a blessing, his hand on Francis' hand. "John told me," Francis said, "that one person he hoped I would see when I passed the threshold would be Father Freddie Chase." As young priests, both John and Francis had known and revered this teacher of the Boston Archdiocese. "You remember my telling you?" Francis reminded me. "He was a dear confessor friend of mine, when I was in the seminary." I certainly did, and I remembered Francis' appreciating that a fine-art painting of a nude woman hung on Father Freddie Chase's bathroom wall.

Mulling over these exchanges with Father Mike and John led Francis to suddenly remember that "Father Fred himself, this very sophisticated scholar," he made it emphatic – "was dedicated to the proposition that angels are very much a reality. Yes," he said, "Father Chase saw nothing superstitious about angels. To him angels were real." His emotion was strong. "Freddie Chase just welled up from my memories of him!" he said with visible joy. It gave me pleasure to see Francis heartened, reminiscing about his seminary confessor.

JESUS AT OUR THIRD CHRISTMAS DINNER

The next morning when our close friend Celeste came for a last visit, Francis seemed at first either asleep or withdrawn, so we spoke quietly. But he surprised us by inviting us not to whisper; he wanted to listen to our

222

conversation. Then he himself spoke, telling us how, on occasion, he had been called to minister to former parishioners when they were dying. One of them had asked him to give the homily at her funeral. Francis told Celeste that as homilist he was proud he had walked in procession with the ministers at Woodford's Congregational Church, once Bill's church.

That night we had our third dinner to the background music of Hildegard of Bingen's "Canticle of Ecstasy." We took pleasure in another of Meg's delectable meals. Again I placed Dr. Devlin's recorder on the tray to catch Francis' actual words.

"Oh!" Francis said, "These delicate pieces of tofu, so specially seasoned – and dipped in that sauce – this is definitely gourmet eating!"

I laughed, concurring with "Mmm," of my own. "Meg outdoes herself every time," I said. "Imagine this – seven different dressings so far!"

Francis confessed it was quite a new eating experience for him. "And certainly," he went on, "if you insert this eating experience in my Catholic tradition, it's part of a long list of last suppers. You know," he said, "the Last Supper."

The music and his words nourished us.

"What is the Last Supper?" he asked rhetorically. "A communing among friends. There's no better communion than this."

When I offered him some eggs, he said, "Now, you've salivated me with the eggs!" and he then announced, "No biscottis for me tonight! I don't want anything else to displace the taste of our hens' unsurpassed eggs."

Francis changed the subject then. He wanted to talk about why he had called on Bill to companion him. "What I'm going through raises different kinds of questions, you know."

I asked, "What kind of questions?"

"Questions interrelated between the dying experience and my faith, which is from the Roman Catholic Tradition."

Francis told me he had been thinking about this since Bill's visit, the previous day. "When Jesus . . . in my humble understanding, when God . . . inserted Himself in the human condition," he said – "what we call the Incarnation – the very minimal you can make of that is that it raised everyone to a new level. And it wasn't that God raised just Jesus," Francis continued, "Jesus was not alone in being raised to that new level. We were *all* raised in some mysterious way to that new level!"

He paused and added, "And so, it's something one needs to talk about and pray about. I need a pastor to help me integrate these things into what I'm going through in my life, in whatever time I have left," he said. "That's kind of in a nutshell why I need a pastor."

Francis confessed he didn't know a lot about the United Church of Christ, Bill's tradition. "But," he explained, "my understanding is that their view of Jesus' role would be wider than that of the Roman Catholic Church." He went on to say, "I've felt comfortable for many years now, widening my own perspective on Jesus' position, while my own tradition is very limited and rigid in this regard, that is, in its official teaching."

Francis made another point. "And I don't think it's fair, it wouldn't be fair for me, and it wouldn't be fair to a certain well-loved priest in our parish, if I put him in this position of trying to pastor me when I come from a very different part of the Catholic community."

He kept on: "We're all parts of the Catholic community, but we all share at different levels, and we all have different viewpoints and different life experiences." I knew Francis knew he was expressing my views as well.

"I feel totally at ease with my decision," he said, referring to his choice of Bill. Francis reminded me he had already said something to that effect. "I told Bill then, at the end of his course, Poetry of Soul, if I could choose my pastor – you'd be the one."

We had finished our meal a while ago and were still absorbed discussing this subject, the new lens through which we had begun deepening our faith in Jesus.

When I reminded him of our participation in the nationwide virtual Community of John XXIII (an offshoot of *CORPUS*), he told me he had thought about Richard Scaine, a married priest like himself, whose articles in *CORPUS REPORTS* we had read. "I have incorporated that thinking, even in my receiving communion," he said. "It has broadened my understanding in receiving the Eucharist, and what it means to me."

But Francis added, "Still, even with that particular contemporary insight, I still feel the need to maintain these very definite roots in my Catholic tradition, even though they're more limiting."

"In Catholicism?" I asked, letting him confirm. "Yes," he underscored, "I'm rooted in my Catholic tradition, even while needing to branch off from those roots."

"That's why we have that bumper sticker on our refrigerator," I said, "God is too big to fit into just one religion."

Francis smiled nodding and then looked at me with an expression of calm acceptance. "In my life now, not knowing how much time I have left, I've been ruminating, thinking about, and praying about all this." I breathed in my gratitude. "It's been moving along. It has to, so I have to look at . . . you know – what does all this mean?"

Francis paused for a moment and said, as if to sum up, "Yes, I have someone companioning me now, someone of my own choosing. He came to this service . . . presumably led by the Spirit – the Spirit that led me."

FRIENDS AT OUR FOURTH CHRISTMAS DINNER

The next morning, a Tuesday, Francis' will to live was strong, even though he called it a struggle. "My own energy," he said, "is pulling me toward living, if I can surface enough."

And he did "surface" enough. By evening we enjoyed what felt like another banquet. Meg's Christmas leftovers provided us an equally elegant meal. Francis visibly reveled in it. For background music, this time, among other CD's we liked, I put on one we especially prized – Alan Shavarsh Bardezhanian's "From Kef to Classical." After hearing Alan and his Middle Eastern Ensemble perform at "New Year's Portland" early in the twenty-first century, we had become followers of this oud virtuoso, going to many of his concerts. This fourth-dinner tete-a-tete would turn out to be the liveliest and the longest – two hours altogether. It was interrupted, however, by Francis' need for short rests during which I checked email for more messages which I would read to him when he awakened.

Francis smacked his lips over Tuscan kale and indicated he wanted to tell me about his morning. "When I awaken," he explained, "I'm very conscious the area is narrowing, the area where I can be as fully conscious as I am of all the loves in my life – you, Elaine, and our friends. When I start to prepare for my remaining days here," he went on, "I try to push back those barriers causing the narrowness." He wanted "to expand light into the day" he said, "and hope times will go on and things evolve."

I asked him if he had any sense how he felt the previous night when he said, "It's not time yet." He spelled out how, often his energy was such that he would just as soon lie back and rest again. He gave the example of waking up at ten or eleven P.M., having missed supper. "I just don't want to fall back into that kind of schedule again," he said, adding he wanted instead to keep to a normal three-meal-a day basis rather than "let things get totally out of control. No, I don't want that to happen again," he repeated.

It had happened earlier, but when I started talking to him about emails, for example, to Norman – "important emails like that," he called them – it had motivated him to go ahead to see which ones he could answer. "I was glad to use what energy I had to reconnect with people who went out of their way to send me a message." Francis then confided, "You didn't know this, Elaine but it's because of you that I rallied. You'd say:

'Emails now,' or 'Time to eat now,' – and I would recover!"

On the other hand, earlier that day, because he was too tired, I had instead, given him a haircut, a beard trim, and a pedicure. "That was the right thing to do then," he said, thanking me. "I was resting, and you were ministering to me. It was very restful, very loving! I could feel your cutting around my lips and chin, and moving up to my head. I was totally, lovingly with you that whole time. It was such a loving experience we had together!"

I remembered all right. I had taken photos of Francis lying on the hospital bed's incline, with my mother's plastic cape surrounding his head, not noticing then the gauntness of his face. Now, looking back at those photos I can see how close he was to death.

After this recall of our intimate exchange, it was time for dessert. Francis said, "I'd like one of Francesco's ginger cookies. Would you get me a saucer?" I placed both before him and munched on one myself.

"Aren't they – Susannah and Francesco – special in our lives!" I exclaimed. "Remember how we connected?" I recalled for him the time we had walked with Tom Sturtevant and the Veterans for Peace contingent during a Veterans Day Parade. We had had lunch afterwards with Tom's daughter Susannah and her husband Francesco. From then on, Susannah was my yoga student and both of them, our good friends. "They even followed us into the permaculture community." Francis remembered.

"We love you very much," I declared aloud, spontaneously holding up my cup of tea as if to toast their very presence.

Francis followed suit, "You're part of our love community. Absolutely right – both of you! You're both dear to us," he said, adding, "goodbye."

In a reminiscing mood, I then thought of Joe and Claire who thirty-seven years before had come to our small wedding. I was reminded of a children's song: "Make new friends, but keep the old. One is silver, the other gold." Susannah and Francesco were new friends, and Joe and Claire friends from long ago. We mused over how their lives and ours had inter-

227

acted over the years. I told Francis how I appreciated Claire's *joie de vivre* and how moved I had been during Joe's retirement dinner celebrating his thirty-four years as Executive Director of Shalom House (an agency offering support and housing to adults with severe mental illness). In listening to Joe's talk that night about his work there, "I saw an even deeper Joe," I told Francis.

By now we were both in tears. "Joe and Claire," I announced, as if they were present, too, "we celebrate your friendship and what it has meant to us all these years!" Francis endorsed this also: "We thank you for being in our lives. Bye Joe and Claire." And then we both lifted our tea cups to toast them.

Having finished dessert, Francis was ready for a rest. I removed the tray from his lap and brought it to the kitchen to wash the dishes. Alan Shavarsh Bardezhanian's Middle Eastern music, "From Kef to Classical" was taking its turn.

When I returned to the room, the dishes done, Francis was stirring awake again. "It nourishes your soul doesn't it, Dear," I said. "That wonderful music nourishes your soul and mine in recalling those rich days in our lives." I knew he already knew what I had been thinking – from the music alone. "What joy we've had together, my Beloved," I said, adjusting his pillows. "What joy, my Love!" His face shone as he nodded. "I see that twinkle in your eyes."

Then Francis started to sing along with the Middle Eastern music. I could hear (and the audiofiles caught) the soft drumming sound of his hand keeping beat.

We were silent now. Only silence could hold all this. We were in a kind of cocoon, safe together from the suffering of the world, even though we were on the brink of his death. Both our lives would be hurled into new worlds – mine without his physical presence and he . . . where? Where is that "place" death leads into?

But for now, we were still physically together. The unforgettable memories of our married life were transferred to this present moment. It felt celestial, even if we were aware those joys were revisiting us in the room where he lay dying.

Then the phone rang. Francis awoke. Unbelievably, it was Claire, about whom we had just been speaking. "I don't want to intrude," she said over the speaker phone. "Joe and I were *just* thinking about you. I'm wondering if you'd like us to bring you a Maine shrimp salad I made this evening." Of course we agreed.

"Francis is moving his head with the background oud music," I told her, raising the volume so she could hear. "Remember this?" I asked. "You were there at that birthday party. Joe gave the toast." She assured me she remembered that night.

I told Claire that earlier this evening, we had been toasting certain friends, in their absence, right out loud.

"And after that," I said, "while Francis was napping, I've been here at the typewriter making a list of the people to notify." We all knew, during the moment of silence that followed, what I meant.

When Claire changed the subject telling us her nephew was surprised that she didn't know how to text, we all laughed and joked about youth's fixation on their devices. "Yeah, it's alien to me too," Francis admitted.

"Okay then, I'll pop in tomorrow," Claire said. "Love you," Francis called out. Moments later he was asleep. I went back to my typing.

When Francis awakened, I read him some incoming emails of note. There was one from Lesley Hoey, one of our yoga teachers at Portland Yoga Studio who had now become a physical therapist. Her friend Dr. Steven Goldbas, an osteopathic physician, had offered to come with her as his assistant to give Francis treatments twice a week – "for the time that you and Francis still have together." Lesley explained that MMO – "manipulative medicine osteopathy" – was a powerful palliative tool for the dying.

Realizing that Dr. Zorsky, Francis' own regular osteopathic physician, might or might not be able to make it, since he lived out of town, Francis agreed he would like them to come.

The other email for Francis came from Martin Steingesser. In the 1970's, Martin, a Maine poet, had visited my English class at Thornton Academy. Francis and I had also demonstrated with him for peace during the Iran-Contra years. I read: "Dear Francis and Elaine – Light travel to you into the new year." Francis was moved by his thoughtfulness. Since hearing news of Francis' cancer, Martin had been mailing him a poem neatly printed on a card, many times a week.

Francis dictated this for me to type on his behalf: "Dear Martin, this is a historic moment for me. It's the first time I've received the gift of poems from a poet laureate. I have admired you for many years as the poet of our community, but never did I dream I'd be the recipient of a poem addressed to my very own self. I honor your gift with great respect. Thank you, Martin – Francis."

Francis sighed in satisfaction, saying, "Friends in my life tonight! It could never be like this in a nursing home compared to all that's involved living in our own home." Francis made the next move. "Even though I came alive with Martin's note, it's time to get me ready for bed."

I flossed his teeth then and brought him a basin of water and a towel to rinse and dry his hands. When I returned from emptying the catheter, Francis mentioned the light in the chicken coop. "Yes, it goes on when it's colder," I explained, looking outside. "It's so windy, it's as if someone's at the door. Shall I give you a massage before you sleep for the night?" I asked. "I won't refuse," he said. When I finished, he thanked me and added, almost crying, "It's so beautiful – our tender exchanges!"

I could tell Francis wanted to tell me something else. "Tonight I had the feeling, when I woke up," he said, "that you injected a new life and energy in me – just this whole thing, your taking care of me like this, getting me ready for bed," he said.

"It's the love and the physical touch," I said.

"Yes," he affirmed, "when you start ministering to me like this, my energy widens in a marvelous way. It just widened perceptively," he emphasized.

I told Francis that Lynn, Lee, and Rowan would be coming tomorrow, and that I had three books to give to Rowan. "Visits from them don't tire you," I said, repeating what we had noticed before.

"Yes, because they're our little family," he said.

"You don't have to perform," I said. "I could even massage you while we talk with them."

"Sure," he said. "And it's good for Rowan also to see," I added, "that I, *memere*, am taking care of *pepere*. She can see the love."

I took another last look at emails and told Francis there were three messages: The first came from Lesley, reporting that Dr. Steve would consult with Dr. Kevin before coming to give him a treatment. Martin's email read: "Ah, dear Francis and Elaine. You both sing as poets yourselves. I'll be sending a poem a day. Love and hugs to you. Martin." And Susan had written about her visit with Francis that morning: "I'm grateful for this gift I'll take with me to my end. He is close to the point of letting go. Francis' way of conveying this to others is remarkable."

Francis' eyes welled up. "I'm ready for the night now."

FAMILY TIME – MADE GLAD

Three days before he started to die, I asked Francis, "What keeps you wanting to live?" He answered, "The joy is holding me here." The truth of his answer was borne out by his question at lunch that noon. As I placed the tray before him – barley mushroom soup, fish, and some delicious Nutty Wafers loaded with pumpkin and sunflower and sesame seeds, he asked, "This is all strengthening food, isn't it?"

It meant a lot to Francis that this dessert (and a bagful of other good-ies) had been brought by our friend, Dr. Ann. We had something in com-mon with her and her late husband. Alex was a Presbyterian minister, and Ann, a former nun. It was Alex I met first as the director of the Clinical Pastoral Education course I had taken in 1989. Our friendship developed after that, just when Francis' adult onset diabetes had struck. Alex' own ex-perience handling diabetes had helped Francis. After Alex' unexpected death in 1999, which shook us, Francis and I regularly met with Ann for lunch. Since working for the homeless keeps this "street doc" busy, we would choose a restaurant near her workplace to meet with her. Ann un-derstood what we were going through.

Joy was visible on Francis' face the next day also when Lynn and Lee came with Rowan for our family time. Francis was beaming when our five-year old, who had taken pleasure the last time in climbing onto his bed, did it again. She referred to the "pee bag" which hung on the opposite side from where she sat, but got to work tinkering with raising and lowering the upper part of the hospital bed. Francis enjoyed her fascination with it, as she sat next to him.

We exchanged Christmas gifts and then ate together the meal Lynn and Lee had brought. During dinner, I told them about a new development with Francis. "It's been happening especially when he awakens in the morn-ing," I said. And I quoted for them the words Francis used to express his feeling of being "torn between one reality and another" during the previous three mornings. First it was "hard to take," I quoted. "Then he called it a 'struggle,' and the next morning," I added, feeling alarmed myself in re-porting this – "he even used the word 'terrified.'"

Lynn looked thoughtful when she told us about an article she had read, just four days before in the *New York Times*. Although it was an article on palliative care for the patient, it seems that some of the panic experienced by patients at the end of life could be chemically induced. I was grateful to hear this, since it threw light on Francis' experience.

If his early morning anxiety was chemically induced, should he take another drug for that anxiety? Even before hearing of this article, I had asked myself the same question after a hospice nurse's admission that even anti-anxiety medications can cause anxiety.

Fortunately, in succeeding days Francis' painful feelings abated. I was sure that both Bill's visits and the chants had something to do with this. I told Lynn and Lee how relieved Francis felt to have Bill as his pastor. He had come the previous afternoon, I told them, adding that after Bill and I had sung for Francis the hymn "I Heard the Voice of Jesus Say . . ." – Francis told us he especially liked the line "and he has made me glad."

As Lynn and Lee were leaving, Rowan, realizing she had not said goodbye to Francis, called out and ran back to his bed to give him a hug. She was wearing Lee's gloves and Francis' new ski hat which I had just given to Lee. What a scene that was! Rowan's right hand lay on Francis' left shoulder, and her left touched his head, resting on the pillow. Francis' left hand was on his heart, and his right hand touched Rowan's right cheek and temple as if to draw her closer to his right cheek. A smile was on her face; bliss, on his.

After they left, Francis rested a while, for by then his energy was low. When his bedtime preparations were completed, he asked me to sing again the hymn I had sung to him with Bill that morning. "I heard the voice of Jesus say / Come unto me and rest." I could see that that line he had quoted – "and he has made me glad" gave him strength. So I sang it for him again.

I lighted the homemade candle that Abraham Sussman, our Sufi friend, had given Francis a few weeks earlier. Then I anointed his forehead with the oil that had been blessed and used to anoint participants at Shrine Sunday's healing-oil ritual the previous August. We had assembled with the family there in Canterbury, New Brunswick, only four and a half months before, for Francis' last of our annual McGillicuddy family reunions.

Francis had started an annual tradition for himself, beginning in the 1990's, to visit the old uninhabited homestead on the land where he was born, had spent his childhood, and where the Franciscan Shrine was built. He'd stop for a short visit with his sister Jo in Houlton, but move on, and once arrived in Canterbury, briefly visit a few people in the area. It was as if he was making his own personal pilgrimages. Francis told me he wanted to go there alone, because he liked "to commune with the ancestors." Now, he would soon be one of them.

MORNING INTO EVENING OF NEW YEAR'S EVE

"Who knows if it's time yet or not?" I wrote to family and friends later in the morning of New Year's Eve. "He's got a foot in two worlds."

For this reason, the hospice team was on hand to help us. Their chaplain, Jennifer, had suggested that she call every morning at nine o'clock to check on Francis so that we two could be present with him, over the speaker phone. He had readily agreed.

"Today it's still there," he said about this bipolar tug on him. "I'm very weak this morning. My energy is pulling me away from eating," he said. "There's no panic right now because you're right here in the flesh to talk with me, the three of us." Francis explained that this gave him more strength to keep going into the outer world.

The hospice booklet given us listed various signs of approaching death. When I told Bill about the term "disorientation," he suggested instead, "a *different* orientation," which Francis also preferred. But when Jennifer proposed the expression "an inward focus," he said, "Yes, that's it."

At this point, I asked Francis if he *wanted* to "keep going into the outer world," and he said yes. At lunchtime, however, after he asked me if he should force himself to eat, and I said no, reminding him that his nurse Pam had said that the choice to eat or not should feel like a natural thing

234

to do, he decided not to eat. But I calculated his decision might have something to do with timing. Since the home-health aide was due to arrive at 1:00 P.M. for his bath, he might have wanted to rest ahead of time. When Francis said, "Not now," that confirmed my guess. But it was clear, there was a progression here.

It was a busy day already for a dying man. After our talk with Jennifer, niece and nurse Jane had come to help me with the list of people to call at the end. Then Bill came. During his short visit, Francis lay in silence, eyes closed, but his increasingly beatific smile showed he was listening and responding to Bill's and my singing two hymns, "Dona Nobis Pacem," and once again, "I Heard the Voice of Jesus Say," interspersed with Bill's reading the Good Shepherd psalm, "Though I walk through a valley of deepest darkness, I fear no harm, for You are with me."

I was grateful Francis had time to rest again because Dr. Kevin telephoned to say he would be coming to our home late afternoon, snowy weather or not. He wanted to give Francis his last treatment of cranial osteopathy.

When he arrived with his partner, Martha, I greeted them at the door and ushered them into Francis' room. Francis was visibly moved by our friend's act of kindness. Martha sat on the stuffed chair watching from one side, and I, from the other, as Kevin wheeled the hospital bed away from the wall. Now he could cup Francis' head in his hands. For the most part, the treatment is done in silence. The silence this time had a deep undercurrent. After they left, Francis fell into a long deep sleep.

NEW YEAR'S EVE – OUR LAST SUPPER

When Francis awoke, again, I told him his sister, Mary, of Saint John, had emailed him a prayer. "She said she uses it every day," I noted, adding that I had thanked her and told her it reminded me of the prayer my mother had taught me as a child, which she also prayed as her sister, Rachel, was dying. I read both prayers to Francis who seemed comforted by them.

Would Francis be too tired after such a full day to take supper with me? When I asked him, however, he accepted. "But it's got to be something very easy on my stomach, Dear."

"Oh, I'm so glad you're eating!" I said, eager for his words, since in spite of all the activity, he had slept most of the day. "You wouldn't take lunch. So why did you change your mind?" I asked.

"Partly because I don't want to give up," he said. "I don't want to go back to sleep right now."

"For me?" I asked. "For us," he said, giving me a long look.

"Francis," I began, hesitantly, "we . . . talked about having last suppers . . ."

"Un-huh, yes," he said in a weak, scratchy voice.

"And we've had several last suppers, haven't we?"

"Yes," he answered.

"We never know when . . . when it's going to be *the* last supper," I said.

"No, we don't know . . . we don't know," he said, going on, "and . . . sometimes it starts off to be just a little spark. Sometimes the last supper starts off . . ." and he repeated this. (I could see he was very weak) ". . . to be a little spark and then when you kind of carefully embrace the little spark, it turns into something bigger."

I agreed. "That might be enough to hope for, for tonight."

"It might turn into something bigger," he said a third time. "We just have to wait and see. We have to be very patient."

"Yes," I said. "You tell me when you want another bite, Darling."

"I'll have another bite now."

I brought the fork to his lips and waited a bit before bringing up the expression he had used, "I like the way you put it – about 'the little spark.'"

"Yeah, well," he said, "I never thought of myself as a poet. But I *do* have a poetic soul." He mused about the difference between being an actual poet and having a poetic soul, and concluded, "If a distinction can be made, I probably have a poetic soul. I've always been and will always be . . . a poetic soul."

I considered, and immediately came back – "Yes, you *are* a poetic soul!"

"It's been consistent with me," he said. "It has guided a lot of my decisions throughout my life."

We went on reminiscing. "I hope I'm not wearing you out," I said.

"It's not a question of wearing me out now," he said. "All I'm doing is using the little energy that comes my way. And tonight that energy is very precious. It's not in abundance tonight, let's put it this way." I could see what he meant.

"No, it's not in abundance," he repeated, "but whatever measure of it I have can help me with whatever thoughts come in my direction." He turned to me. "You know, today it was a struggle, a real struggle to get myself awake long enough to eat. But I overcame the exhaustion long enough to get something in my stomach."

"Do you know what helped you?" I asked. "Having finally gotten enough rest?"

Francis explained, "If I hadn't made a supreme act of the will, I wouldn't be eating anything now. I would have collapsed."

I knew when that had happened – after Dr. Zorsky had left. "I made this effort, and you encouraged me," Francis said, quoting me: "'Want to try this hot and sour soup?' You led the way by tempting me to try some, and I said, 'well, yes, I'll try.' It went on from there," he continued. "And I'm glad I did. You're a very good person to help draw me out, you know. You're excellent at that – drawing me out, helping to motivate me."

I smiled.

"So, is this New Year's Eve?" he asked. When I confirmed it was he said, "Oh yeah – New Year's Eve!"

"Want another bite?" I asked, "Just tell me when you're ready. I don't want to push you," I said, adding, "I've never tried to push you in our marriage, Dear, you know that. And even if I had, you wouldn't have let me anyway." He laughed with me, agreeing, "No."

The Armenian Middle Eastern music was playing now. "Oh, that music!" I said, but asked,

"Are you fearing, or thinking you won't always be able to continue doing this?"

"Oh, yeah," he said.

"And how does that feel to you? I asked.

"What's that again?" he asked, unsure.

I had noticed some of Francis' words here and there were mumbled, unclear. There were a lot of pauses in his speech. I could see he was making a supreme effort to be with me. "For us," he had said. But I resumed:

"When you look ahead and realize you won't be able to keep up with these last suppers . . ."

He interrupted me – "Oh, no! – I'm becoming reconciled to it. I don't expect to go on forever."

"Oh, good," I said, relieved.

"Unless I . . . unless I'm mistaken, this is a more minor one tonight."

"A more minor what?" I asked. Since he was having difficulty pronouncing the words and his voice was weak, I wasn't clear what he was trying to say.

"A minor supper," he said. "It's minor in energy."

"Yes, I see," I said. "Minor in content," he added. "It's a very small window . . . a very small . . ."

"Yes," I encouraged him, since again his speech was slow.

"A small window into what?" I said, trying to help him.

"A small window that I'm allowed to have . . . into the world. Yeah," he said, satisfied he'd got it out. "It's small."

"Is it still a joyous thing still?" I asked. "You said yesterday it's the joy that's holding you."

"There's not . . . less joy tonight," he said, "but the energy is less. Yes, definitely less energy. Yet," he went on – "there's some comfort there. When you took me in tonight," he said, "I could still feel some comfort. I can relax back into the comfort zone now. So it's not all bereft. No, I'm not bereft."

Hearing this, my distress witnessing his diminishment lessened, but I wanted to be sure.

"Is some of the terror leaving?"

"Yes, I would say so, yeah."

"Oh, I'm so glad about that, my Darling!" I said.

Now we could relax and let Alan Shavarsh Bardezhanian's Middle Eastern Music bring us – as it had two nights ago with his oud – a little bit of heaven.

"That music tears your heart out, doesn't it?" I told Francis.

His head was already nodding with the music's rhythm. And again, he began to sing along because this music held our treasured memories.

We had been present on the night when Alan and his Middle Eastern musicians had celebrated the release of this one and only acclaimed CD. We had bought it directly from him and then taken part in the gala dinner.

That haunting music had also graced, in the same year, our own celebration of Francis' seventy-fifth birthday. We had rented for the night, not far from Portland Yoga Studio, the entire small, choice Bella Cuchina Restaurant. People representing

At Francis' 75th birthday party.

all aspects of Francis' life – family, parish, priesthood, peace, yoga, Dances of Universal Peace, and just plain good friends – had filled all the tables. Among other choice CD's as background music for this birthday party, it seemed to us there was more joy in the room when Alan's music was on.

Elaine standing near Francis.

On that night of his seventy-fifth birthday, after Joe's toast, Francis had given a little talk, and I had recited Shakespeare's "Let me not to the marriage of true minds admit impediments." Everyone in the room had looked radiant, as if we were all caught up in a joy bigger than all of us.

Francis' little talk.

Francis and I were nonetheless aware, in looking at my McGillicuddy in-laws walking past the buffet table, that Lou, his oldest, surviving brother, was standing alone. His wife, Dina, was home. The cancer she had overcome once, had returned. We were aware she was seriously ill, but we didn't know that Dina would die at home, two days later.

Saying goodnight to Sue Ewing.

240

"You're right on with the melody, the rhythm, and the beat!" I affirmed, watching Francis. "You haven't lost your sense of pitch," I added, surprised at his alertness.

"What a melody, huh!" he said, continuing to hum with an even stronger voice.

"Oh my Dearest," I said, giving him a kiss after positioning the supportive bolster at his back – "My Beloved, I've always been so happy living with you. . ."

"Mmm," he murmured lovingly.

"Yes," I said "I've always been happy with you – from the beginning when I fell in love with you forty-one years ago!"

Francis then fell asleep. I turned to family and friends through email: I told them that Francis was especially weak tonight, and so, not knowing how much longer he would be able to speak, I was cherishing every self-disclosure my dying husband Francis was sharing with me. Mentioning that he knew very well I was emailing them, I could honestly say, I confided, that Francis was sharing these with them as well.

I assured them also – though grieved to see him and his voice, too, so weakened in such a short time – that it was a comfort to witness a growing spiritual strength in him. "Before my eyes, in the last three months," I said, "I've witnessed the truth of St. Paul's observation: "...we do not lose heart. On the contrary," I quoted, "though outwardly our bodies are dying, inwardly our spirits are being renewed every day." (II Corinthians 4:16)

NEW YEAR'S DAY – LETTING GO

On New Year's Day, although Francis silently welcomed with a nod my chanting the Lord's Prayer in Aramaic, he also told me, "Let me be for a while. Everything takes effort." Then when his nurse Pam called to see if we had questions, Francis asked whether he should give in, "I feel like sinking back and see where this rest takes me." Pam encouraged him, "As long as you have no concerns nor fears . . ."

Francis told her that whatever concerns he might have were very minor and that his "need to sink back" was greater than anything else. "Elaine and I have searched our souls together," he said. "I just feel it's a good time to let it happen." So Pam told him to go ahead and allow himself to let go into God's hands.

When Jennifer called, she encouraged him, too, telling him to "surrender into God's space" and to let himself be "enveloped in God's Love. Your own wisdom will arise," she told him so that "whatever seeds of wisdom you've cultivated will now flower, producing the fruits of your spiritual work."

Jennifer told us that she felt "very very assured" about Francis, specifically because he had allowed the fears to come up. Sometimes, she explained, dying people say "I have faith, so I don't have fear," but because they push back the fear instead of looking at it, it comes up later.

After this conversation – with very few exceptions – Francis did not speak on this New Year's day. He remained in a deep world of his own – letting go.

At eleven as pre-arranged, Lesley arrived with Dr. Steve, a friend and colleague of Dr. Kevin who had given Francis a cranio-osteopathic treatment the previous afternoon. Seeing Francis smiling blissfully and giving numerous non-verbal signs that this treatment was most welcome to him, we wept; and, moved by what the moment called for, I sang for Francis. When Lesley told me two months after Francis' death that she had seen his lips moving in sync with mine as I sang "Set me as a seal upon your heart . . ." I wept again.

I cannot explain as Steve did, what he felt in Francis' body, but I grasped the main idea. In contrast to the faster rhythm in the "earthly body," as Steve called it, the rhythm in Francis' body was much slower. "At that level, then," Steve noted, "the treatment interfaces with body and soul." He also told me that he could feel "coming and going in Francis' body," and that there was no fear in it. "He has comfort," he said. I wept with relief. Most moving of all: "In Francis," Steve said, "the physical and the spirit body are saying goodbye to each other."

In the early afternoon, Carolyn Ehringhaus arrived. She was a yoga student and massage therapist who had experience giving massage to the dying. Carolyn had come twice a week during the month of December. Already appreciating the importance of massage for Francis, I welcomed her help. Of course he was silent during this last massage. (Carolyn told me later she wasn't sure if Francis was aware of even just her presence.) So what a surprise for both of us, when, as she started to massage his foot, he said, "That feels so good!" [7]

Francis surprised me again in the evening as I sat working at the computer next to him. Dr. Devlin had instructed me to continue checking his blood sugars and giving him insulin, as long as he was still living. So when it was time, I reached for Francis' finger, pricked it, and took a drop of blood. I did not expect him to, nor did he, awaken. But then, after fussing unsuccessfully with his glucose meter, I left the room to fetch another from a bathroom drawer. When I returned, Francis opened his eyes and watched me fumbling with that one. When, after a little finagling, the new, unused, simpler model worked, Francis smiled at me and said: "You are a miracle woman, and you're going to sweep me into paradise!"

Rather quickly, then, as if he were in a hurry to get back into his deep communion within, he said: "I feel so good! So good! I don't know which step this is along the way. But whatever step it is, I embrace it. I don't know

---

[7] Some months after Francis died, Carolyn emailed to say this about Francis: "With feebly spoken words, when he was able, eyes and facial expression when not, Francis expressed a deep appreciation to me, which means to you for arranging for his various caregivers. What I experienced that day was profound, but insignificant compared to the meaning of your massaging and caring for Francis at this time in his life. I do believe that he fought that last day to be with you longer."

if it's the earliest step or not – no, I don't know, but I embrace it. I do embrace it! Now let me rest."

I was, as they say – "floored" – stunned. His words were gifts. Francis was giving me one gift after another – loving words that would nourish me for a lifetime.

THE DAY FRANCIS STARTED TO DIE

On the morning of January 2, Francis had difficulty breathing. Coughing up mucous helped, but it became obvious by early afternoon that his lungs kept refilling. I reported it to Lenora Trussell, the weekend hospice nurse who prescribed Ativan to calm the expected panic from shortness of breath. She would arrive, she said, later that afternoon.

Almost to the minute, an email arrived from Saadi (Dr. Neil Douglas-Klotz), the person who had created the melody for the Song of Songs passage which I would sing for Francis as he passed – "Set me as a seal . . . for love is strong as death." He, Halima, and Abraham had just made a recording of this chant, and he was sharing it with us electronically as an MP3. I played it then for Francis, more than once, until Lenora arrived. (I shared the MP3 with family and friends the next day.) Jane, Francis' niece, also a nurse, came separately in her own car. It was late afternoon.

Lenora observed Francis and declared she was very pleased to see how gently he was breathing – how peaceful he looked. Except for the sedative, Ativan, she judged that Francis did not need to be medicated further, in addition to his fentanyl patch and PCA pump.

In her presence, then, and Jane's, I sang for Francis, as I had earlier in the day, the chant he had asked me to sing. Lenora pointed out several ways in which Francis was being "very responsive." She told me that when my own eyes were closed, at some moments while I was singing, "Francis opened his, and moved his mouth in an attempt to sing along with you."

Lenora paused and added, "He doesn't want to leave. No wonder, with you singing for him like this – why *would* he want to leave?"

Lenora told Jane and me something she had observed from years of being a hospice nurse: When, before birth, we're in the womb, our lungs are filled with amniotic fluid. At death, when the lungs begin filling with fluid, it feels like coming home. This completing of the circle, from birth to death is soothing to the dying, Lenora said. Jane and Lenora then left. Jane promised to come back, in spite of the snowstorm. She was gone for three hours.

Francis and I were alone now. We had three hours alone together. I left his bedside for only a few minutes to heat up an already prepared supper, but promptly returned to eat it while near him. Once done, putting aside my plate, I took off my shoes to sit next to him on the bed. I sat facing him.

Francis was calm, alert, aware. His smile was radiant, his eyes luminous, communicating to me ineffable things. I took both his hands in mine. He immediately returned my hold, his hands warm, his grasp firm. I told him I was handing him over into Jesus's hands, ready to receive him. Our eyes held one another in his smile of bliss. Francis then lay back to rest.

After Jane's return, around 7:30 P.M., Francis' movements became restless, so she called the hospice nurse on duty. It was a different nurse who decided to call Dr. Inhorn. Jane and I carried out our instructions to medicate Francis every hour orally with liquid morphine until it was obvious he did not need more. He looked very peaceful as we took turns watching, but then, there were no more smiles. No matter. Francis' last smile, like all the smiles of his life for me and others, was engraved forever in my mind and heart.

DEATH THE EXPERIENCE OF A LIFETIME

Jane and I saw the sudden change in Francis' countenance when it happened. Suddenly, he was no longer in his body. He had left. Francis stopped breathing at 1:25 A.M., less than two hours into the next day, January 3, 2010 – a Sunday.

There was a "nor'easter" that night. Francis knew ahead of time who the carefully chosen friends were whom I had called to help me wash and anoint his body with oil after he died. He was grateful we would be honoring his body in this way before the undertakers came to take it. Three people were able to get through the storm to join Jane and me: Dr. Ann Lemire and two nurses, Bridget Franciose, and Barbara DeCoste. We enclosed Francis' body in the set of pale-green flannel sheets that Susannah had given us for his hospital bed. They were now his shroud.

It was Francis' smile that greeted me when I awoke the next morning, the official day of his death. When Lenora called to inquire what had happened, I told her we had administered morphine as the night wore on. She said that sometimes what looks like agitation in a dying patient is excitement about dying itself.

Halima and Abraham Sussman's email commending me for choosing to wash and anoint Francis' body with oil deserves to be quoted:

> *All love and power to you both. . . . In many parts of the world it is completely natural to stay with, wash, and prepare the body of someone we love who has died. It is part of a mid-wiver process. And can be a part of what I call good dying. Good and healing for everyone. When my parents died, I washed and cared for their bodies at home. We sat with each of them until it felt right and finished. hours. No reason to rush anything. It pleased me greatly that they were only touched by people who loved them, and that I could be present for the slow separation of body and spirit, cooling of body. It felt like one more gift of life. 'Naked I come from my mother's*

womb, and naked I return therein.' It was enormously healing for me and my family. I still feel it all these years later. There is a real sense of passage that is integrating to experience and witness. With another friend, we sang her on her way out of her body. Quite an amazing experience of accompanying. Midwifery is an apt description.

The veil between birth, life, and death is one of the great mysteries. We all travel this path. As a good friend put it, Death is the experience of a lifetime!

INTERMENT

Francis did not hesitate to call things by their names. Because his body was cremated, and since cremains include many bone shards, it was literally Francis' bones we surrendered to Mother Earth on May 22, 2010, a sunny Saturday. Twenty-one of us family and friends gathered on the Goulet-McGillicuddy plot at the Notre Dame Cemetery in Springvale, the town where I was born and the cemetery where I will be buried near Francis, with the rest of his cremains added to mine.

Francis' nephew and godson, Reverend Terence Curry, S.J. led his uncle Francis' interment. We sang two hymns by David Haas, befitting Francis. The opening hymn "You Are Mine" ends with: "I will call your name, embracing all your pain, stand up, now walk, and live," and the closing line of the second hymn includes its title: "We are called to act with justice, we are called to love tenderly, we are called to serve one another, to walk humbly with God."

Terry recited some prayers between the hymns, and I proclaimed the passage from St. Paul's Letter to the Romans 8:35-36; 37-9:1:

"Who shall separate us from the Love of God?

247

Will anguish or distress, or persecution or hunger?
Or nakedness, or danger, or the sword?
No, in all these things we overcome
overwhelmingly
through Him who loved us.
For I am certain of this:
that neither death nor life,
nor angels, nor principalities,
nor things present, nor things to come,
nor powers, nor height, nor depth,
nor any other creature
will be able to separate us
from the Love of God
made visible in Christ Jesus."

Lynn, Lee, and Rowan's presence heartened me. Six-years old, now, Rowan sang along with her dad, crouched on the grass for her to see the words, as he pointed them out. I was glad the words might reassure her, new to the reality of death. At some moment between our songs, Rowan suddenly walked over to me standing facing Terry. The box of Francis' cremains, flanked by flowers, lay between us on the ground. I took Rowan in my arms, and was in turn, reassured.

TREE PLANTING

For the planting of our "Francis" tree the next day, thirty-five people gathered on our front lawn under sunny blue skies. This ritual, too, would be simple.

Lynn, Lee, and Rowan stood next to me facing our home while friends fanned out along the lawn, with a few on the porch, facing us and Avalon

Road. Abigail, our neighbor's grandchild and Rowan's playmate, stood next to Rowan who stood in front of the tree with the same name – Rowan. For the first time since its planting three years earlier, in 2007, this tree displayed a large white blossom at its crown.

Elaine at the tree planting.

Shawn, our arborist had already dug the hole for this other hallowed tree, Stewartia pseudocamellia, now the center of our attention. Along with the pile of rich humus already laid there, I added a special note by Dr. Sheila, sent me for this purpose. Sheila had written, "Made from flowers and plants, it will nourish the tree."

I had saved some of Francis' cremains to place at the base of his tree. I knew that cremation is, indeed, allowed in the Catholic Church, but I was also aware that saving some of his cremains for this (and to keep within my home) *might* be frowned upon. I was proceeding with it, nevertheless. Directly, I remembered a certain remark Francis had made before he died. Buoyed up by this unexpected recall, I felt reconfirmed in the rightness of my action.

Rowan assisting with care.

I knelt to lay Francis' cremains into the small pit awaiting the tree, stood up, looked around, and spontaneously decided I would tell our friends about this sudden recollection which, just now, had emboldened me. "I didn't dare 'publish' in my letters to family and friends," I admitted for all to hear, "this comment Francis made a few days before he died, but it's this: Francis asserted he would not let himself be controlled all the way to the grave." There were both laughter and tears that afternoon.

Shawn shoveled the pile of earth back into the cavity, and explained to us that this Japanese Stewartia pseudocamellia tree, already twenty-feet tall, slim and graceful, would grow very slowly to a height of forty feet and a girth, twenty feet wide.

To express my intention, I said in a clear voice, "Our planting is not meant only to honor Francis' memory, but to symbolize and celebrate love that keeps on growing.

I then read as one, these two passages from Rilke's *Letter to Countess Margot Sizzo-Noris-Crouy, Epiphany*, 1923:

> *I am not saying that we should love death, but rather that we should love life so generously, without picking and choosing, that we automatically include it (life's other half) in our love. This is what actually happens in the great expansiveness of love, which cannot be stopped or constricted. . . .*
>
> *Death is our friend precisely because it brings us into absolute and passionate presence with all that is here, that is natural, that is love. . . . Life always says Yes and No simultaneously. Death (I implore you to believe) is the true Yea-sayer. It stands before eternity and says only: Yes.* [8]

Our friends were then invited, if they wished, to speak about what Francis meant to them. Jaynie Schiff-Verre's spoke first and suggested that we do what Quakers do after someone speaks: They listen, and wait a few

---

[8] *A Year with Rilke; Daily Reading from the Best of Rainer Maria Rilke*, translated and edited by Joanna Macy & Anita Barrows, (HarperCollins).

breaths before another speaks, to honor what was said and the person who shared it.

Beloved as Francis was, and loving us, in the stories we shared about him, he came alive among us. We were one with each other and the birds whose songs filled the silent intervals. Finally, I read this poem of Rilke's from the same book, *A Year With Rilke: The Book of Hours II*:

> *To the Beloved*
>
> *Extinguish my eyes, I'll go on seeing you.*
> *Seal my ears, I'll go on hearing you.*
> *And without feet I can make my way to you*
> *without a mouth I can swear your name.*
> *Break off my arms, I'll take hold of you*
> *with my heart as with a hand.*
> *Stop my heart, and my brain will start to beat.*
> *And if you consume my brain with fire,*
> *I'll feel you burn in every drop of my blood.* [9]

Our own work of tree planting completed, we turned now to another event – a picnic in our . . . (it felt unnatural to think "my") backyard. We came together near the deck and the glass door under the grapevines. Some sat in lawn chairs near the chicken coop, and others at the large wooden table set near the blueberry bushes, at the base of the Canadian hemlocks.

---

[9] Ibid., 250.

EPILOGUE
Appointment with Our Past

In the process of writing the first two chapters of this love story, I was drawn as by a magnet to revisit Francis' and my "underground" attic apartment. When my friend Gloria and I decided to meet for lunch somewhere between her home and mine, I seized the opportunity to suggest Augusta.

We chose a May date in 2012, shortly after *Sing to Me and I Will Hear You – The Poems* was published. It was a cool spring day when I drove north. Since this was a drive Francis had made weekly before I moved to Portland to be near him, I put myself in his place, remembering he'd bring along a bottle of wine and a side of roast beef to save some of my grocery dollars.

Gloria and I met at a recently built Thai restaurant located near the small airport compound close to where Francis and I used to walk at night. I saw trucks sitting in a row facing the restaurant with extra grey buildings behind them, absent in my day. They blocked out the natural scenery.

Although I had earlier thought of including Gloria in my plan to find and revisit the apartment after lunch, I was actually glad, after all, that she needed to get back home instead. We had had a good visit but yes, it was better for me to be alone now, for this appointment with my past.

Driving past the cemetery, I was pleased to see that the greenery here was undisturbed. I had forgotten how steep this hill is at the top end of Winthrop Street. While driving slowly down the hill, I was looking on the left side for Elm Street where the large white house that had held my old apartment, I expected, still stood. The scenery was improving. In fact, I noticed street signs reading: Historic District. After spotting my street, I deliberately, for now, drove further down to see if the Department of Human Services building where I had worked, was still there. Parking the car, I walked down the hill to discover that it was not only closed, but boarded up. But noticing that across the street, a building had been torn down with the granite in piles, I remembered reading about improvements initiated in the town, that is, a project seemed in progress to restore the waterfront within view down the hill from where I stood.

Then I took a photo of the closed-down building, and slowly walked back in the direction of Elm Street. In a little notebook, I jotted down the names of a few streets I had forgotten. And there, on the same side of the street as Elm Street, up ahead, was the Lithgow Library, more massive than I had remembered, but a handsome building. I walked on the other side of the street to get a frontal view which I photographed. Then I got in my car and drove, just three streets up, to Elm Street. The house itself, no. 14, was not as close to Winthrop Street as I had thought it was. But the moment I saw it – the third building to the left – the whole scene quickly came back to me.

I knew this particular house at 14 Elm Street was the house. The tell-tale tree in front of it vouched for that. So did the mini-porch outside what used to be my attic window. I drove by it, to the end of the short street to see where "Aunt Edie" had lived, the elderly woman I had regularly visited. Of course she was gone now, but the house across her street which looked uninhabited, with a for-sale sign on the lawn, was a good place to park my car. That done, I walked back toward no. 14.

It certainly had a lot of additional porches attached to the side. Just as I got near it, a van arrived, stopped near the front porch, and its door opened automatically, as if it were a bus. Unclear what this meant, I walked past the house and saw a man in the driveway whose wild look would have frightened a child, as he somewhat frightened me, so I walked on to observe the house from a distance. Then, with the van sitting there, obviously waiting for someone to appear, I walked to the open door and inquired, what I was beginning to guess, "Is this a group home?" The driver said "Yes," pointing to the side of the building, adding, "There's an office there." Noticing another man standing in the front of the building looking as self-absorbed as the first, who nevertheless had tried to talk with me before I had walked on – I was confident by now, to walk toward the side door where the first man had stood, to inquire.

As I was arriving, one of the women, whom I deduced worked there, was leaving. "I used to live here," I said, quickly explaining my presence, "and I stopped by, hoping to see the house again, and maybe even the attic apartment I had rented." Then, seeking more information, I added, "The van driver told me this is a group home now." With a cordial smile she verified it was, "Yes, eight people live here." Then, without hesitating, even as we talked, she had turned around and opened the screen door to invite me in. After speaking to another woman with short dark hair, she said, "Danielle, this woman has questions to ask. Go ahead and show her around." She smiled at me and left the building.

Danielle then telephoned yet another person, Kathyrn, who came around the corner within minutes. I told them both my story, but succinctly, not to use up too much of their time. I included my background and Francis' and how, while waiting for the Vatican in Rome to make a decision on the issue of optional celibacy, we had had an "underground" relationship. And this building had been our primary meeting place. "That was forty-one- years ago," I reported, adding with a smile, "You weren't even born then." Danielle responded, rolling her eyes: "I certainly had not been born yet!" I could tell she was even younger than Kathryn, a blond young woman who told me she had been working here for many years. My voice caught when I told them I was writing a memoir, a love story, now that my first book of poems was being published this month. With eyes brimming, they took down the web address of the blog where I had posted my letters to family and friends about Francis' last days, for anyone to read. Then Kathryn motioned me to follow her. "You mean," I exclaimed, "you'll let me go upstairs to the very attic space that was my...I mean our apartment?" I hardly believed my good luck. "It's not a problem," she added. "That's where my office is."

As we walked up the carpeted stairs and turned into another narrow hall, Kathryn and I were comparing notes, I, describing the direction the original stairs had led from, and she, speculating how the renovations had been completed. It was obvious to me, the moment she opened the door, that it was indeed the same attic space I had occupied. I was pleased she allowed me to take photos of this very simple, unassuming wide-open office space and meeting room. The bathroom was the same size as I remembered it, but the kitchen had been expanded, subtracting some of the space from the once larger room which had served as my bedroom and office. I could see Kathryn's desk near the old attic window, and another desk near it. Two long tables, side by side surrounded by chairs, served their purposes for group or individual counseling. We talked some more and then descended together to the first floor where Danielle awaited us. By the time I said goodbye, repeating my gratitude for their gracious reception, the two women and I exchanged eye contact and warm handshakes.

After walking back to my car at the end of Elm Street, I started up my Toyota wagon for the ride back home to Portland. I was satisfied, and more, by what I had learned. The seventy-five minute drive home gave me time to ponder. Known as "Motivational Services Inc., this group home at 14 Elm Street in Augusta, Maine, in existence for about thirty years, served as a psychiatric rehabilitation house. In a word – it was a mental health facility. How fitting Francis' and my "place of tenderness," as he had called it, became a house of healing!

TRIBUTES

I cannot express my reaction to the news of Francis' death. I sat here remembering the interview I did with you, and your asking me when it was over what I thought. I told you that the audience would certainly learn about the important work that Francis and you had done and were doing, but what struck me the most was the beautiful love you had for each other. It was demonstrated in every glance, every touch, every consideration you extended to each other to make sure both your voices were heard. – S.H.

He was, without any doubt, a shining star in the active way he lived his principles. He struck me, every time I had the pleasure of seeing him, as being the kind of thorough-going grown-up we all aspire to be: gentle and confident, able to engage sincerely and comfortably with anyone, either lightly or seriously, as the occasion called for. He stood up for folks who could not speak up well for themselves. Francis leaves inspired memories. – S.V.Y.

The two most important things he taught me – to always do what is right. – P.H.

Francis was an inspiration to me, living, in the best spiritual sense, what I envision an authentic Christian life to be. He was also a "good father" to many of us. What a great soul he was! Our community has felt a significant loss. I'm adding my small voice to the collective. – R.L.

I will never forget how he hugged me each time we got together. This is special because most men in our society are reluctant to hug another man, so he made a great male role model. I also liked his sense of humor. Sometimes I can be too serious, but he frequently got me to laugh. – C.R.

Fifteen years ago, my wife and I met him at a vigil in Monument Square. It was cold. He had a sign. He introduced himself and embraced me with a hug I came to know was his trademark. He was smiling that sweet smile. "What an endearing man," my wife said. Endearing is the right word. – J.W.

Always the rock for Elaine, always kind to all, he is now a leader in how to let go with courage, grace, faith and love. He taught us all the most valuable lesson we might ever need. – M.G.

I was moved to see Francis' special obituary in the newspaper and flooded with such good memories of who and how he was, I want to write you. As a member of Community Psychiatry at Maine Medical Center, I worked with him many times. His humanity, caring and determination to better the lives of those he served shone through always, but my favorite memory is of a training experience we had. He and I were lying at right angles on the floor of some church hall, arm wrestling! The idea was gender equality or empowerment or something, but I remember our joyful competitiveness, a woman versus a man, and the fact that I actually made some headway but he didn't let me win. – P.M.

He was a source of inspiration because he modeled the values he espoused. – T.W.

My fondest Francis memories include his vibrant smile and hearty laugh – from Camp days to more recent summer family reunions. – S.C.

I like to reflect on the life experiences we shared together growing up on the farm. I looked up to him as an older brother for guidance. I remember it was he who pushed for higher education for me with my parents, and that step in attending St. FX has enriched my life experience greatly. – C.M.

Francis during a retreat in 2005.

Francis is a prince – always was. His passing was very inspiring, sobering, and a light on the path, all at the same time. – T.M.

I always learned deeply from him, even when there were no words spoken. – C. L.

He taught me the important things. As I watch my little boy, I know how fast I will become the old man. But I will show him by example how to live well, how to love well, and how to die well, as I learned from Francis. – D.W.

I write with admiration for Francis' patience and unbowed humor in his daily encounters with pain. In my last visit, even when already suffering, he yet listened patiently to my stories, asked discerning questions, and added his own insights to enrich the narration. Francis is one of those great souls who shine in our midst, making the world more nonviolent, just, wise and good simply by being their beautiful, godly selves. – G.H.

I will always have the image of Francis that I have witnessed many times – his translucent and sparkling pale blue eyes with a radiant smile. – MEQ.

When I think of courage, I think of Francis singing in the face of pain. – C.Q.

Today, I went for my last run of the year in Evergreen Cemetery. As I ran up the hill in the back of the cemetery, I thought of the times Francis would be walking down the hill towards me. We would both stop, and talk about Thomas Merton, peace/war, and politics. I relished those conversations and admired his gentle manner. I was inspired by his acts of courage. – M.B.

Every once in a while, a vision of Francis's face shines forth, his twinkling eyes and beautiful smile. I remember all the times I said to him "Hi handsome!" – P.W.

I kept an eye on him in yoga class to make sure I could keep up with him, and I usually didn't. I loved his presence in yoga class and the sweet way he always consented to demonstrate a pose. – D.H.

I remember Francis for his sharp wit, kindness and the quiet sense of decency that marked his interactions with all whom he met. He reminded me so much of my own Irish relatives. – J.S.

He was a wonderful man and so good to me for many years – always so understanding and easy to talk to. I really enjoyed working with him. – S.K.

I don't think there was ever a person who was not touched in some way by his presence. He lived his life fully and shared openly his spirit with the generosity and caring of a whole human being. As a gentle and quiet man, his actions spoke much more than any words could say. – R.L.

In the newly formed Lifeline Program at USM, Francis and I would go out for runs together, about three miles. For me there was no warming up period with him. I liked him right away. It wasn't long before I admired and looked up to him. He was easy to be with and I greatly respected his points of view. – D.T.

It feels to me a huge hole has been created in this world. Francis was a treasure, very calm, very loving, emanating warmth and kindness always. I sensed he did not have a mean fiber in his body. – C.A.

To know Francis was to love him. And who knew him better or loved him more than Elaine? He is smiling that sweet smile of his eternally. – J.W.

Credits for Illustrations

Elaine G. McGillicuddy, a native Mainer, is a retired high school English teacher. She lived in Missouri, New York, Massachusetts, and Waterville, Maine, during the 15½ years she was an Ursuline nun. In 1968, while Campus Minister at Colby College, she met and later married Francis A. McGillicuddy after he left the clerical priesthood. She has a B.A. in English from the College of New Rochelle, New York, an M.A. in Religious Studies from Providence College, Rhode island, and is a certified Iyengar Yoga teacher, leader of the Dances of Universal Peace, and permaculture designer. Widowed in 2010, McGillicuddy lives a largely monastic life at home in Portland, Maine.

While working on her third book, *Sing to Me and I Will Hear You – The Uncollected Poems and Journals*, she is on sabbatical from teaching yoga at Portland Yoga Studio, which she co-founded with Francis in 1989. www.elainemcgillicuddy.com